Teacher's Book

A RESOURCE FOR PLANNING AND TEACHING

Level 4 Imagine

Senior Authors

J. David Cooper
John J. Pikulski

Authors

Kathryn H. Au
Margarita Calderón
Jacqueline C. Comas
Marjorie Y. Lipson
J. Sabrina Mims
Susan E. Page
Sheila W. Valencia
MaryEllen Vogt

Consultants

Dolores Malcolm
Tina Saldivar
Shane Templeton

INVITATIONS TO LITERACY

Houghton Mifflin Company • Boston

Atlanta • Dallas • Geneva, Illinois • Palo Alto • Princeton

Literature Reviewers

Librarians: **Consuelo Harris,** Public Library of Cincinnati, Cincinnati, Ohio; **Sarah Jones,** Elko County Library, Elko, Nevada; **Maeve Visser Knoth,** Cambridge Public Library, Cambridge, Massachusetts; **Valerie Lennox,** Highlands Branch Library, Jacksonville, Florida; **Margaret Miles,** Central Library, Sacramento, California; **Danilta Nichols,** Fordham Library, New York, New York; **Patricia O'Malley,** Hartford Public Library, Hartford, Connecticut; **Rob Reid,** L.E. Phillips Memorial Public Library, Eau Claire, Wisconsin; **Mary Calletto Rife,** Kalamazoo Public Library, Kalamazoo, Michigan

Teachers: **Linda Chick,** Paloma School, San Marcos, California; **Virginia Crowl,** Leisure Park Elementary School, Broken Arrow, Oklahoma; **Sandra Ferenz,** Centerville Elementary School, Lancaster, Pennsylvania; **Sherry Krause,** San Miguel Elementary School, Santa Rosa, California; **Peggy Nixon,** Midway Elementary School, Sanford, Florida; **Wendi A. Wu,** East Columbus Elementary School, Columbus, Ohio

Program Reviewers

Virginia Crowl, Leisure Park Elementary School, Broken Arrow, Oklahoma; **J. Alan Fink,** Lincoln Elementary School, Oskaloosa, Iowa; **Peggy Nixon,** Spring Lake Elementary School, Altamonte Springs, Florida; **Lynn Sherwin,** Cedar Hills Elementary School, Jacksonville, Florida; **Judy Thum,** Paul Ecke Central School, Encinitas, California; **Wendi A. Wu,** Wickliffe Elementary School, Columbus, Ohio

Be a Writer Feature

Special thanks to the following teachers whose students' compositions are included in the Be a Writer features in this level:

Judy Thum, Paul Ecke Central School, Encinitas, California; **Pamela Ziegler,** Washington Elementary School, Fargo, North Dakota; **Nancy Simpson,** Friday Harbor Elementary School, Friday Harbor, Washington; **Steve Buettner,** Hammond Elementary School, Laurel, Maryland; **Sandra Grier,** Taylors Elementary School, Taylors, South Carolina; **Cydelle Greene,** Calusa Elementary School, Miami, Florida

Printed in the U.S.A.

ISBN 0-395-91451-5

123456789-WC-04 03 02 01 00 99 98

Credits

Cover photography by Tracey Wheeler.

Photography: Tony Scarpetta Photography pp. 81K, 107L

Tracey Wheeler Studio pp. 40G, 40H, 59D, 59L, 59M, 81D, 81K, 81M, 81N, 107D, 107K, 107M, 113C

Banta Digital Group pp. 38A, 39A, 40A, 40B, 40C, 40D, 41A, 59K, 59L, 59M, 59N, 63A, 81G, 81K, 81L, 81M, 91E, 91G, 107K, 107L, 107N, 113C

Cosmo Condina (Tony Stone Worldwide), p. 41D; Courtesy of Eloise Greenfield, p. 91G; Courtesy of Bud Howlett, p. 63A; Cathlyn Melloan (Tony Stone Worldwide), p. 91J; Mairo Ruiz/© Time Magazine, p. 41A

Illustration: John Dunivant, Title Page

Acknowledgments

Special thanks to David E. Freeman and Yvonne S. Freeman for their contribution to the development of the instructional support for students acquiring English.

IT'S COOL. IT'S SCHOOL.

Performance Standards

During this theme, all students will

- *Recognize how fiction selections relate to real experiences they have had at school*
- *Write a personal narrative*
- *Make inferences based on information in a selection*
- *Predict the outcome of a selection*
- *Sequence the events of a selection*
- *Revise writing with an emphasis on using complete sentences*

Launching the Program

Managing Instruction

Grouping

Group the students in different ways to meet individual needs .

- **Whole class** instruction for concepts all students need to learn.
- **Small groups** of three or more for meeting special skills needs.
- **Cooperative groups** with partners for completing a common task.
- **Individual activities** for focusing on a special need or individual choices.

INTERACTIVE LEARNING

Previewing the Literature

Cooperative Learning

Invite students to look through their anthologies with partners and to complete the graphic organizer. Discuss students' responses and reactions.

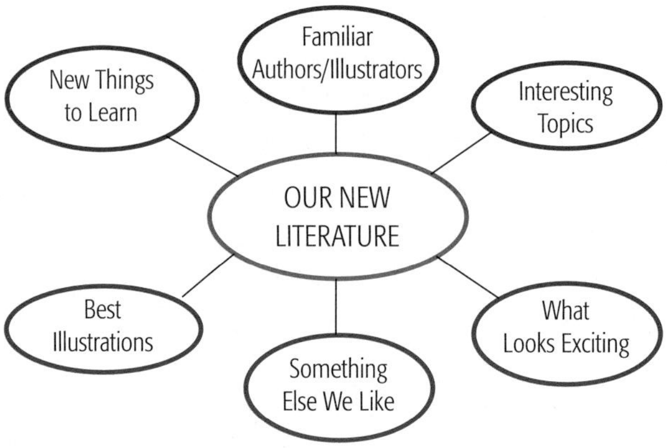

Discussing Themes

Direct the students to the table of contents, noting that the literature is organized in groups that go together called themes–**It's Cool. It's School., Meet the Challenge,** etc. Ask volunteers to read the theme titles. Have the class select one theme to preview. Divide the class into small groups. As students look through the theme, bring out the following points in discussion:

- Each theme is different and has a variety of selections.
- Students are encouraged to respond to the literature.
- Information is given about authors and illustrators.
- Student writers share their work in **Be a Writer.**

Project

Making a Poster About My Interests

Invite students to make posters that tell about their interests by drawing and gluing pictures on a piece of paper. Suggest that they use pictures that show:

- what they like to do for fun
- what their hobbies are
- what sports they play or enjoy watching
- what kind of books they like to read
- what television shows or movies they like to see
- what they like to do on vacations

Put the students' names on the backs of the posters and display them for others to see. You may want to make and display your own poster. As everyone gets to know each other, have students guess which poster belongs to which person.

Materials

- magazines
- safety scissors
- construction paper
- markers or crayons
- glue

Managing Assessment

Getting to Know Your Students

Question: How can I use this introductory time to get to know my students and their strengths?

Answer: Try these ideas:

- Look at each student's poster to identify interests and attitudes.
- Note how students express themselves during small-group and whole-group discussions.
- Note how students work with each other in completing the activity.
- Note students who are excited about the literature and seem familiar with particular authors and illustrators.
- Observe students' writing, looking for strengths and things to improve. (See Responding, page 35A and Reading-Writing Workshop, page 36A).
- Observe students' reading, looking for strengths and things to improve in comprehension (responding and discussing) and fluency (oral reading).

Give the *Baseline Group Test* or the *Informal Reading Inventory*, if needed. See *Teacher's Assessment Handbook*.

Portfolio Opportunity

Save students' posters for a record of their interests and favorite activites.

A Literacy-Centered Classroom

INTERACTIVE LEARNING

A Reading-Writing Area

Discuss with students the importance of having a place in the classroom where reading and writing get special attention.

Brainstorm with students a list of things the Reading-Writing area might have:

- books to check out
- comfortable chairs and pillows
- a rug or carpet
- a display area for things written about books students have read, as well as student-written books
- tables and bookshelves
- writing materials
- magazines and newspapers
- a checkout system for books
- plants, posters, or other items to decorate the area

Create the Reading-Writing area in your classroom by having students help decide what your space will allow. Have students sign up to be responsible for certain tasks such as arranging book displays, organizing writing materials, etc.

Add to and change the area throughout the year.

Literacy Areas Across the Curriculum

Discuss with students how they use reading, writing, listening, speaking, viewing, and thinking skills in every subject and in everyday life.

Brainstorm with students other areas the classroom might include to help them become more literate:

- a listening area
- a viewing area
- a science and social studies area
- a math table
- an area for creative projects
- a computer area

Create other areas by having students help decide what space the class will use the most. Assign groups of students to help arrange the areas.

Add to and change the areas throughout the year.

Independent Work

Making an Independent Reading-Writing Chart

Explain to students that each day there will be a time for independent reading *and* independent writing. Ask students to share their ideas about what everyone should do during these times. Record responses on a chart to display in the classroom. Encourage students to keep a copy of the chart in their journal or writing folder. During discussion bring out points such as those listed at right.

Reading	Writing
• Everyone reads during reading time. • Select reading materials before the special time. • The teacher may talk and read with the students. • Keep a record of books read. • Share with a friend what has been read.	• Everyone writes during writing time. • Write stories, letters, cartoons, and other things. • There may be teacher/student conferences. • Have a folder to keep writing. • Share your writing with a friend.

Making a Journal

Materials
- writing paper
- construction paper
- old wallpaper sample books
- notebooks

Discuss with students the purposes of journals. Point out that they can use their journals as a place to write their thoughts, questions, and feelings about what they have read. Help them see that journals are also a good place to keep lists of interesting words, things they have written, and things they want to read or write.

Invite students to create their own journals and decorate the covers. Plain notebooks or stapled pages of notebook paper can be covered with construction paper or wallpaper samples. Have students divide their journals into sections:

- Reading
- Vocabulary
- Writing
- Independent Reading
- Books I Would Like to Read
- Things I Would Like to Write

The Great Yellowstone Fire
How did the fire-fighters feel?
How did they keep from getting lost?

Managing Instruction

Independent Reading and Writing

Schedule daily time for independent reading and independent writing. Build time up to 15–20 minutes per day for each.

Journals

There are many different ways to use journals.

Encourage students to:
- record thoughts and/or feelings about what they read
- write responses
- keep a list of new/interesting words
- write predictions or questions about their reading
- list things they would like to know more about, including nonfiction topics
- list books that others have mentioned that may be interesting
- correspond with those who are reading the journal

Start a written dialogue by writing responses to students' journal entries. Invite students to write back with their next journal assignment.

Have students read a partner's journal and write a response.

INTRODUCTORY SELECTION:
Hurray for Ali Baba Bernstein

Award Winning Author
- **Sunshine State Young Reader's Award**
- **Kentucky Bluegrass Award**
- **South Carolina Children's Award**

by Johanna Hurwitz
illustrated by John Dunivant

Other Books by the Author

Busybody Nora
Class President
Class Clown

Selection Summary

Ali Baba Bernstein, a nine-year-old fourth grader, lives in New York City; his best friend is Roger Zucker. In "Ali Baba and the Mystery of the Missing Circus Tickets," Roger's family plans to go to the circus for his birthday, but Roger's sister Sugar comes down with chicken pox. Roger asks Ali Baba to go in her place. Then disaster strikes—Mrs. Zucker can't find the circus tickets. Ali Baba deduces that they are in Mrs. Zucker's raincoat pocket. But one of the guests at the Zuckers' the night before has accidentally taken the coat with the tickets in it. The boys begin a search for the right raincoat and are ultimately successful. Several tan coats are returned to their rightful owners, and Roger and Ali Baba go off to the circus.

FIVE-DAY PLANS
5-Day Planner
See pages 2–3 of the *Five-Day Lesson Plans* booklet.

Lesson Planning Guide

	Strategy Instruction	Meeting Individual Needs	Lesson Resources
1 **Introduce the Literature** *Pacing: 1 day*	**Preparing to Read and Write** Introducing a Reading Strategy, 16A **Prior Knowledge/Building Background,** 16A **Selection Vocabulary,** 17A • miraculously • miserable • mysterious • consolation • accidentally • plaid • triumphantly	**Other Choices for Building Background,** 17A	***Literacy Activity Book,*** Reading Strategies, p. 1; Vocabulary, p. 2 **Transparency,** Vocabulary, IS–1
2 **Interact with Literature** *Pacing: 1–3 days*	**Reading Strategies,** 18 **Predict/Infer,** 19 **Think About Words,** 23 **Self-Question,** 25 **Monitor,** 27 **Evaluate,** 29 **Summarize,** 33	**Choices for Reading,** 18 **Students Acquiring English,** 21 **Extra Support,** 19, 29 **Challenge,** 35 **Minilessons** Predict/Infer, 19 Think About Words, 23 Self-Question, 25 Monitor, 27 Evaluate, 29 Summarize, 33	**Reading-Writing Workshop,** 36A-36G ***Literacy Activity Book,*** Comprehension Check, p. 3; Prewriting, pp. 4–5; Revising, p. 6 The Learning Company's Ultimate Writing & Creativity Center software
Reading-Writing Workshop *Pacing: 3 days*	**About the Workshop,** 36A **Plan Your Writing,** 36C **Prewriting,** 36B–36C **Drafting,** 36D **Revising,** 36D–36E **Proofreading,** 36F **Publishing and Sharing,** 36G	**Students Acquiring English,** 36D **Minilessons** Prewriting, 36C Drafting, 36D Revising, 36E Proofreading, 36F Publishing and Sharing, 36G	The Learning Company's Ultimate Writing & Creativity Center software ***Literacy Activity Book,*** Prewriting, pp. 4–5; Revising, p. 6

The Introductory Selection provides an opportunity for students to settle into a new school year in a literacy-centered environment. This is also a time for teachers to get to know their students through informal observations of reading and writing.

Formal instruction begins with the first selection of the theme It's Cool. It's School. See page 31B.

Introduce the Literature

Preparing to Read and Write

INTERACTIVE LEARNING

Introducing a Reading Strategy

Have students work with a partner to brainstorm what they think good readers do as they read. Share and discuss students' ideas.

Direct partners to compare their ideas to the checklist on *Literacy Activity Book* page 1. As students review the checklist, bring out the following points.

- Good readers use these strategies whenever they read.
- Different strategies are used before, during, and after reading.
- As readers are learning to use strategies, they must think about how each strategy will help them.

Ask students to read the points under each strategy and discuss what they mean. Suggest that students use this checklist as they read.

Literacy Activity Book, p. 1

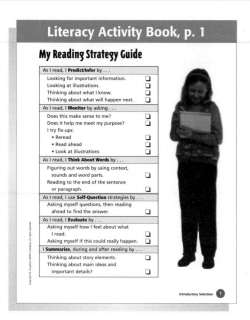

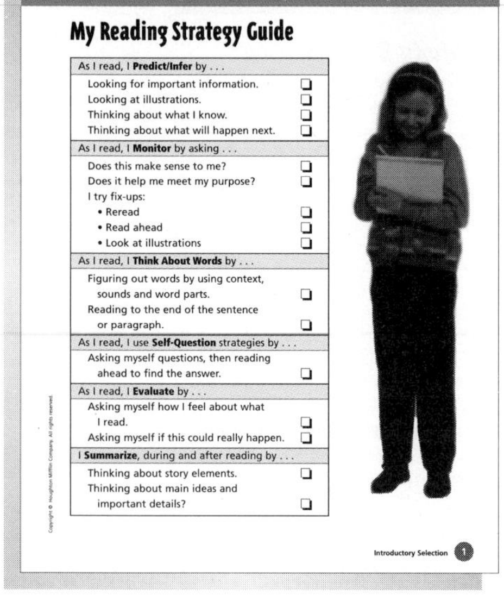
My Reading Strategy Guide

As I read, I **Predict/Infer** by . . .
- Looking for important information. ❑
- Looking at illustrations. ❑
- Thinking about what I know. ❑
- Thinking about what will happen next. ❑

As I read, I **Monitor** by asking . . .
- Does this make sense to me? ❑
- Does it help me meet my purpose? ❑
- I try fix-ups:
  - Reread ❑
  - Read ahead ❑
  - Look at illustrations ❑

As I read, I **Think About Words** by . . .
- Figuring out words by using context, sounds and word parts. ❑
- Reading to the end of the sentence or paragraph. ❑

As I read, I use **Self-Question** strategies by . . .
- Asking myself questions, then reading ahead to find the answer. ❑

As I read, I **Evaluate** by . . .
- Asking myself how I feel about what I read. ❑
- Asking myself if this could really happen. ❑

I **Summarize**, during and after reading by . . .
- Thinking about story elements. ❑
- Thinking about main ideas and important details? ❑

Introductory Selection 1

Prior Knowledge/Building Background

Key Concept: **Understanding how to look for something that is lost**

Cooperative Learning

Ask students to tell you what they know about looking for things that have been lost. Discuss different methods of finding lost things. List ideas on the board. Then ask students why each method might or might not be effective.

Looking for Lost Things

Things That Get lost	Ways to Find Lost Things	How Effective is This Method

Managing Instruction

Reading Strategies

At the beginning of and throughout each selection, students will be directed in thinking about each of the reading strategies.

In this selection, minilessons are provided to give practice with each strategy. Use these as needed to help students learn the strategies.

Other Choices for Building Background

Quick Write: Puppy or Pencil

Ask students to think about whether they would look for a lost puppy and a lost pencil in the same way. Have students write in their journals how they would look for each item.

Teacher Read Aloud

MEETING INDIVIDUAL NEEDS

Students Acquiring English Read aloud the first paragraph on page 22 of *Hurray for Ali Baba Bernstein.* Have students give the names of the items in the purse in their primary language.

Graphic Guide

Have students draw and fill in the first two columns of a Pre-Reading Guide like the one shown. Have them return to the chart after reading to fill in what they've learned about looking for lost items.

Graphic Guide

What I know about looking for lost things	What I think I will learn from the story about looking for lost things	What I have learned about looking for lost things

Transparency IS–1

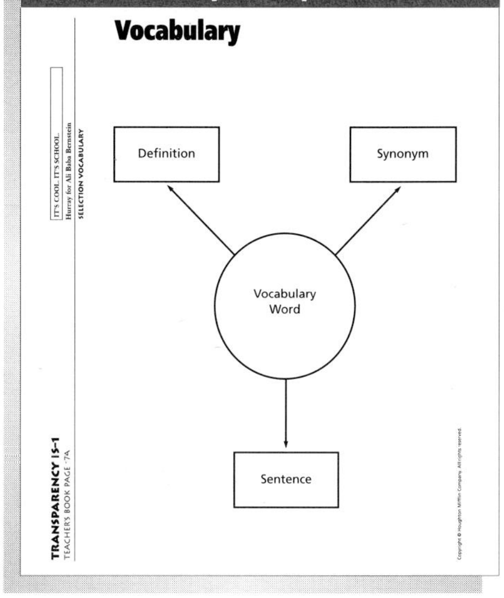

Literacy Activity Book, p. 2

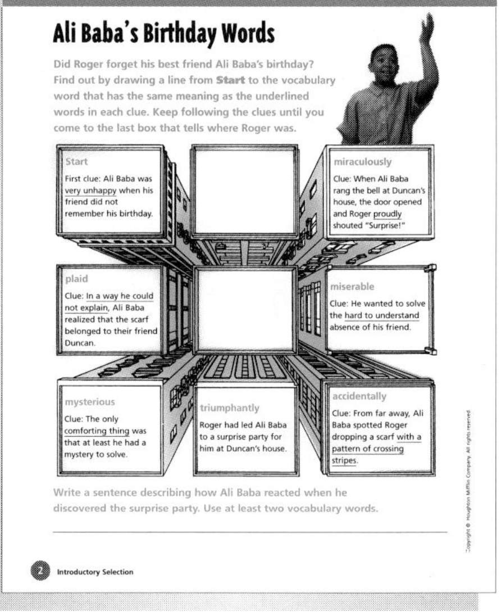
Ali Baba's Birthday Words

Did Roger forget his best friend Ali Baba's birthday? Find out by drawing a line from **Start** to the vocabulary word that has the same meaning as the underlined words in each clue. Keep following the clues until you come to the last box that tells where Roger was.

Start
First clue: Ali Baba was very unhappy when his friend did not remember his birthday.

miraculously
Clue: When Ali Baba rang the bell at Duncan's house, the door opened and Roger proudly shouted "Surprise!"

plaid
Clue: In a way he could not explain, Ali Baba realized that the scarf belonged to their friend Duncan.

miserable
Clue: He wanted to solve the hard to understand absence of his friend.

mysterious
Clue: The only comforting thing was that at least he had a mystery to solve.

triumphantly
Roger had led Ali Baba to a surprise party for him at Duncan's house.

accidentally
Clue: From far away, Ali Baba spotted Roger dropping a scarf with a pattern of crossing stripes.

Write a sentence describing how Ali Baba reacted when he discovered the surprise party. Use at least two vocabulary words.

2 Introductory Selection

Copyright © Houghton Mifflin Company. All rights reserved.

INTERACTIVE LEARNING

Selection Vocabulary

Key Words

miraculously
miserable
mysterious
consolation
accidentally
plaid
triumphantly

Display Transparency IS–1. Explain to students that they can learn more than definitions alone as they acquire vocabulary words. Then have them work in groups to complete the transparency diagram for each word. Definitions that may help are: miraculously–in a way that cannot be explained; miserable–very unhappy; mysterious–hard to explain or understand; consolation–a comforting thing, person, or event; acciden-tally–without meaning to; plaid–cloth with a pattern of crossing stripes; triumphantly–successfully.

Vocabulary Practice: Have students complete *Literacy Activity Book* page 2.

Interact *with* Literature

Reading Strategies

- ▶ **Predict/Infer**
- **Monitor**
- **Think About Words**
- **Self-Question**
- **Evaluate**
- **Summarize**

Teach/Model Have students look back at their Reading Strategies Guide on *Literacy Activity Book* page 1. Review how these strategies can help them improve their reading. Ask volunteers to tell how each strategy could help them with the story.

Predicting/Purpose Setting Invite students to look at the pictures. Ask them if they can predict what they think might happen in the story.

Choices for Reading

Give students a choice or assign them a way to read the selection:

Independent Reading	**Cooperative Reading**

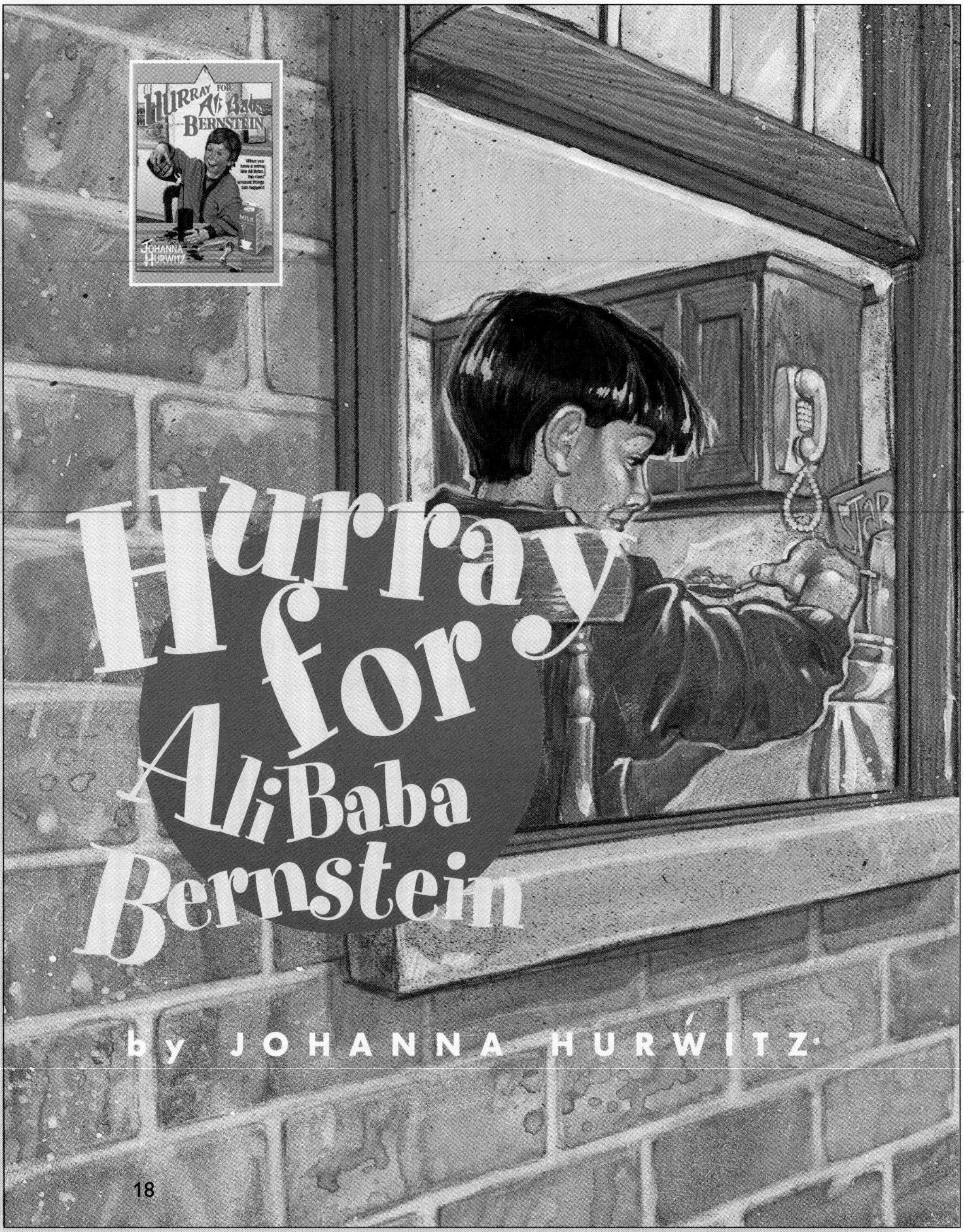

Ali Baba and the Mystery of the Missing Circus Tickets

On the Sunday morning when Ali Baba was nine years, eleven months, and four days old, his best friend, Roger Zucker, was ten years old. As a birthday treat, Roger's parents had bought three tickets to the circus. Originally the plan was for both parents to take Roger. But then Roger's little sister, Sarah, who was nicknamed Sugar, got the chicken pox. So Mrs. Zucker said that she would stay home with Sugar instead of leaving her with a baby-sitter. And that meant there was an extra ticket. Roger phoned at nine-thirty in the morning and invited Ali Baba to go with him and his father.

"Super!" shouted Ali Baba into the telephone. What great luck that Sugar had gotten the chicken pox!

19

MINILESSON

Predict/Infer

Teach/Model

Ask students if they try to figure out what will take place next in a story as they are reading. Point out that good readers use pictures and text details to predict what might happen, and that they also infer things that the author doesn't say directly. Discuss how readers can also use what they already know to help make predictions.

Practice/Apply

Ask volunteers to read aloud pages 19 and 20. Then have students work with partners to predict what they think will happen next. Have volunteers tell what clues they used to make their predictions, including information they already knew. Remind students to check their predictions as they read.

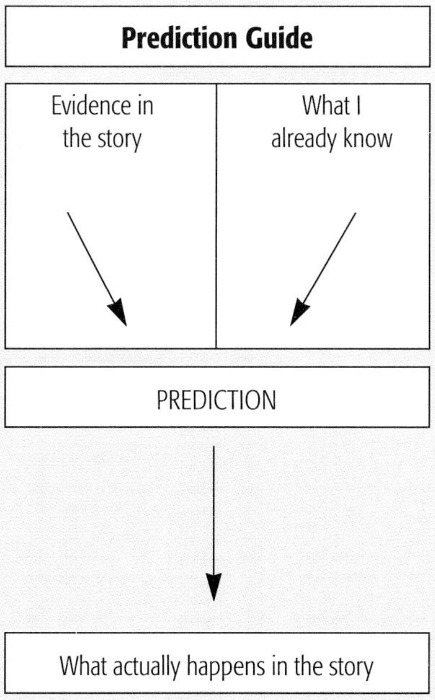

Extra Support

MEETING INDIVIDUAL NEEDS

Have students who need a more visual approach complete a Prediction Guide chart like the one shown at the right.

QuickREFERENCE

Journal

Have students write predictions in their journals to check and revise as they continue reading.

Interact *with* Literature

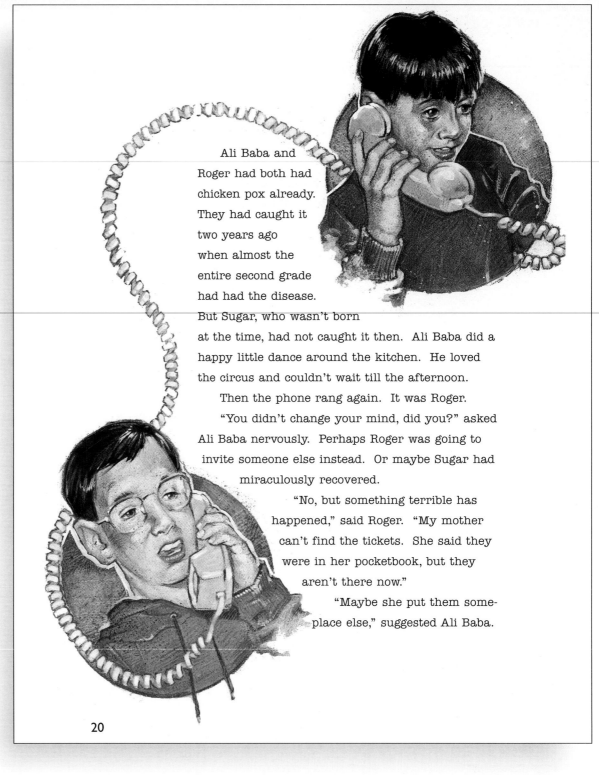

Ali Baba and Roger had both had chicken pox already. They had caught it two years ago when almost the entire second grade had had the disease. But Sugar, who wasn't born at the time, had not caught it then. Ali Baba did a happy little dance around the kitchen. He loved the circus and couldn't wait till the afternoon.

Then the phone rang again. It was Roger.

"You didn't change your mind, did you?" asked Ali Baba nervously. Perhaps Roger was going to invite someone else instead. Or maybe Sugar had miraculously recovered.

"No, but something terrible has happened," said Roger. "My mother can't find the tickets. She said they were in her pocketbook, but they aren't there now."

"Maybe she put them someplace else," suggested Ali Baba.

20

"No. She says she's certain that she put them right in her pocketbook when she bought them a couple of days ago. And she called the ticket office and they told her they've sold out all the tickets. This is the last performance, so we can't go to the circus after all." Roger sounded miserable. "This is turning out to be a rotten birthday," he said.

"Wait," said Ali Baba. "I'm coming over. We'll search your house. If they weren't stolen, we'll find them."

He hung up the phone and raced to get his jacket. "I'm going over to Roger's house," he informed his mother. And then, without any further explanation, he rushed out.

Ali Baba wanted to go to the circus very much. But there was something that he loved even more than the circus. He loved mysteries. And here were both at the same time. A mystery about the tickets, which if he solved it would mean that he would get his afternoon entertainment, too. But he had to work fast. It was already after ten o'clock. The circus was scheduled to begin at two. He had less than four hours to locate the missing tickets.

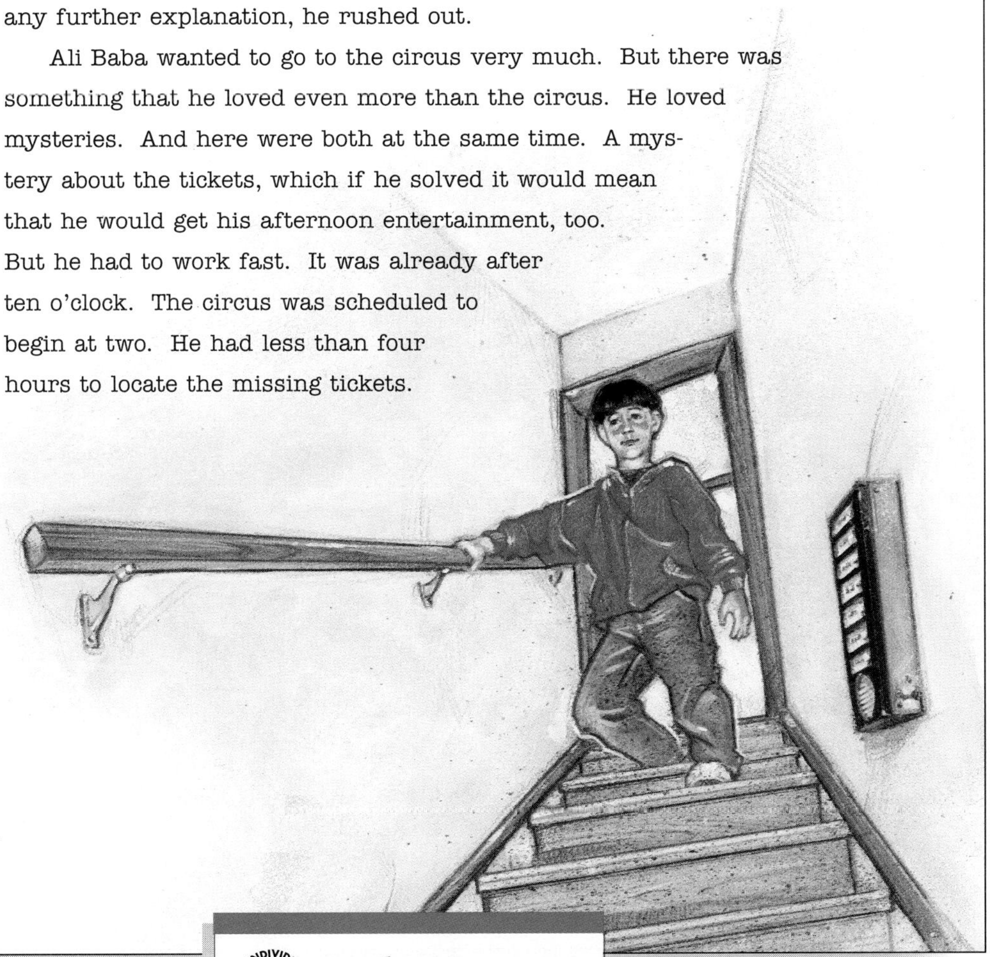

QuickREFERENCE

Multicultural Link

Ali Baba lives in New York City. Discuss with students the many cultures represented by the people who live in New York City. Compare New York's diversity with the various ethnicities represented in your classroom.

Students Acquiring English

MEETING INDIVIDUAL NEEDS

Some students might benefit from a structured preview of the illustrations that show Ali Baba's and Roger's adventures.

Interact *with* Literature

"Are you sure you put the tickets in your pocketbook?" he grilled Mrs. Zucker when he got to Roger's house. Mrs. Zucker was sitting at the kitchen table with the entire contents of her pocketbook spilled onto the table. There were her keys, sunglasses, wallet, a small notebook, a makeup case, and a package of sugarless gum. There were no circus tickets.

"I know!" said Ali Baba suddenly. "You were carrying a different pocketbook when you bought the tickets!"

It was a good idea on his part. His mother had several different pocketbooks, and which one she carried depended on which outfit she was wearing. (And Ali Baba noticed that her keys were almost always in a pocketbook that she wasn't carrying.)

Mrs. Zucker shook her head. "The handle just came off my other bag," she said. "I have to get it repaired or replaced. This is the only pocketbook I've used for the past two weeks."

Roger sighed.

"Where do you leave your pocketbook when you are at home?" asked Ali Baba. "Did anyone touch it? Could Sugar have taken the tickets out? I don't mean she stole them, but she could have taken them to play with, couldn't she?" he asked.

22

Informal Assessment

As students read, make notes about:

- how long they stay on task
- how oral readers decode words
- how they use root words, prefixes, and suffixes to determine meaning

"I keep my pocketbook on a shelf in the closet. She can't reach it," explained Mrs. Zucker. "Besides, even if she could, she wouldn't be able to open the clasp on the bag."

Ali Baba sighed.

"I'm looking to see if there is a good movie playing," called Mr. Zucker from the next room. He had the newspaper open before him and had promised the boys to take them to a film as a consolation. But neither boy wanted a movie. What was a movie compared to the circus?

"Could you have put the tickets in your pocket?" Ali Baba suggested. "Did you look in your coat pocket?"

Mrs. Zucker gasped. "I think you're right!" she said, jumping up. "I think I stuffed the tickets into my raincoat pocket. How silly of me to forget." She jumped up and went to the closet. "See, here they are," she said, pulling an envelope out of the pocket. However, the envelope did not contain circus tickets. There were grocery coupons to get fifteen and twenty cents off on cat food and coffee and things like that.

"How did these get into my pocket?" Mrs. Zucker asked. She

23

MINILESSON

Think About Words

Teach/Model

Mention to students that all readers come across new words. Good readers use clues to figure out how to say the word and what it means. Discuss the following chart.

Hints
1. Think about what makes sense.
2. Read to the end of the sentence or paragraph to see if that helps.
3. Sound out letters or word parts.
4. How does the word begin?
5. How does the word end?
6. What word parts do you know?

Other Clues
1. Look at the pictures.
2. Think of other words that look like the new word.

Think Aloud

As I read I come to the word *consolation*, a word that I don't know. I read the sentence again. I read the next sentence. I know that going to a film is their second choice. I have heard of a consolation prize. That could also be a second choice for not winning. *Consolation* must be another word for not getting your first choice.

Practice/Apply

Have students work with partners to select another word in the story and tell how they could figure out what it means and how to pronounce it.

Interact *with* Literature

inspected the coat closely. "This isn't my coat," she exclaimed.

"Whose coat is it?" asked Ali Baba excitedly. This mystery was getting more and more mysterious.

Mrs. Zucker shrugged her shoulders. "I don't know," she said. "I guess someone took my coat from the closet and left this one instead."

"How can we find out who it was?" asked Roger.

Just then the telephone rang. Mrs. Zucker went to answer it as Roger and Ali Baba stood looking at each other helplessly.

"It's here! I have it!" Mrs. Zucker shouted happily into the phone. "I'll have Roger bring it over to you right away."

She hung up the receiver and smiled brightly. "Your worries are over," she said. "That was Rosie Relkin. She was here last night with some of our friends for coffee and dessert. And she accidentally took the wrong raincoat when she went home. So all you have to do is drop off this one at her apartment and get mine."

"Did you ask her if there were circus tickets in the pocket?" asked Roger.

"Don't be silly," said his mother. "Of course the tickets are in the pocket. You'll see for yourself as soon as you get the coat."

24

Self-Assessment

Ask students how they are helping themselves with their reading. Have them ask:

- Am I understanding the story?
- Am I thinking about words and making predictions?
- Am I figuring out the main idea?
- Do I like the story so far?

"Let's get going," said Ali Baba. "Where does Rosie Relkin live?"

It was only two blocks to Rosie Relkin's apartment. She opened the door as soon as the boys rang the bell. She had been waiting for them.

"Here," said Roger, exchanging the tan raincoat in his arms for the one Rosie Relkin held out. Roger put his hands into the pockets and immediately pulled out an envelope addressed to Kit Conners and a subway token. But there were no circus tickets.

"Where are the tickets? They're not in either pocket," said Roger, mystified. "And what is this letter doing in my mother's pocket?"

"That can't be your mother's coat," Ali Baba said. "It must belong to someone named Kit Conners."

"This isn't my coat, either," said Rosie Relkin, handing back the coat that Roger had given her. "Mine has a red plaid lining. This is blue."

Roger took one raincoat, and Ali Baba took the other. "Who do they belong to?" Ali Baba asked.

"And what about the circus tickets?" asked Roger.

MINILESSON

Self-Question

Teach/Model

Ask students if they have any questions about the story so far. Record their questions on the board. Explain that good readers ask questions as they read and then keep reading to find their answers.

Practice/Apply

Ask volunteers to tell what questions they want to have answered as they read more of the story.

Examples might include:

Will the boys actually find the tickets?

Will the boys get to go to the circus?

What other things could keep them from going?

Will they get to the circus before it starts?

Interact *with* Literature

"I bet Kit Conners took my coat," said Rosie Relkin. "She was at the Zuckers' apartment last night, too."

"What about Mrs. Zucker's coat?" asked Ali Baba. "Where do you think that is?"

Rosie Relkin shook her head. "I don't know," she said. "This is quite a tangle. But I'd really appreciate it if you took this over to Kit Conners's apartment and brought my coat to me. Kit only lives a block away."

"I wonder if we'll ever get to the circus?" Roger sighed as the two boys and the two raincoats went off in the direction of Kit Conners's apartment.

"Maybe Kit Conners has your mother's coat," said Ali Baba. "We've got to find those tickets before two o'clock."

"And we still have to find Rosie Relkin's raincoat for her, too," Roger said.

"You know something?" said Ali Baba. "If I were president of the United States, I would make a law against these tan raincoats. Why does everyone wear the same kind of coat?"

Kit Conners was delighted to see the boys. "Rosie Relkin phoned to tell me you were coming. She said you had my coat. I didn't realize that I had taken the wrong one last night. But I looked now, and sure enough, I've got someone else's."

She took the coat that Roger gave her. "It's mine, all right," she said. "I wonder whose coat I wore home last night?"

26

Informal Assessment

As students read, make notes about how well they stick to the task and whether they seem to be enjoying it. If any students are reading aloud, note how well they decode words.

QuickREFERENCE

Journal

Have students record in their journals what they would do if they were president of the United States and had lost something important.

"It must be my mother's," said Roger.

"It might belong to Rosie Relkin," Ali Baba reminded his friend. "Her coat is still missing, too."

Kit Conners handed Roger a coat that was a clone of the one that he had given her. However, on closer inspection, the lining was different. "It's not Rosie Relkin's raincoat," said Ali Baba. The lining was green plaid.

"I never noticed what color lining my mother's coat had," said Roger. "Up until today it never mattered. But I sure hope the lining of her coat is green plaid and that this is it." He put his hands inside the pockets of the coat that Kit Conners had handed him. "What's this?" he asked.

"Let's see," demanded Ali Baba.

Roger handed Ali Baba a baby's pacifier.

"Does your sister still use one of these?" asked Ali Baba.

"No," said Roger with disgust. "She outgrew it ages ago."

"Margie and George Upchurch were at your house last night," Kit Conners told Roger. "They have a six-month-old baby. I bet this coat belongs to Margie. Let me give you her address."

27

MINILESSON

Monitor

Teach/Model

Explain that when you monitor something, you keep watch over it. Readers monitor their reading to make sure they understand what they read. Discuss how rereading, finding answers to questions, checking predictions, and reading further can help readers understand a selection.

Think Aloud

I can use monitoring to keep track of all the coats that have been mentioned so far. I may want to make a list of how many coats there are, what each coat looks like, what's in its pockets, and who it belongs to. I can complete the list as I read.

Practice/Apply

Have students read pages 28–29 and practice monitoring. Do they understand what is happening, especially with the baby and the pacifier and the last raincoat?

Technology Tip

Students could build a data base listing the owner of each coat, a description of each coat, what was found in the pockets of each coat, etc.

Interact *with* Literature

"Your parents have too many friends," complained Ali Baba.

A minute later the boys were off looking for the street where the Upchurch family lived.

"That can't be my coat," said Margie Upchurch when Ali Baba and Roger Zucker tried explaining about the mix-up of the raincoats the night before. "I wore my coat home," she shouted above the wails of a crying baby.

In the background Ali Baba could see Mr. Upchurch, unshaven and still in his bathrobe, trying to comfort the infant.

"It must be your coat," said Ali Baba. "There was a pacifier in the pocket, and we can see you have a baby."

Mrs. Upchurch looked surprised at this piece of information. "A pacifier?" she asked with delight. "We've been looking all over the house for one of the baby's pacifiers, and they've all disappeared." She examined the object that Roger handed her.

"Let me just go and wash it," she shouted above the baby's cries. A minute later the clean pacifier was in the baby's mouth and all was quiet. Then Margie Upchurch went to her closet and took out still another tan raincoat.

28

Informal Assessment

Ask students to read aloud one of these pages to check decoding. See the *Teacher's Assessment Handbook* for an oral reading checklist.

"I don't know who this one belongs to," she said.

Roger looked at the coat hopefully. "You look," he told Ali Baba. "I'm scared."

Ali Baba wasn't scared at all. He was confident that they had finally tracked down the correct coat. He put his hands into the pockets and triumphantly pulled out a small envelope from one of them. Inside there were three tan tickets for that afternoon's circus performance. The tickets were the same color as all of the coats.

"Hurray! We did it! We found the tickets!" he began shouting. Of all the mysteries he had ever attempted to solve, this had been the most successful.

But there was still one small mystery before the boys.

"Whose raincoat is this?" asked Margie Upchurch, pointing to the other one that was still unclaimed.

MINILESSON

Evaluate

Teach/Model

Explain that good readers evaluate what they read. They do this by asking questions such as:

1. How do I feel about this? Why?
2. Do I believe this could really happen?

Ask a volunteer to tell how he or she feels about the story so far. Explain that in so doing they are evaluating.

Practice/Apply

Ask students to read pages 28–29. Then ask volunteers what they think of these pages. Could these things really happen? What are some other ways to evaluate as they read?

How does the character act and feel?	How do others feel about the character?

Character

What does the character look like?	Do I like this character? Why?

QuickREFERENCE

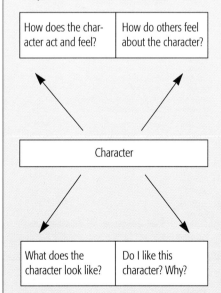

Extra Support

Some students may be more successful at evaluating one part of the story at a time. Have students complete the character evaluation chart at the right.

Interact *with* Literature

"We don't know. It isn't Rosie Relkin's," said Roger. He pulled the envelope with the grocery coupons out of the mystery raincoat. "These could belong to anyone."

"Not just anyone," Ali Baba pointed out. "They must belong to someone who has a cat."

"Muriel and Alfred Thomas were at your house last night," Margie Upchurch told Roger. "And they have a cat," she added. "I can't ever go to their house because I have an allergy to cats. They make my eyes tear and make me sneeze, too." She went off to check the exact address where the Thomases lived.

Muriel Thomas was just as surprised as Mrs. Upchurch to discover that she had taken the wrong raincoat the evening before. She traded coats with Roger, giving him a coat with a red lining in exchange for the one he carried with a blue lining. And then the boys retraced their steps and returned to Rosie Relkin's apartment.

"Thank goodness you found it!" Rosie Relkin said, clutching her raincoat as if it were a very precious item.

Ali Baba thought that was very funny. It wasn't as if she had lost something unique. All the coats looked the same — what difference did it make what color the lining was? Once you put the coat on, no one could see the lining inside.

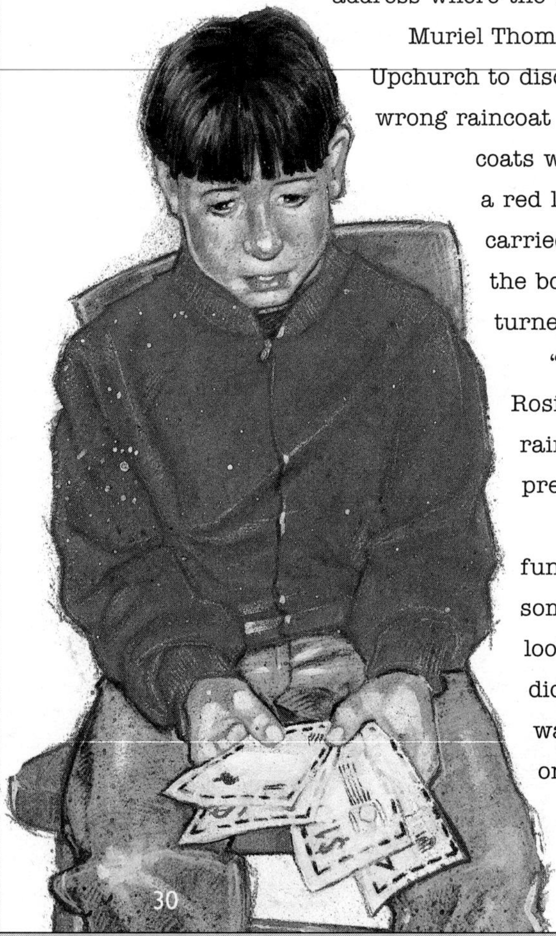

30

Self-Assessment

Ask students to talk about reading the story. Have them answer questions about the experience:

- Did I think reading the story was easy or difficult? What made it easy/difficult?
- Which adult did I like best? Why did I like that particular adult?

To the boys the unique coat was the one with the circus tickets in the pocket. Ali Baba and Roger Zucker ran all the way back to the Zucker apartment.

"I'm glad you got my coat from Rosie Relkin," said Mrs. Zucker when she saw the boys.

"We didn't get it from Rosie Relkin," announced Roger.

"What do you mean?" asked Mrs. Zucker.

"It will take too long to explain," said Roger. "We've got to hurry if we're going to get to the circus on time."

But there was still enough time for Ali Baba to phone home and tell his parents that he was going off to the circus with Roger. They also had time enough to admire Sugar's chicken pox and to eat a quick lunch. And finally Mr. Zucker, Roger, and Ali Baba were off to the circus.

Interact *with* Literature

"How does it feel being ten?" Mr. Zucker asked his son as the three of them rode downtown on the bus.

"I don't know," Roger complained. "I've been too busy this morning to think about it."

"We sure solved a big mystery," said Ali Baba proudly. He felt like a real private eye. Imagine, a mystery and a circus all on the same day. **It was super!**

Johanna Hurwitz

Meet the Author

Books and stories played a big part in Johanna Hurwitz's life even before she was born — her parents met each other in a bookstore in New York City. Hurwitz grew up in an apartment stuffed with books and says that some of her "happiest early memories are of being read to by my parents."

When Hurwitz was eight, she began telling stories to her two-year-old brother William. William's interest in her stories, Hurwitz says, was important in "sparking my writing career." Hurwitz also loved the public library, and at the age of ten decided to be a librarian. At the same time, she decided to become a writer.

She did succeed in becoming a librarian by the age of twenty-two, but she was almost forty before she published her first book, *Busybody Nora.*

Hurwitz has written more than thirty books for young people. You may have read or heard of *School Spirit, Class Clown,* and *The Adventures of Ali Baba Bernstein.*

John Dunivant

Meet the Illustrator

John Dunivant has been drawing ever since he can remember. When he was six, he saw the movie *Star Wars* and began to concentrate on drawing creatures and spaceships. Later, when he received a book of the paintings and drawings that were used to plan the film, he says, "I realized 'grown-ups' do this too," and began to think of art as "my destiny."

When Dunivant does illustrations, such as the ones he did for this selection, he tries to imagine himself in the situations described in the story. He usually listens to music when he works, often the soundtrack from — you guessed it — *Star Wars.*

33

MINILESSON

Summarizing

Teach/Model

Explain that a summary tells the main parts of the story. To summarize a story like *Hurray for Ali Baba Bernstein* a reader thinks about story elements–characters, setting, plot, and theme. Draw the chart and use the Think Aloud to help students fill it in.

Characters
Setting
Plot Event 1 Event 2 Event 3, etc.
Theme

Think Aloud

I know that Ali Baba and Roger are the main characters. They live in New York City and want to go to the circus. However, they can't find the circus tickets. The action in the story–the plot–is made up of the search for the missing tickets. The story ends happily after the boys track down several coats that had been accidentally swapped. The theme has to do with thinking things through and sticking to a task: hard work pays off. Now I can summarize the story.

Practice/Apply

Ask volunteers to give a summary of the story. Then have students work with partners to write a summary of another well-known story.

Interact *with* Literature

More About the Author

Johanna Hurwitz

When Johanna Hurwitz is creating a character, she visits schools and watches what real children do and say. Then she uses her considerable story-telling skills to turn her observations into an Ali Baba Bernstein, a busybody named Nora, or a class clown named Julio.

Hurwitz was born in New York City in 1937, the oldest of two children. She attended Queens College and then worked as a children's librarian. Later she became a lecturer on children's literature. She published her first novel, *Busybody Nora*, in 1976, and has gone on to write more than thirty other juvenile novels. Hurwitz does not plan to write adult novels; she likes writing about childhood. She says, "There is an intensity and seriousness about childhood that fascinates me." Hurwitz is married with two grown children. She lives in Great Neck, New York.

RESPONDING

That's the

Draw a Map

Which Way Did He Go?

Use the details from the story to help you draw a map of Ali Baba's neighborhood. Label all the places where he and Roger stopped in their search for the tickets. Then draw the route that the boys followed as they went from one house to the next.

Write a Letter

You Do the Explaining

When Mrs. Zucker asked Ali Baba and Roger how they found her coat, Roger replied, "It will take too long to explain." How would you explain what happened? Write a letter to Mrs. Zucker telling her how Roger and Ali Baba found her coat with the tickets.

34

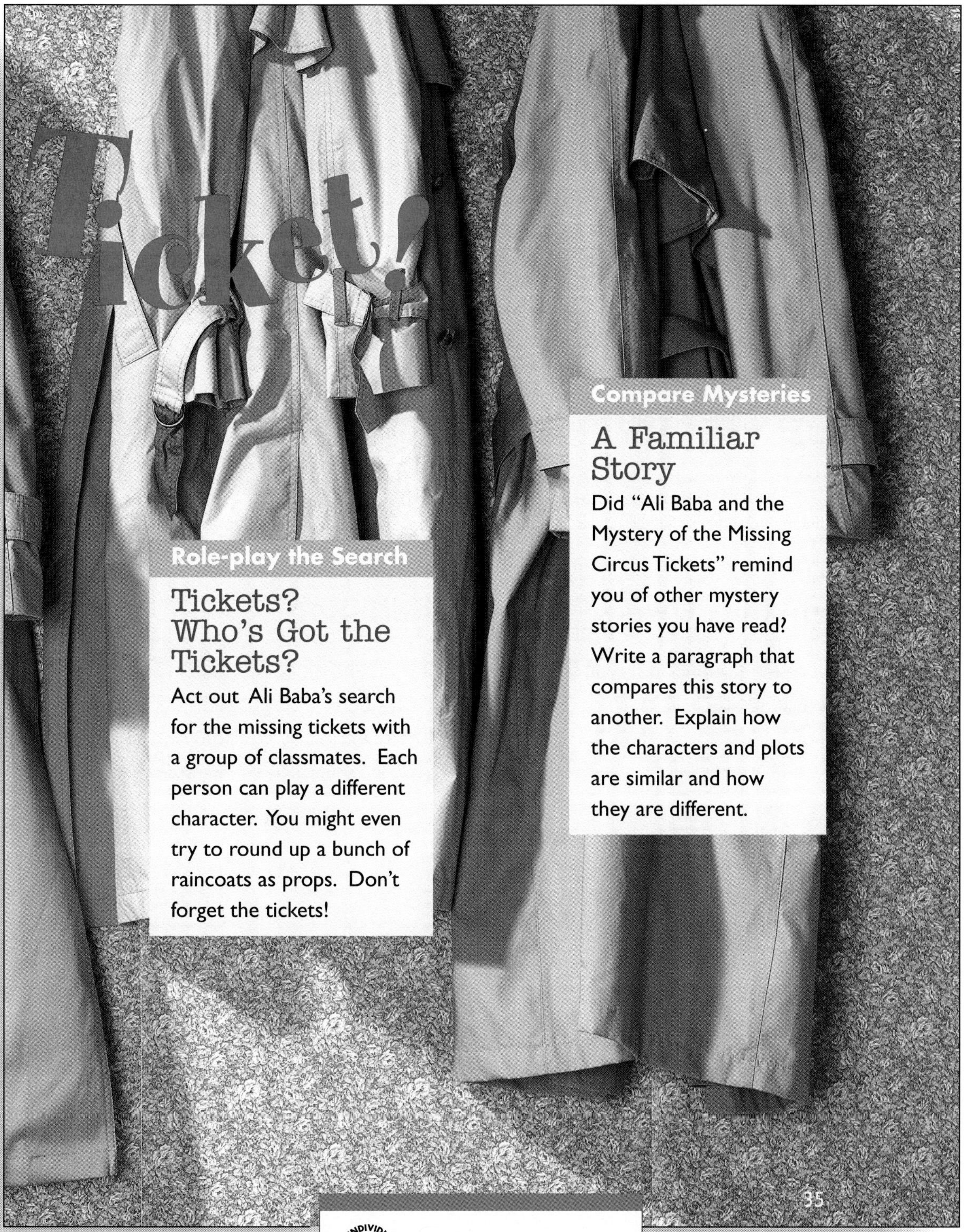
Ticket!

Role-play the Search

Tickets? Who's Got the Tickets?

Act out Ali Baba's search for the missing tickets with a group of classmates. Each person can play a different character. You might even try to round up a bunch of raincoats as props. Don't forget the tickets!

Compare Mysteries

A Familiar Story

Did "Ali Baba and the Mystery of the Missing Circus Tickets" remind you of other mystery stories you have read? Write a paragraph that compares this story to another. Explain how the characters and plots are similar and how they are different.

35

Responding Activities

Personal Response

Have students write a journal entry using one of the following prompts.

1. What was your favorite part of the story? Why did you like it best?
2. Did you feel the mix-up with the raincoats could have really happened?
3. Why did you or didn't you like the story?

Anthology Activities

Students can choose one of the activities on Anthology pages 34–35 to do alone or with a partner.

QuickREFERENCE

Home Connection

Have students interview someone older at home to find out about a time he or she lost something that was very important. Share and discuss their findings.

Challenge

MEETING INDIVIDUAL NEEDS

Invite students to write about a time when they lost something.

Informal Assessment

Use student responses and the comprehension check on page 36 to assess general understanding of the story. If you need more information about each student's comprehension, have them individually retell the story. See *Teacher's Assessment Handbook.*

Responding *(continued)*

Comprehension Check

Use *Literacy Activity Book* page 3 and/or the following questions to check comprehension:

1. Besides the idea of going to the circus, why does Ali Baba want to look for the tickets? (He loves a mystery.)
2. Why was it possible for each of the adults to have taken the wrong coat? (The coats were nearly identical.)
3. Where did Ali Baba and Roger find the clues that led them to the owner of each coat? (in the coat pockets)

Managing Instruction

Literature Discussion Circles

- Develop with students a set of guidelines for behavior during Discussion Circles.
- Divide the class into groups of 3 to 5; let students select their group occasionally.
- Give students prompts to direct discussion:

  How is this book like others you have read?
  Would you like to solve mysteries?
  Tell about a time you solved a mystery.
- Allow 3-5 minutes for discussion. Move among groups to observe and participate.

Portfolio Opportunity

- For a record of selection comprehension, save *Literacy Activity Book* page 3.
- For a writing sample, save each student's personal response.

More Responding Activities

Literature Discussion

- What surprised you in the story?
- What do you think Mrs. Bernstein learned?

Write a Poem

Have students work in pairs to write a poem about *Hurray for Ali Baba Bernstein.*

Design Your Own

Invite interested students to design their own tickets to the circus.

Retelling

If you need more information about each student's comprehension, have them individually retell the story. See *Teacher's Assessment Handbook*.

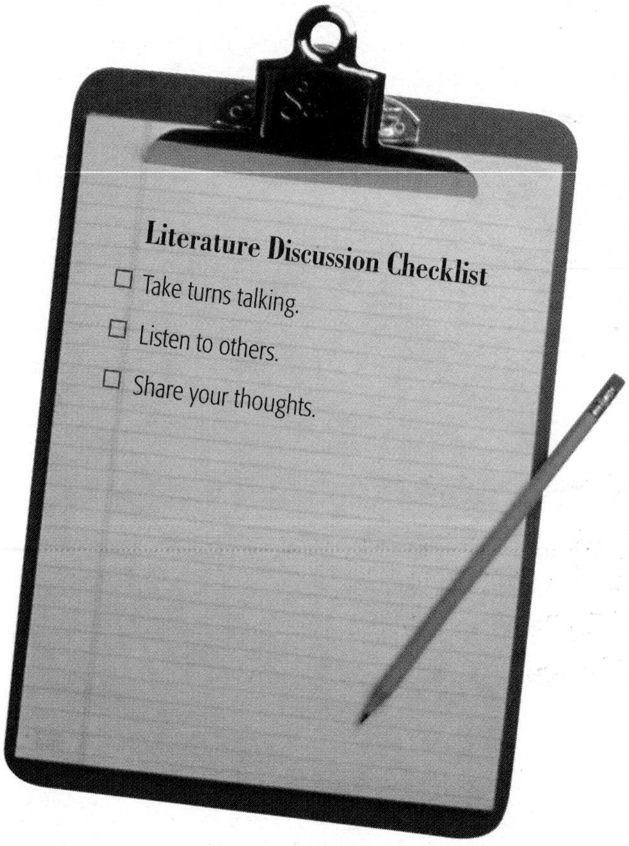

Literacy Activity Book, p. 3

Reading-Writing Workshop

A CLASS BOOK

About the Workshop

The Reading-Writing Workshops throughout *Invitations to Literacy* are designed to help you guide students through a writing project, using the writing process. Within the guidelines for each workshop, students can develop writing on topics they choose themselves. Minilessons offer brief, point-of-use instruction on specific points about writing. In this introductory workshop, students write and publish a class book about their favorite activities. The minilessons focus on the stages of the writing process to build background on the process approach.

In this and other workshops, keep these points in mind:

Writing Process
Encourage students to use the writing process as a guide, not as a rigid sequence of steps.

Selecting Topics
Give students freedom to select their own topics. Each workshop suggests ways for them to get ideas for topics to write about.

Switching Topics
Allow students to abandon an unsatisfying or frustrating piece and begin again with a new topic or a different approach.

Work Environment
Provide a classroom atmosphere where students feel comfortable working at their own pace.

Minilessons
Use minilessons as needed for whole-class or small-group instruction.

Peer Support
Encourage students to help each other throughout the process, especially in peer conferences.

Publishing
Celebrate students' writing by providing many different opportunities for publishing and sharing. Help students create such occasions.

Independent Writing
Provide time each day for students to write independently as well as time to continue their workshop activities.

Connecting to *Hurray for Ali Baba Bernstein*

Ask students to tell about a time when they were unable to do an activity they really wanted to do. How did they respond to the situation? Have students think of other ways Ali Baba and Roger could have spent the afternoon.

Reading-Writing Workshop
A Class Book

Warm-Up

Shared Writing

Brainstorm with students a list of their favorite things to do. Elicit that this information will help classmates get to know each other. Suggestions might include going to the circus or the movies, reading a book, or playing with friends. Record responses on the chalkboard.

Discuss possible ways of sharing the information with each other and with visitors to the classroom. Guide students to see that writing a class book would be a good way to put together all the information about themselves. Continue brainstorming about what else could go in the book.

Prewriting

LAB, pp. 4, 5

Choose a Topic

Students narrow their topic choices, discuss them, and select their topic.

- **Narrow the Choices** Invite students to choose three topics that interest them and that they would like to write about.
- **Talk and Think About It** Have partners explore their topic choices, answering these questions about each one: Why do I want to write about this topic? What will it tell people about me? Can I write several paragraphs about it?
- **Settle on a Topic** Bring the class back together. Ask each student to choose one of their topics to write about.

Help with Topics

Side by Side

Students may want to write about an activity they can do either alone or with someone else. Encourage students to think about how the activity changes in each situation.

Use Your Imagination

Invite students to write about something they have never done but would like to do. Ask them to explain the appeal of a new activity.

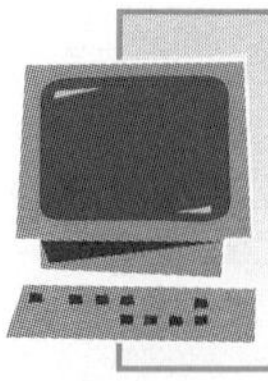

Students can use The Learning Company's new elementary writing center to brainstorm and organize their ideas.

Prewriting *(continued)*

Plan Your Writing Students plan their page, listing and organizing their ideas on the graphic organizer before writing a first draft.

- **Main Idea and Details** Ask students to jot down their main ideas. Under each idea, have them write details that go with it.

Help with Planning

Cut It Out

Students can rearrange their ideas by cutting and pasting them in a new order.

Students using a word processor can use the Cut and Paste features to reorganize ideas.

Put It In Order!

Talk about ways to put ideas in the best order. Encourage students to think about what makes sense, what should come first, and what is the most important part.

Literacy Activity Book, p. 4

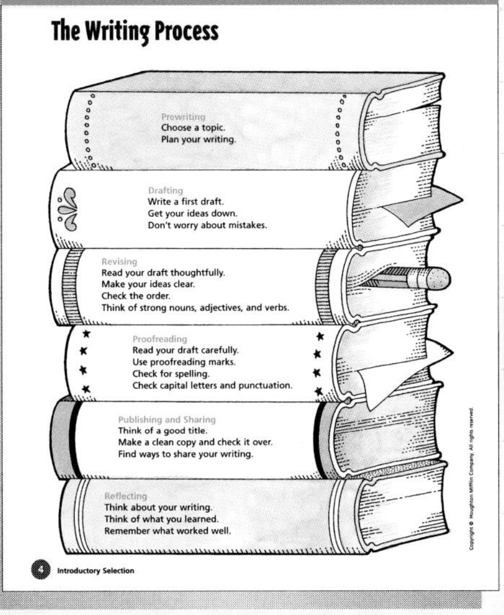

The Writing Process

Prewriting
Choose a topic.
Plan your writing.

Drafting
Write a first draft.
Get your ideas down.
Don't worry about mistakes.

Revising
Read your draft thoughtfully.
Make your ideas clear.
Check the order.
Think of strong nouns, adjectives, and verbs.

Proofreading
Read your draft carefully.
Use proofreading marks.
Check for spelling.
Check capital letters and punctuation.

Publishing and Sharing
Think of a good title.
Make a clean copy and check it over.
Find ways to share your writing.

Reflecting
Think about your writing.
Think of what you learned.
Remember what worked well.

4 Introductory Selection

Copyright © Houghton Mifflin Company. All rights reserved.

Literacy Activity Book, p. 5

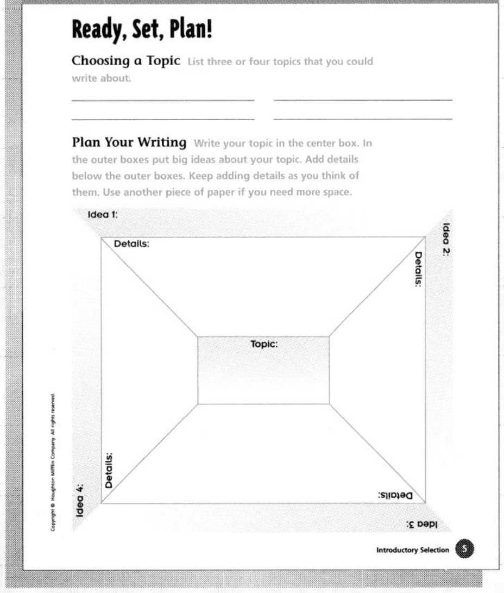

Ready, Set, Plan!

Choosing a Topic List three or four topics that you could write about.

Plan Your Writing Write your topic in the center box. In the outer boxes put big ideas about your topic. Add details below the outer boxes. Keep adding details as you think of them. Use another piece of paper if you need more space.

Idea 1:
Details:
Idea 2:
Details:
Topic:
Idea 3:
Details:
Idea 4:
Details:

Introductory Selection 5

Copyright © Houghton Mifflin Company. All rights reserved.

MINILESSON

Prewriting

LAB, p. 4

Use *Literacy Activity Book* page 4 to review the writing process. Students can use this page as a reminder not to try to do everything at once.

Discuss with students how to get started writing. Elicit that a good topic is one you're interested in, know something about, or want to learn about. Ask how to get ideas:

- brainstorm
- make lists
- look at pictures
- answer partner's questions
- make a cluster or web of activities
- make a Venn diagram to compare and contrast

You may want to model one of the prewriting strategies for your own page of the class book.

Next, discuss what to do with a topic once it's chosen.

- list ideas and details
- make a cluster or web
- think about a good order

Continue modeling your own prewriting. Emphasize to students that there isn't a right or wrong method. They can try different ways and see what works best for them and their topic.

Reading-Writing Workshop *(continued)*
A Class Book

MINILESSON

Drafting

Ask students to compare two ways of making cookies: 1) with a recipe and the right ingredients or 2) without a recipe and using whatever you find. Compare prewriting with planning to cook something. Now that students have a recipe (their plan), writing a first draft should go smoothly.

Be sure students understand the term *first draft*. Emphasize the word *first* and that drafting is simply getting ideas into words and down on paper. Assure them they'll have plenty of time to make changes and corrections when they revise and proofread.

Discuss these guidelines for drafting:

- Think about your purpose and who your readers will be.
- Write down your ideas quickly.
- Don't worry now about spelling or punctuation.
- If you get stuck, do more prewriting.

Self-Assessment

Have students evaluate what they have written, using the Revising Checklist on *Literacy Activity Book* page 6.

Drafting

Students use their prewriting notes to write a first draft.

- **Getting Ideas Down** Remind students that the purpose of a first draft is to get ideas on paper. They shouldn't worry about mistakes now.

Help with Drafting

Tips for Drafting

Have students write on every other line to allow space for corrections later. Writing on only one side of their paper will also allow them to cut and move sentences during revising. Reassure students that it's all right if their first draft is messy.

Keep Writing!

MEETING INDIVIDUAL NEEDS

Students Acquiring English Encourage students to keep writing, even if they're unsure about how to say something. They should feel free to ask a classmate questions if they need to.

Revising

LAB, p. 6

Students revise their drafts and discuss them in writing conferences.

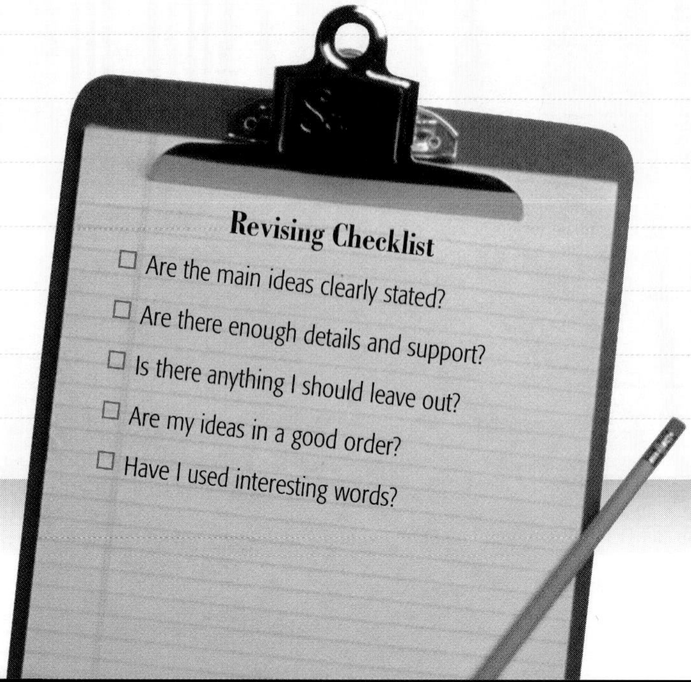

Revising Checklist
☐ Are the main ideas clearly stated?
☐ Are there enough details and support?
☐ Is there anything I should leave out?
☐ Are my ideas in a good order?
☐ Have I used interesting words?

Revising *(continued)*

Writing Conference

Cooperative Learning Invite students to read aloud their revised draft with you or a partner. When they've listened to a partner's writing, they can use these questions, which appear on *Literacy Activity Book* page 6. You may need to modify the questions to make them specific to the type of writing your students are doing.

Questions for a Writing Conference

- What is the best thing about this piece?
- Does it stay on the topic?
- Does it seem well organized?
- Does it help me learn about what this person enjoys doing?
- What additional information would I like to know?
- What information seems unclear?
- Does the piece of writing end in a strong way?

Help with Revising

Out with the Old

Remind students not to be tied to everything they've written down. Encourage them to take out whole sentences or completely change the order of their ideas.

Writer to Writer

Remind students to be positive and helpful in their writing conferences. Encourage partners to ask one another questions and to make suggestions.

MINILESSON

Revising

LAB, p. 6

Provide a sample of writing from your own draft page for the class book. Be sure that your sample is in first draft form, needing revision.

- Ask volunteers to suggest ways to revise your writing. Model how to use questions to guide revision. Have students help you think of interesting words and to find areas that are unclear.
- Use students' suggestions for revisions by using arrows and crossing out words. Have a volunteer read the revision aloud.
- Discuss how the revisions have made the writing clearer. Remind students that revising helps readers know what the writer really means.

Literacy Activity Book, p. 6

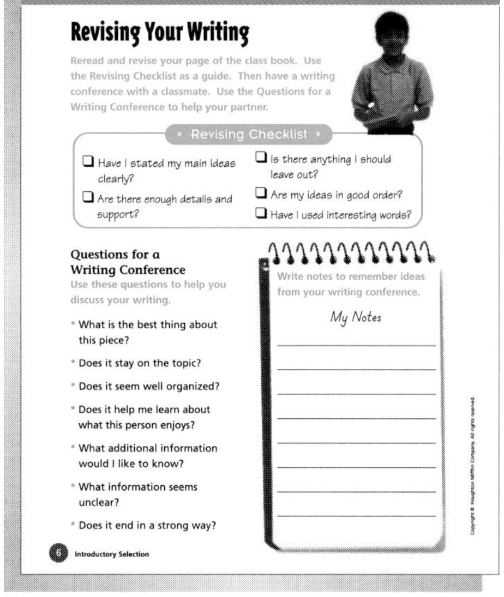
Revising Your Writing

Reread and revise your page of the class book. Use the Revising Checklist as a guide. Then have a writing conference with a classmate. Use the Questions for a Writing Conference to help your partner.

Revising Checklist

- ❑ Have I stated my main ideas clearly?
- ❑ Are there enough details and support?
- ❑ Is there anything I should leave out?
- ❑ Are my ideas in good order?
- ❑ Have I used interesting words?

Questions for a Writing Conference

Use these questions to help you discuss your writing.

- What is the best thing about this piece?
- Does it stay on the topic?
- Does it seem well organized?
- Does it help me learn about what this person enjoys?
- What additional information would I like to know?
- What information seems unclear?
- Does it end in a strong way?

Write notes to remember ideas from your writing conference.

My Notes

6 Introductory Selection

Reading-Writing Workshop *(continued)*
A Class Book

MINILESSON

Proofreading

Congratulate students on their revising efforts. Tell them now is the time to check for mistakes in spelling, punctuation, and grammar. Discuss why it is important to make their work as error free as possible.

Review proofreading marks with students. They can refer to the list in the Handbook at the back of the *Literacy Activity Book*. Write these marks on the chalkboard.

- ¶ Indent new paragraph
- ^ Add something
- Take out something
- ≡ Capitalize
- / Make lowercase letter

Next, write this sentence on the chalkboard without the corrections.

i like going to the
cirkus, but my favrite
thing do is _______.

(In the corrected version, "i" is marked for capitalization, "c" replaces the "k" in "cirkus", the comma is replaced by a period, "o" is added in "favrite", and "to" is inserted after "thing".)

Ask volunteers to make any necessary corrections, using proofreading marks. Then have them complete the sentence.

Proofreading

Students proofread their revised drafts, correcting errors in spelling, grammar, and capitalization.

Grammar and Spelling Connections

- **Checking Sentences** Remind students to check that each sentence begins with a capital letter and ends with the right punctuation.
- **Proper Nouns** Have students check that names of particular people and places begin with capital letters. Have them also check to see that they don't have unneeded capital letters.
- **Spelling** Have them check each word for spelling. Encourage them to use a dictionary to check spelling of less familiar words.

Help with Proofreading

Proofreading Marks

Refer students to the proofreading marks in the Handbook at the back of the *Literacy Activity Book*. They may need to practice making paragraph symbols and delete marks.

Checklists

A proofreading checklist is also at the back of the *Literacy Activity Book*. Encourage students to add to their checklist when they find mistakes in their own writing.

Double-Check It

Remind students to proofread their revised draft at least twice to be sure of catching all errors.

Publishing and Sharing

Students make a clean copy of their writing and combine pieces to form the class book.

- Have the class decide on a title and discuss how they want their finished book to appear.
- ***Cooperative Learning*** Invite volunteers to form teams to design a cover, write a table of contents, and make illustrations for the book.
- Discuss ways of making the book available to new students, classroom visitors, and parents.

Ideas for Publishing and Sharing

Making Copies

Ask students how multiple copies of the book could be made. Volunteers might photocopy the inside pages and have each student make a cover for one of the copies.

A Book Tour

Have students suggest ways to share their book with readers outside their classroom.

Parents' Night

If your school holds a parents' night or an open house, copies of the class book might be distributed.

MINILESSON

Publishing and Sharing

- Ask a volunteer what the word *publish* means. Invite students to list things that are published. Use the classroom as a starting point, but also include real-world publications, such as newspapers, magazines, newsletters, posters, brochures, and calendars, along with many kinds of books.
- Review with students the list of people who might use their class book. Tell them that all their hard work has a purpose when they share it with readers.
- Invite students to suggest other kinds of writing they may do this year and the ways they can share their writing with readers beyond the classroom.

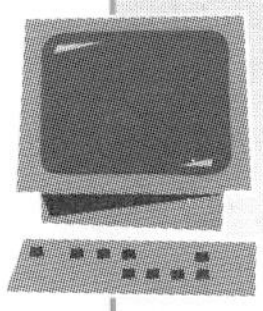

Students using The Learning Company's new elementary writing center can use the multimedia presentation feature to create a multimedia version of their work.

Selection Wrap-Up

Managing Assessment

Portfolios

Question: How can I get students interested in portfolios?

Answer: Try these suggestions:

1. If possible, share an example of a portfolio from another class or a previous year. Model for students how you might evaluate the contents:

- Compare two pieces of writing from different times during the year. Point out ways in which the student's work improved over time.
- Discuss a piece of work the student selected for inclusion in the portfolio. Point out what it shows about the student's interests and strengths.

2. Explain that a portfolio includes many different samples of a student's work. Discuss how a variety of work samples provides a better picture of student's growth than, for example, a single test score.

3. Note that during the first theme students will make collection folders to hold all their work, and that later they will take part in selecting samples of their work to be put in their portfolios. They will be doing this for the other themes throughout the year.

ASSESSMENT

Reflecting/Self-Assessment

Ask students to show what they did during the reading of *Hurray for Ali Baba Bernstein.* Use prompts such as these to help them think about their work: How well did you understand the story? How did you use strategies to help your reading? What worked well in your writing? What didn't work so well? Did you take part in class discussions? Did you listen attentively to others when they spoke? Have students copy and fill in the graphic organizer below. Help individuals identify strengths and areas for improvement.

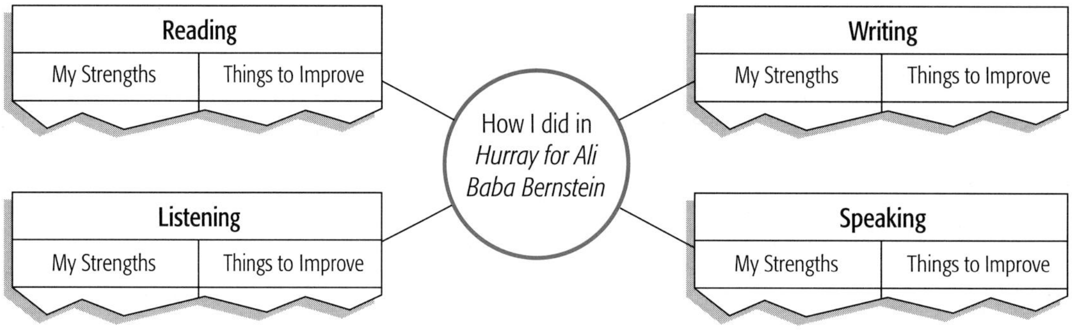

Discussing Literacy Assessment

Explain to students that during the year you and they will use many ways to evaluate their growth as readers, writers, speakers, and listeners. List some of these ways on the board:

- observing daily work in class
- checking *Literacy Activity Book* pages
- listening as students read aloud
- listening during class discussions and speaking activities
- checking written work, especially from Reading-Writing Workshops
- comparing examples of past and present work
- meeting with students to discuss their work
- assigning Performance Assessment activities
- giving tests

Invite students to save one piece of work they did during *Hurray for Ali Baba Bernstein*. (See Managing Assessment note on left.)

IT'S COOL.
IT'S SCHOOL.

Table of Contents

THEME: It's Cool. It's School.

Anthology *LITERATURE FOR WHOLE-CLASS INSTRUCTION*

School's Open: Check It Out!

Now Playing at a School Near You

LITERATURE FOR SMALL-GROUP INSTRUCTION

PAPERBACK PLUS

EASY

Freckle Juice
by Judy Blume

In the same book . . .
- a comic strip
- a science experiment
- fun facts about freckles
- a poem about a bad day

PAPERBACK PLUS

AVERAGE/CHALLENGING

Yang the Youngest and His Terrible Ear
by Lensey Namioka

In the same book . . .
- poems about baseball
- a profile of a young violinist
- an experiment to test acoustics

SOAR TO SUCCESS!

THE INTERMEDIATE INTERVENTION PROGRAM

Level 4 Books
A collection of books with teacher support for small-group intervention

Bibliography

Books for Independent Reading

- Multicultural
- Science/Health
- Math
- Social Studies
- Music
- Art

VERY EASY

Miss Nelson Is Missing!
by Harry Allard
Houghton 1985 (32p); also paper
The kids in Room 207 wonder what happened to their nice teacher.

A One-Room School
by Bobbie Kalman
Crabtree 1994 (32p)
All aspects of a one-room school are explained and illustrated.

Tanya's Big Green Dream
by Linda Glase
Macmillan 1994 (47p)
Tanya needs a project for her school's Earth Day celebration.

Handtalk School
by Mary Beth Miller
Four Winds 1991 (32p)
Photographs from a residential school for the deaf.

Count Your Money with the Polk Street School
by Patricia Reilly Giff
Bantam 1994 (80p); also paper
Ms. Rooney's class is saving money to take a trip.

Crow Boy
by Taro Yashima
Viking 1955 (40p); Puffin 1976 paper
A special talent helps a shy boy adjust to school.

EASY

Benny and the No-Good Teacher
by Cheryl Zach
Bradbury 1992 (76p)
Benny is disappointed to be in Mrs. Rumphill's class.

My Great-Aunt Arizona
by Gloria Houston
Harper 1992 (32p); also paper
Arizona taught generations of children about the faraway places she never got to see.

Hannah
by Gloria Whelan
Random 1991 (64p); Random 1993 paper
A clever teacher helps blind, nine-year-old Hannah become self-sufficient.

Herbie Jones and the Class Gift
by Suzy Kline
Putnam 1987 (96p); Puffin 1989 paper
Herbie and his pal must find a way to earn money for their teacher's gift.

Elaine and the Flying Frog
by Heidi Chang
Random 1991 (64p); also paper
Getting involved in a science project helps Elaine adjust to her new school.

I'm George Washington, and You're Not!
by Steven Kroll
Hyperion 1994 (64p)
Marty's stage fright could ruin the school play.

Author's Day
by Daniel Pinkwater
Macmillan 1993 (32p)
When author Bramwell Wink-Porter visits a school, the children think he's someone else.

Ramona Quimby, Age 8
by Beverly Cleary
Morrow 1981 (192p); Dell 1992 paper
Ramona adjusts to a new school year. **Available in Spanish as *Ramona empieza el curso.***

I Thought I'd Take My Rat to School: Poems for September to June
by Dorothy M. Kennedy
Little 1993 (64p)
Brief, often humorous, school poems by many well-known poets.

AVERAGE

My Name Is María Isabel
by Alma Flor Ada
Macmillan 1993 (64p)
María does not want to be called Mary. **Available in Spanish as *Me llamo María Isabel.***

Amber Brown Goes Fourth
by Paula Danziger
Putnam 1995 (101p)
Without her best friend Justin, Amber is certain fourth grade will be awful. **Available in Spanish as *Amber en cuarto y sin su amigo.***

Serious Science: An Adam Joshua Story
by Janice Lee Smith
Harper 1993 (80p)
Adam Joshua comes up with an invention he thinks will save the world.

Figment, Your Dog, Speaking
by Laura Hawkins
Houghton 1991 (160p) paper
Marcella's dog Figment helps her make new friends in school.

Wayside School Is Falling Down
by Louis Sachar
Lothrop 1989 (172p); Avon 1990 paper
Adventures of the students who attend the thirty-story Wayside School.

The Beast in Ms. Rooney's Room
by Patricia Reilly Giff
Dell 1988 (80p) paper
A teacher helps Richard discover he likes to read. **Available in Spanish as *La bestia en la clase de la señorita.***

The New One
by Jacqueline Turner Banks
Houghton 1994 (107p)
Twins Judge and Jury can't decide whether to befriend a new girl in their class.

Earthquake in the Third Grade
by Laurie Myers
Clarion 1993 (63p)
How can John and his classmates get their teacher to stay?

Muggie Maggie
by Beverly Cleary
Morrow 1990 (80p); Avon 1991 paper
Maggie does not want to learn cursive writing.

The Sub
by P. J. Petersen
Dutton 1993 (86p)
Two boys switch seats to fool the substitute teacher.

AVERAGE *(continued)*

The Hundred Dresses
by Eleanor Estes
Harcourt 1944 (80p); Voyager 1974 paper

Wanda's classmates wonder why she always wears the same blue dress. **Available in Spanish as *Cien vestidos.***

Degas, the Ballet, and Me
by Tom van Beek
Checkerboard 1993 (48p)
Anne-Marie records in her diary her interest in Degas' art.

The Skirt
by Gary Soto
Delacorte 1992 (64p); Dell 1994 paper
Miata has lost the folklórica skirt her mother loaned her.

Much Ado About Aldo
by Johanna Hurwitz
Morrow 1978 (96p); Penguin paper
Class projects involving insects lead Aldo to vegetarianism.

Fourth Grade Rats
by Jerry Spinelli
Scholastic 1991 (144p); Apple 1993 paper
Being in the fourth grade is not always easy.

The Chalk Box Kid
by Clyde Robert Bulla
Random 1987 (64p) paper
Gregory's chalk box garden helps him to adjust to changes in his life.

School Spirit
by Johanna Hurwitz
Morrow 1994 (144p)
Julio and his friends try to keep the school board from closing their school. See others in series.

Toad Food and Measle Soup
by Christine McDonnell
Puffin 1984 (112p) paper
Five funny stories about Leo's everyday experiences in school.

Lazy Lions, Lucky Lambs
by Patricia Reilly Giff
Dell 1985 (80p) paper
Richard and his friends develop writer's block when asked to write an essay. **Available in Spanish as *Leones perezosos, corderos afortunados.***

Going to School in 1876
by John J. Leoper
Atheneum 1984 (85p)
What going to school was like a century ago.

CHALLENGING

King Kong and Other Poets
by Robert Burch
Viking 1986 (160p)
A poetry contest allows Marilyn to tell her class about her unusual life.

Yellow Bird and Me
by Joyce Hansen
Clarion 1986 (128p); also paper
Doris helps Yellow Bird, the class clown, with his reading problem.

The Great Science Fair Disaster
by Martyn N. Godfrey
Scholastic 1992 (176p) paper
Marcie knows disaster will follow when her dad, the principal, plans a science fair.

The Cybil War
by Betsy Byars
Viking 1981 (144p); Puffin 1990 paper
Friends Simon and Troy both admire their classmate Cybil.

Darnell Rock, Reporting
by Walter Dean Myers
Delacorte 1994 (160p); Dell paper
After Darnell reluctantly joins the school paper, he wants to do a story on a homeless man he has befriended.

Beetles, Lightly Toasted
by Phyllis Reynolds Naylor
Macmillan 1987 (144p); Dell 1989 paper
Andy competes with his cousin in an essay contest.

There's a Boy in the Girls' Bathroom
by Louis Sachar
Knopf 1987 (224p) paper
Bradley is a bully with no friends until a new kid helps him to change his behavior.

Books for Teacher Read Aloud

Sideways Arithmetic from Wayside School
by Louis Sachar
Scholastic 1992 (96p) paper
Fifty hilarious stories, each filled with brain teasers.

The Show-and-Tell War and Other Stories About Adam Joshua
by Janice Lee Smith
Harper 1988 (176p); also paper
Five humorous stories about Adam Joshua's school adventures.

Children of the Dust Bowl
by Jerry Stanley
Crown 1992 (86p); also paper
Story of the Arvin Federal Camp and teacher/counselor Leo Hart.

Technology Resources

Software

Great Start Macintosh or Windows CD-ROM software. Includes story summaries, background building, and vocabulary support for each selection in the theme. Houghton Mifflin Company.

Spelling Spree™ Macintosh or Windows CD-ROM software. Includes spelling, vocabulary, and proofreading practice. Houghton Mifflin Company.

Channel R.E.A.D. Videodiscs "Suspended in Space" and "The Ordinary Princess." Houghton Mifflin Company.

Internet: Education Place (www.eduplace.com) Visit the Reading/Language Arts Center in the Teachers' Center to find projects, games, and theme-related links and activities.

Teacher's Resource Disk Macintosh or Windows software. Houghton Mifflin Company.

Writing Software The Learning Company's Ultimate Writing & Creativity Center. Macintosh or Windows software. The Learning Company®.

Video Cassettes

Schools Nat'l Geo

How to Conduct Yourself in School Aims

Skills for Classroom Survival Nat'l Geo

Alice in Wonderland by Lewis Carroll. Media Basics

The Hundred Dresses by Eleanor Estes. Am. Sch. Pub.

Crow Boy by Taro Yashima. Weston Woods

Audio Cassettes

Sideways Stories from Wayside School by Louis Sachar. Listening Library

The Chalk Box Kid by Clyde Robert Bulla. Am. Sch. Pub.

Crow Boy by Taro Yashima. Weston Woods

Ramona Quimby, Age 8 Beverly Cleary. Listening Library

Fourth Grade Celebrity by Patricia Reilly Giff. Listening Library

Audio Tapes for *It's Cool. It's School.* Houghton Mifflin Company.

AV addresses are on pages H7–H8.

Theme at a Glance

Selections	Reading: Comprehension Skills and Strategies	Reading: Word Skills	Writing and Language Arts: Responding	Writing and Language Arts: Writing
Tales of a Fourth Grade Nothing	✓ Predicting Outcomes, 45 Genre: Realistic Fiction, 47 Making Inferences, 51 Fact and Opinion, 53 Reading Strategies, 44, 46, 48, 52	✓ Structural Analysis: Base Words, 59E	Personal Response, 58 Literature Discussion, 58 Selection Connections, 58 Home Connection, 58	Humorous Dialogue, 55 ✓ Writing a Sentence, 59C
I'm in Another Dimension **Ten Minutes Till the Bus** **Last Night**	Reading Poetry, 60 Predict/Infer, 61			Write a Poem, 61
Classroom Peanuts	Reading Comic Strips, 62 Genre: Comic Strip, 63			Story Map, 63 Draw a Comic Strip, 63
I'm New Here	✓ Sequence of Events, 65 Problem Solving/Decision Making, 69 Predicting Outcomes, 71 Genre: Narrative Nonfiction, 77 Reading Strategies, 64, 68, 70, 74, 76	✓ Structural Analysis: Inflected Forms, 81E	Personal Response, 80 Literature Discussion, 80 Selection Connections, 80 Home Connection, 81	Varying Sentence Types, 67 Journal Writing, 81C
This is School? Cool!	Predict/Infer, 82			Application Essay, 83
Lucas Cott Does Raisin Bread Arithmetic	Venn Diagram, 84 Predict/Infer, 85 Sequence of Events, 86			Summary, 87
Childtimes	Thinking Critically, 88	Vocabulary: *famous* and *infamous,* 89		Write a Letter, 88 Emphasizing Strategies, 89
Reading-Writing Workshop **Be a Writer: The Day I Was a Hero**				Personal Narrative, 90–91F Good Beginnings, 91A Supplying Details, 91B Dialogue, 91C
Koya DeLaney and the Good Girl Blues	✓ Making Inferences, 95 Sequence of Events, 101 Reading Strategies, 94, 96, 100, 102	✓ Structural Analysis: ✓ Compound Words, 107E	Personal Response, 106 Literature Discussion, 106 Selection Connections, 106 Home Connection, 107	Thoughts vs. Dialogue, 99 Writing Messages, 107C
Alice & Alex	Narration, 108 Genre: Play, 109 Colloquialisms, 110 Idea Map, 111			

✓ ***Indicates Tested Skills.*** *See page 40F for assessment options.*

Theme Concept

School offers the challenges and rewards of life: friendship, problems, humor, and personal growth.

Pacing

This theme is designed to take 4 to 6 weeks, depending on your students' needs.

Multi-Age Classroom

Grade 3–What a Day!
Grade 5–Try to See It My Way

Cross-Curricular

Spelling*	Grammar, Usage, and Mechanics	Listening and Speaking	Viewing	Study Skills	Content Area
✓ Short Vowels, 59H	✓ Subjects and Predicates, 59I	Committee Report, 59K; Campaign Speech, 59K	Creating Posters, 59L; Working Together Collage, 59L	✓ Showing Information Graphically, 49, H2	**Social Studies:** Transportation Beginnings, 59M; Scavenger Hunt, 59M **Art:** Design a Vehicle, 59N **Math:** Speed and Distance, 59N
					Music: Set a Poem to Music, 61 **Math:** Number Sentences, 61
			Comics in Newspapers, 62		
✓ Spelling Long *a* and Long *e*, 81H	✓ Kinds of Sentences, 81I	Introducing Yourself, 81K; Words from Other Languages, 81K	Watching a Video about School, 81L; What We Don't See, 81L	Parts of a Book, 81N, H3	**Social Studies:** El Salvador Quiz Show, 81M; Travel Poster, 81M; Informational Interview, 81N **Arts:** Tell a Story, 81N
					Math: Distance on a Map, 83
		Role-Playing, 86		Graphs, 87, H4	**Math:** Create Food Activities, 87
		Discussion in Pairs, 88 Putting on a Play, 89			
Words Often Misspelled, 91E					
✓ Spelling Long *i* and Long *o,* 107H	✓ Run-on Sentences, 107I	Rhyme and Rhythm, 107K; Tape Recording, 107K	Body Language, 107L; Games Demonstrations, 107L		**Health:** Take Your Pulse, 107M; Fitness and Exercise, 107M; Field Day, 107N **Math:** Estimate two Minutes, 107N
Theme Assessment Wrap-Up: Spelling Review, 113B		Reader's Theater, 113			**Art:** Design, 113

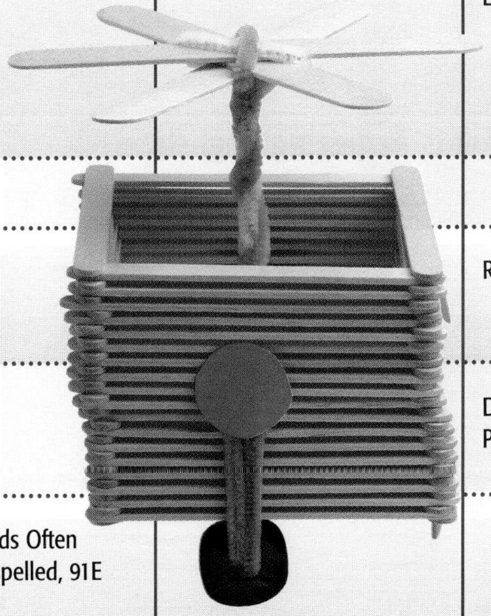

* *Additional spelling lists with practice, Literacy Activity Book (LAB), pp. 291–296 (optional)*

Meeting Individual Needs

Students Acquiring English
Activities and notes offer strategies to help students' comprehension.

Challenge
Challenge activities and notes stimulate critical and creative thinking.

Extra Support
Activities and notes offer strategies to help students experience success.

Through Literature...

Instructional Reading

Anthology
Level 4, pp. 36–113

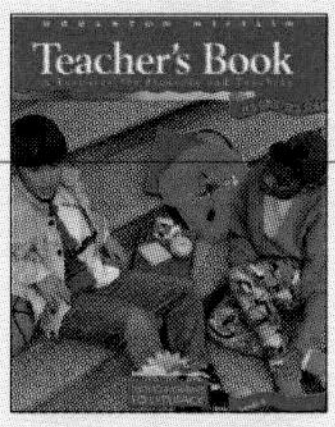

Teacher's Book
It's Cool. It's School.

Supported/Independent Reading

Average/Challenging Paperback Plus
Yang the Youngest and His Terrible Ear
by Lensey Namioka

Easy Paperback Plus
Freckle Juice
by Judy Blume

Bibliography
Teacher's Book, pp. 40A–40B

Extra Support/Students Acquiring English

Great Start™ CD-ROM software
It's Cool. It's School.

Audio Tapes
for It's Cool. It's School.

SOAR TO SUCCESS!
The Intermediate Intervention Program

Extra Support Handbook
Level 4, pp. 11–23, 104–111

Students Acquiring English Handbook
Level 4, pp. 56–81, 240–247

Language Resources:
Chinese, Hmong, Cambodian, Vietnamese

Extension/Challenge

Teacher's Book
- Theme Projects
- Communication Activities
- Cross-Curricular Activities

Home/Community Connections
Level 4

Internet: Education Place
www.eduplace.com

Through Instruction...

Teaching Choices Reading, Writing, Language Arts, Cross-Curricular

Teacher's Book
Choose among skill Minilessons, Interactive Learning Lessons, and Reteaching Lessons and activities to meet students' needs.

Literacy Activity Book
Level 4, pp. 7–42

Extra Support/Students Acquiring English

Extra Support Handbook
Level 4, pp. 11–23, 104–111

Students Acquiring English Handbook
Level 4, pp. 56–81, 240–247

Channel R.E.A.D. Videodiscs
- "The Ordinary Princess"
- "Suspended in Space"

Extension/Challenge

Teacher's Book
- Spelling Challenge Words
- Performance Assessment

Internet: Education Place
www.eduplace.com

Spelling Spree CD-ROM

The Learning Company's Ultimate Writing & Creativity Center software

Planning for Assessment

Performance Standards During this theme, all students will learn to

- *Recognize how fiction selections relate to real experiences they have had at school*
- *Write a personal narrative*
- *Make inferences based on information in a selection*
- *Predict the outcome of a selection*
- *Sequence the events of a selection*
- *Revise writing, with an emphasis on using complete sentences*

Informal Assessment

Informal Assessment Checklist, pp. H5–H6

- Reading and Responding
- Predicting Outcomes, Sequence, Making Inferences
- Writing a Sentence
- Word Skills and Strategies
- Grammar
- Attitudes and Habits

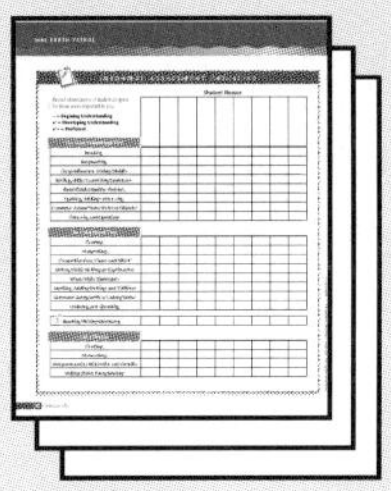

Literacy Activity Book

- Selection Connections, p. 8
- Comprehension Check, pp. 10, 20, 33
- Comprehension Skills, pp. 11, 21, 34
- Writing Skills, pp. 12, 22, 35
- Word Skills, pp. 13, 23, 36

Reading-Writing Workshop

- Personal Narrative, pp. 90–91F
- Scoring Rubric, p. 91F

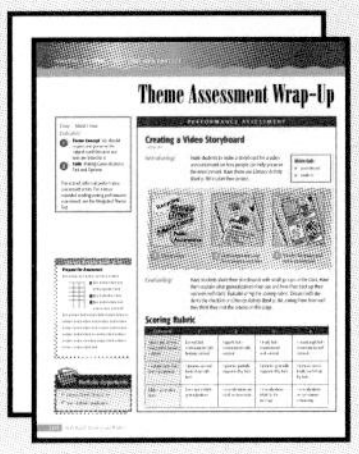

Performance Assessment

- Creating a Skit, p. 113A
- Scoring Rubric, p. 113A

Retellings–Oral/Written

- *Teacher's Assessment Handbook*

Formal Assessment

Integrated Theme Test

Test applies the following theme skills to a new reading selection:

- Reading Strategies
- Predicting Outcomes, Sequence, Making Inferences
- Word Skills and Strategies
- Writing Fluency
- Grammar and Spelling (optional)
- Self-Assessment

Theme Skills Test

- Predicting Outcomes, Sequence, Making Inferences
- Base Words, Inflected Forms, Compound Words
- Writing Skills
- Study Skills
- Spelling
- Grammar

Benchmark Progress Test

- Give a Benchmark Progress Test two or three times a year to measure student growth in reading and writing.

Managing Assessment

Theme Checklists

Question How can I best use the Informal Assessment Checklist?

Answer The Informal Assessment Checklist can help you keep track of informal observations you make throughout the theme. These tips keep it simple to use:

- The Checklist has individual and group forms. Use the group form to monitor most students. Use the individual form for students who are a focus of concern.
- Don't try to check all categories for all students. For many students, occasional checks during a theme will be sufficient to document their progress or to note any difficulties in particular areas. For students needing more support, plan more observations, focused on the categories of concern.
- Some teachers keep the Checklist on a clipboard and make notes as they teach. Others take a moment at the end of the day or week to reflect and record their observations. Experiment to find the way that works for you.

For more information on this and other topics, see the *Teacher's Assessment Handbook*.

Portfolio Assessment

The portfolio icon signals portfolio opportunities throughout the theme.

Additional portfolio tips:

- Introducing Portfolios to the Class, p. 113B
- Selecting Materials for the Portfolios, p. 113B
- Grading Work in Portfolios, p. 113B

Launching the Theme

Literacy Activity Book, p. 8

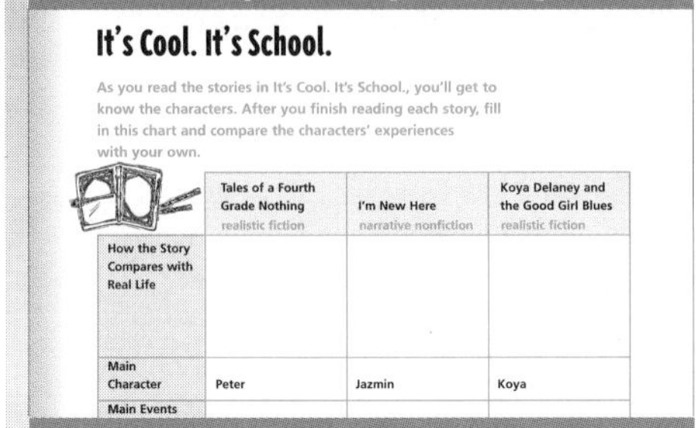

It's Cool. It's School.

As you read the stories in It's Cool. It's School., you'll get to know the characters. After you finish reading each story, fill in this chart and compare the characters' experiences with your own.

	Tales of a Fourth Grade Nothing (realistic fiction)	I'm New Here (narrative nonfiction)	Koya Delaney and the Good Girl Blues (realistic fiction)
How the Story Compares with Real Life			
Main Character	Peter	Jazmin	Koya
Main Events			

Literacy Activity Book, p. 7

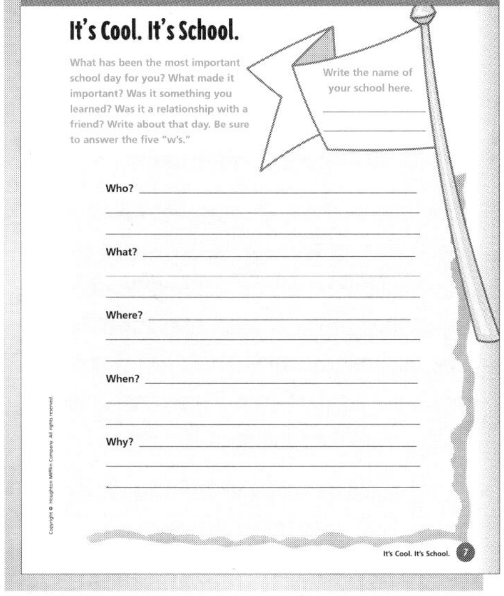

It's Cool. It's School.

What has been the most important school day for you? What made it important? Was it something you learned? Was it a relationship with a friend? Write about that day. Be sure to answer the five "w's."

Write the name of your school here.

Who? ______

What? ______

Where? ______

When? ______

Why? ______

Copyright © Houghton Mifflin Company. All rights reserved.

It's Cool. It's School. 7

Selection Connections

Invite students to complete *Literacy Activity Book* page 7. Then discuss the Selection Connections chart on *Literacy Activity Book* page 8. Note that students will return to the chart after reading each selection and at the completion of the theme.

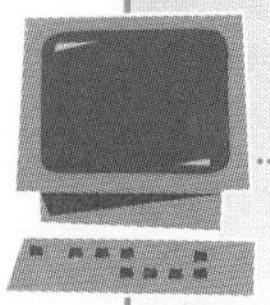

See the Houghton Mifflin **Internet** resources for additional activities.

See the **Teacher's Resource Disk** for theme-related support material.

INTERACTIVE LEARNING

Theme Concept School offers the challenges and rewards of life: friendships, problems, humor, and personal growth.

Setting the Scene

Introduce the title: "It's Cool. It's School."

Discussion prompts:

- What are some things you like about school? (making friends, learning about new things)
- What learning activities are you involved in outside of school? (sports programs, music lessons, language classes)
- What do you want to be when you grow up? What will you need to learn about to do this? (Answers will vary.)

Students Acquiring English If there are students who have been to school in another city, area, or country, invite them to compare their former schools to their present one. Also, make sure students acquiring English understand the theme title by having them paraphrase it.

Quick Write

Write the theme concept on the board, and ask students to write as many words and phrases as they associate with the concept. Then have students gather in small groups to share and categorize their ideas.

Interactive Bulletin Board

MEETING INDIVIDUAL NEEDS

Invite students to draw self-portraits and hang their pictures on a bulletin board. Encourage them to use a variety of media. When new students join the class later in the year, add their pictures to the display. If some students move away, have them write their new addresses beneath their self-portraits before they go.

Choices for Projects

Capture the Spirit of Your School

Materials
- felt
- glue
- safety scissors
- wooden dowels

Discuss with students what makes their school unique. Then challenge groups of students to capture that spirit in one of the following ways:

- create a new school logo
- write a new school slogan
- choose a new school mascot
- make a school pennant

To make a pennant, follow these steps.

1 Cut a long triangle out of felt.

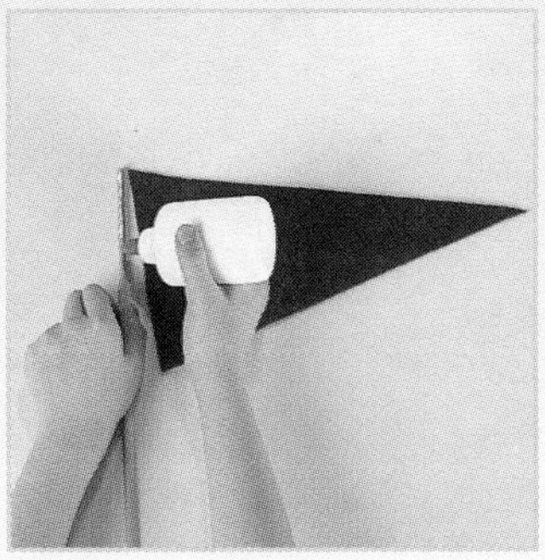

2 Apply two or three lines of glue to the dowel.

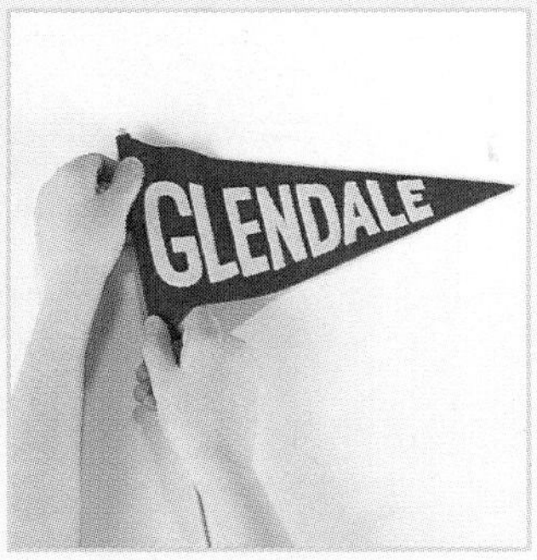

3 Roll the dowel into the wide end of the triangle.

Create a Time Line of Your School

Have students research the history of their school and create a time line highlighting the important events. Suggest that groups of students interview teachers or school administrators about the school's history. You may wish to assign a specific time period to each group of students.

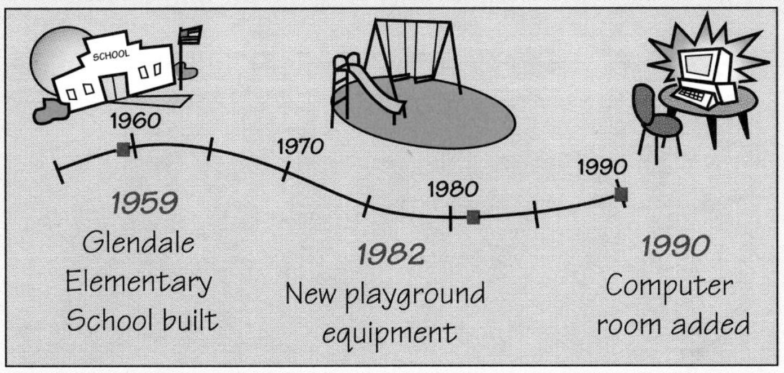

After groups pool their knowledge, have students insert photos and drawings of important events and write a caption for each. Display the completed time line in a prominent location.

Independent Reading and Writing

Plan time each day for independent reading and writing. For independent reading, provide books from the Bibliography on pages 40A–40B; allow students to select books on any subject; or encourage students to read the Paperbacks Plus for this theme:

Easy reading: *Freckle Juice* by Judy Blume

Average/challenging reading: *Yang the Youngest and His Terrible Ear* by Lensey Namioka

For independent writing, encourage students to choose their own writing activities. For those who need help getting started, suggest one or more activities on pages 59D, 81D, and 107D.

See the *Home/Community Connections Booklet* for theme-related materials.

Portfolio Opportunity

- Save *Literacy Activity Book* page 8 to show students' ability to compare selections.
- The Portfolio Opportunity icon highlights other portfolio opportunities throughout the theme.

SELECTION: Tales of a Fourth Grade Nothing

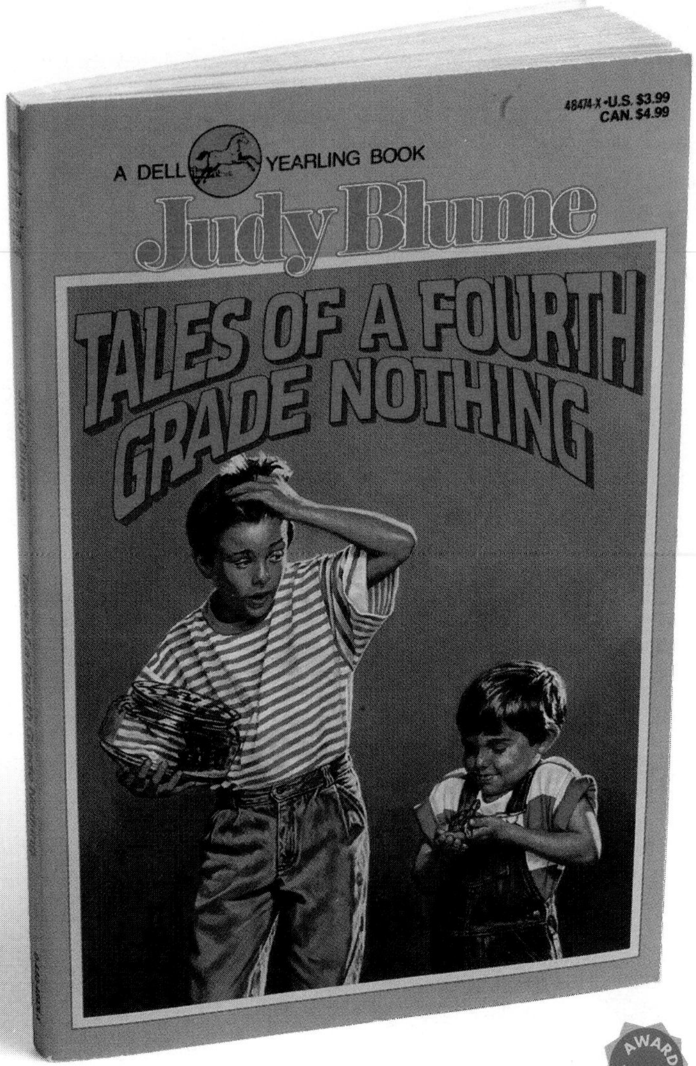

by Judy Blume

An award-winning author

- **Arizona Young Reader's Award**
- **Georgia Children's Book Award**
- **Charlie May Simonton Award**
- **Massachusetts School Children's Book Award**

Other Books by the Author

Freckle Juice

Fudge-a-Mania

Otherwise Known as Sheila the Great

Selection Summary

Peter Hatcher, his parents, his two-year-old brother Fudge, and his pet turtle Dribble live in an apartment in New York City. In this episode, Peter is working with classmates Sheila and Jimmy on a school project about city transportation. According to their plans, Sheila will copy their work into a booklet; Peter and Jimmy will make a poster; and they will all give an oral report. Peter and Jimmy finish the poster and store it under Peter's bed. Fudge finds the poster, however, and scribbles all over it; Peter and Jimmy must start over. Peter uses what he learns about his feelings toward Fudge to work things out with his classmates, and their final project is a success.

5-Day Planner

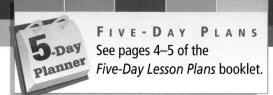

FIVE-DAY PLANS
See pages 4–5 of the *Five-Day Lesson Plans* booklet.

Lesson Planning Guide

	Skill/Strategy Instruction	Meeting Individual Needs	Lesson Resources
1 **Introduce the Literature** *Pacing: 1 day*	**Preparing to Read and Write** Prior Knowledge/Building Background, 41C **Selection Vocabulary,** 41D • project • committee • arranged • solution • method • schedule **Spelling Pretest,** 59H • class • plan • desk • still • check • dull • cost • trust • snip • knock	**Support in Advance,** 41C **Students Acquiring English,** 41C **Other Choices for Building Background,** 41C **Spelling Challenge Words,** 59H • topic • traffic • sketch • whisper • script	***Literacy Activity Book,*** Vocabulary, 9 **Transparencies:** Building Background, 1–1; Vocabulary, 1–2 **Great Start** CD-ROM software, "It's Cool. It's School." CD
2 **Interact with Literature** *Pacing: 1–3 days*	**Reading Strategies** Self-Question, 44, 48 Predict/Infer, 44, 52 Think About Words, 46 **Minilessons** ✓ Predicting Outcomes, 45 Genre: Realistic Fiction, 47 ✓ Study Skill: Showing Information Graphically, 49, H2 Making Inferences, 51 Fact and Opinion, 53 Writer's Craft: Humorous Dialogue, 55	**Choices for Reading,** 44 **Guided Reading,** 44, 46, 50, 56 **Students Acquiring English,** 43, 47, 48, 51, 52, 55, 59 **Extra Support,** 45, 51, 57 **Challenge,** 50, 58	**Reading-Writing Workshop:** Personal Narrative, 90–91F ***Literacy Activity Book,*** Selection Connections, 7–8; Comprehension Check, 10 **Audio Tape** for It's Cool. It's School.: *Tales of a Fourth Grade Nothing* The Learning Company's Ultimate Writing & Creativity Center software
3 **Instruct and Integrate** *Pacing: 1–3 days*	✓ **Comprehension:** Predicting Outcomes, 59A ✓ **Writing:** Writing a Sentence, 59C ✓ **Word Skills and Strategies:** Structural Analysis: Base Words, 59E **Building Vocabulary:** Vocabulary Activities, 59G ✓ **Spelling:** Short Vowels, 59H ✓ **Grammar:** Subjects and Predicates, 59I **Communication Activities:** Listening and Speaking, 59K; Viewing, 59L **Cross-Curricular Activities:** Social Studies, 59M; Art, 59N; Math, 59N	**Reteaching:** Predicting Outcomes, 59B **Activity Choices:** Dialogue, Transportation Project, Persuasive Paragraph, 59D **Reteaching:** Structural Analysis: Base Words, 59F **Activity Choices:** Synonym Concentration, Transportation Words, Vocabulary Notebook, 59G **Challenge Words Practice:** 59H **Reteaching:** Subjects and Predicates, 59J **Activity Choices:** Listening and Speaking, 59K; Viewing, 59L **Activity Choices:** Social Studies, 59M; Art, 59N; Math, 59N	**Reading-Writing Workshop:** Personal Narrative, 90–91F **Transparencies:** Comprehension, 1–3; Comprehension Reteaching, 1–4; Writing Skills, 1–5; Grammar, 1–6 ***Literacy Activity Book,*** Comprehension, 11; Writing, 12; Word Skills, 13; Building Vocabulary, 14; Spelling, 15–16; Grammar, 17–18 **Audio Tape** for It's Cool. It's School.: *Tales of a Fourth Grade Nothing* **Spelling Spree** CD-ROM The Learning Company's Ultimate Writing & Creativity Center software

✓ ***Indicates Tested Skills.*** *See page 40F for assessment options.*

Introduce *the* Literature

Preparing to Read and Write

Support in Advance

Use these activities for students who need extra support before participating in the whole-class activity.

Cooperation Categories

Assign students a category such as sports. Have them list three examples of people working together (for example, under sports, *baseball*).

Management Tip
During support in advance, the rest of the class may write in their journals.

Students Acquiring English

Working at a classmate's home may be an unfamiliar concept. Compare this with playing at a friend's house.

INTERACTIVE LEARNING

Prior Knowledge/Building Background

Key Concept When working together, people learn a great deal about themselves and others.

Planning a Project Ask students if they have ever worked with others to accomplish a goal. Divide the class into small "committees" whose task is to plan a booth for the school carnival. Using Transparency 1–1 as a guide, ask students to brainstorm steps and guidelines for the project. Complete the transparency as groups present their ideas. Discuss why organization and communication are important in group projects.

Transparency 1–1

Goal: Sample answer: To plan a face-painting booth for the school carnival
Materials Needed: Sample answer: Boards, nails, hammer, paint, face paints, brushes

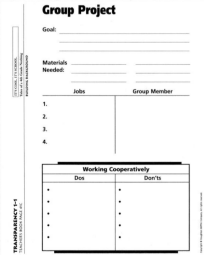

Transparency 1–1

Group Project

Goal:

Materials Needed:

Jobs	Group Member
1.	
2.	
3.	
4.	

Working Cooperatively

Dos	Don'ts
•	•
•	•
•	•
•	•
•	•

IT'S COOL. IT'S SCHOOL. Tales of a 4th Grade Nothing BUILDING BACKGROUND

TRANSPARENCY 1–1 TEACHER'S BOOK PAGE 41C

Great Start
For students needing extra support with key concepts and vocabulary, use the "It's Cool. It's School." CD.

Other Choices for Building Background

Ways of Working Together

Students Acquiring English Ensure that students are familiar with the meaning of the word *cooperation* by inviting them to list or illustrate ways that people work together in their own lives and communities. Post these examples on a bulletin board entitled "Cooperation in Action."

Pantomime

Extra Support Ask students to think of the kinds of transportation they would expect to see in a large city. Have students try to guess these modes of transportation as volunteers pantomime them.

Spelling

You may want to give the Spelling Pretest on page 59H before students read the selection.

Daily Language Practice

Use the sentences on page 59J as daily practice of the spelling and grammar skills taught in this theme.

INTERACTIVE LEARNING

Selection Vocabulary

Key Words

committee

arranged

method

project

schedule

solution

Display Transparency 1–2. Demonstrate how the word grid can help students explore the meaning of each vocabulary word. In box one, under "Word," write *committee*; in box two, write *people working together*; in box three, write *team*; in box four, have students suggest a sentence using the word *committee*. Ask volunteers to help fill in the word grid for the other words. Discuss how each word relates to working together.

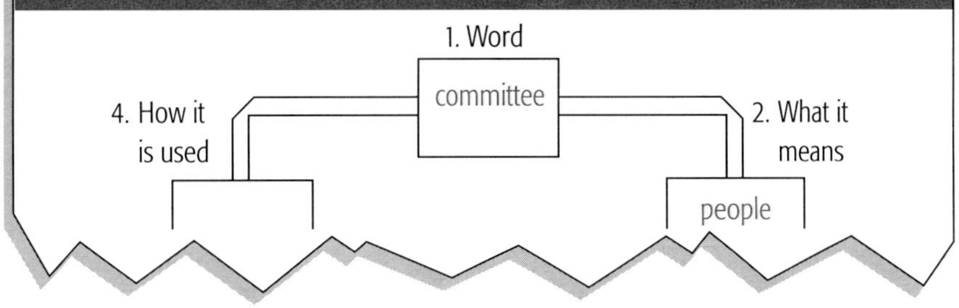

Vocabulary Practice Have students work independently or in pairs to complete page 9 of the *Literacy Activity Book*.

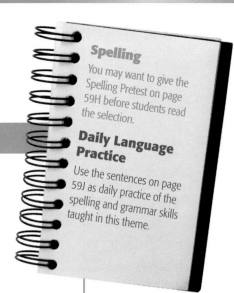

Transparency 1–2

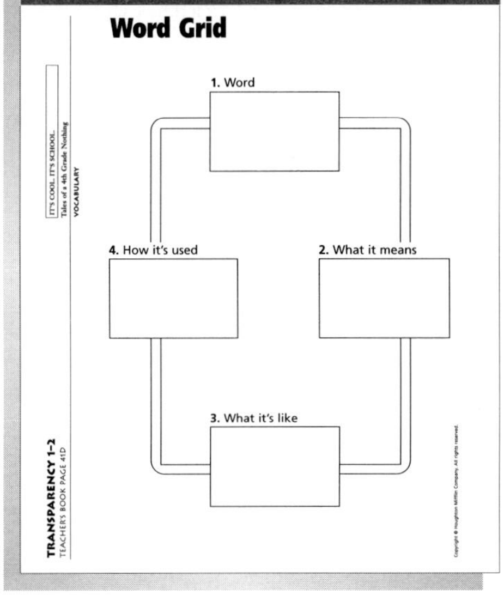
Word Grid

1. Word

2. What it means

3. What it's like

4. How it's used

IT'S COOL. IT'S SCHOOL.
Tales of a 4th Grade Nothing
VOCABULARY

TRANSPARENCY 1–2
TEACHER'S BOOK PAGE 41D

Copyright © Houghton Mifflin Company. All rights reserved.

Science

Teacher FactFile

Monorail

- A monorail is a type of electric train that runs above or below a single track.
- The first U.S. monorail was installed in Houston, Texas, in 1956.
- The Disney parks in California and Florida have monorails that connect parts of the parks, hotels, and parking lots. These monorails ride above a beam, are powered by an electric current, and are stabilized by gyroscopes (wheels or disks that are free to turn in various directions).

Literacy Activity Book, p. 9

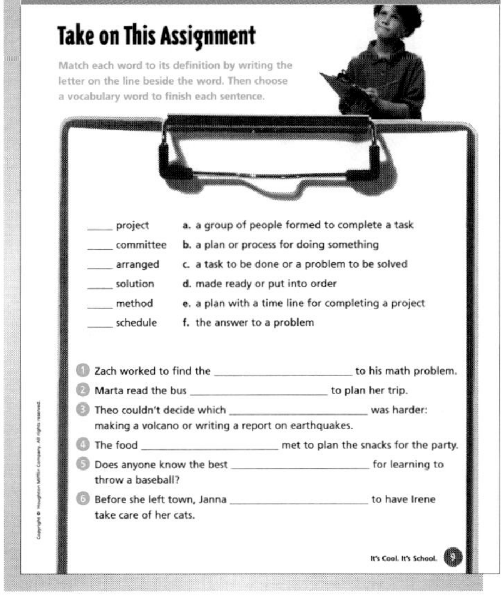
Take on This Assignment

Match each word to its definition by writing the letter on the line beside the word. Then choose a vocabulary word to finish each sentence.

____ project — **a.** a group of people formed to complete a task

____ committee — **b.** a plan or process for doing something

____ arranged — **c.** a task to be done or a problem to be solved

____ solution — **d.** made ready or put into order

____ method — **e.** a plan with a time line for completing a project

____ schedule — **f.** the answer to a problem

1. Zach worked to find the ____________ to his math problem.
2. Marta read the bus ____________ to plan her trip.
3. Theo couldn't decide which ____________ was harder: making a volcano or writing a report on earthquakes.
4. The food ____________ met to plan the snacks for the party.
5. Does anyone know the best ____________ for learning to throw a baseball?
6. Before she left town, Janna ____________ to have Irene take care of her cats.

Copyright © Houghton Mifflin Company. All rights reserved.

It's Cool. It's School. 9

Interact *with* Literature

More About the Author

Judy Blume

Hailed as one of the finest contemporary writers of children's literature, Judy Blume aims to tell honest stories: "My responsibility to be honest with my readers is my strongest motivation. I am offended by dishonest books. I hate the idea we should always protect children. They live in the same world we do."

Educators and critics seem to agree; they have cited her books for numerous prestigious awards. *Tales of a Fourth Grade Nothing* won the Georgia, South Carolina, and Massachusetts Children's Book Awards in 1977.

Blume was born February 12, 1938, in Elizabeth, New Jersey. She attended Boston University and graduated from New York University in 1960. After rearing her daughter and son full-time for a number of years, she turned to writing as another creative outlet. In addition to her numerous works for children and young adults, Blume has written two novels for adults.

Meet the Author

Judy Blume

Meet the Illustrator

Betsy James

As a child, Judy Blume liked movies, radio shows, and the children's room of her library. "But," she says, "I didn't find real satisfaction in reading until I was older . . . there weren't any books with characters who felt the way I felt, who acted the way I did . . . ." So, when Blume grew up, she decided to write books for children about real life.

In 1966, Blume started writing children's stories, thinking about them while she washed the dinner dishes. For two years her stories were rejected, and she almost gave up. Then she took a course on how to write for children. She loved the course so much she took it twice! Finally her career took off.

Blume has written novels for both children and adults. She won awards for *Tales of a Fourth Grade Nothing* and *Superfudge*, among others. Blume says about her writing that "until you pull it out of your own heart, it doesn't really work."

Betsy James grew up in Salt Lake City, Utah. She liked hiking and camping with her family, and she also liked to read. "I could usually be found up in a pine tree or with my nose in a book," she says. When not reading or hiking, James was drawing. In her family, the children always made their own greeting cards and gifts for relatives.

James went from creating books as gifts to writing and illustrating books for publication. To prepare to illustrate this selection, James read lots of stories by Judy Blume, who lives only fifty miles away from her in New Mexico.

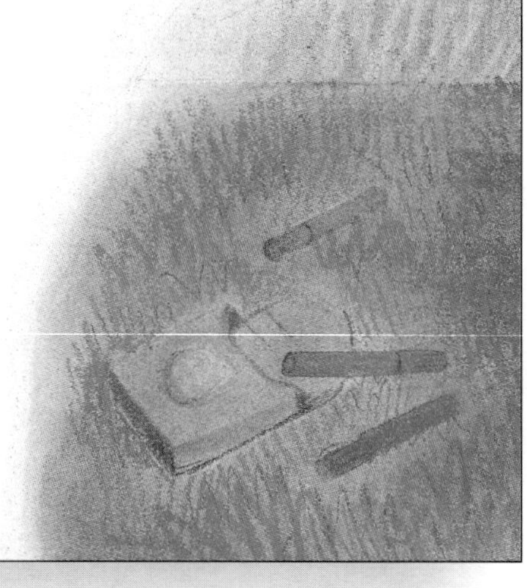

42

Students Acquiring English

Students may have difficulty understanding the meaning of the word *Nothing* in the selection title. Explain that here the word means the same as *nobody*, or a person of no importance.

QuickREFERENCE

MINILESSON

Technology
E-Mail

Teach/Model

Elementary schools and homes around the country are going "on-line." Ask students if they have ever had a "key-pal"–the on-line equivalent of a pen-pal. Discuss with the class how they can collaborate with other classrooms to write stories, talk about current events, or even share opinions about the selections they are reading in this theme. Guide students to understand that when they read and respond to e-mail, they should use appropriate language and be tolerant of other people's views.

- Be polite. Don't say anything that you wouldn't say in person.
- Avoid using all capital letters. It is like shouting.
- Put a smiley face :–) when you mean something as a joke.

Practice/Apply

Invite students to take electronic field trips to other schools using e-mail. These schools might be in their district or in other parts of the country. Have them brainstorm topics to discuss with their key-pals and work collaboratively to send electronic messages. Encourage them to share interesting responses with classmates.

Interact *with* Literature

Reading Strategies

Self-Question
Predict/Infer

Teacher Modeling With a Think Aloud, model how good readers use strategies as they read.

Think Aloud

Before I read the story, I'll read the title, look at the pictures on the first four pages, and self-question by asking myself what I might find out. What are these friends working on? Why are they arguing? Then I can use what I know to predict what might happen in the story.

Predicting/Purpose Setting Suggest that students use their predictions and questions to formulate a purpose for reading and that they adjust their predictions and questions as they read.

Choices for Reading

Independent Reading	Cooperative Reading
Guided Reading	Teacher Read Aloud

Guided Reading

Have students using the Guided Reading option read to the end of page 47 to see if they find answers to their questions.

In January our class started a project on The City. Mrs. Haver, our teacher, divided us up into committees by where we live. That way we could work at home. My committee was me, Jimmy Fargo, and Sheila. Our topic was Transportation. We decided to make my apartment the meeting place because I'm the only one of the three of us who's got his own bedroom. In a few weeks each committee has to hand in a booklet, a poster, and be ready to give an oral report.

The first day we got together after school we bought a yellow posterboard. Jimmy wanted a blue one but Sheila talked him out of it. "Yellow is a much brighter color," she explained. "Everything will show up on it. Blue is too dull."

Sheila thinks she's smarter than me and Jimmy put together — just because she's a girl! So right away she told us she would be in charge of our booklet and me and Jimmy could do most of the poster. As long as we check with her first, to make sure she likes our ideas. We agreed, since Sheila promised to do ten pages of written work and we would only do five.

After we bought the yellow posterboard we went to the library. We took out seven books on transportation. We wanted to learn all we could about speed, traffic congestion, and pollution. We arranged to meet on Tuesday and Thursday afternoons for the next two weeks.

44

Quick REFERENCE

Background: FYI

In an earlier episode, Sheila is watching Fudge as they play in the park. Sheila chases Peter, yelling, "Peter's got the cooties!" Fudge falls and loses his two front teeth. Sheila feels so awful that she quits playing the cooties game.

Our first few committee meetings turned out like this: We got to my place by three-thirty, had a snack, then played with Dribble for another half hour. Sheila gave up on cooties when Fudge lost his front teeth. But it still isn't much fun to have her hanging around. She's always complaining that she got stuck with the worst possible committee. And that me and Jimmy fool more than we work. We only put up with her because we have no choice!

Sheila and Jimmy have to be home for supper before five-thirty. So at five o'clock we start cleaning up. We keep our equipment under my bed in a shoebox. We have a set of Magic Markers, Elmer's glue, Scotch tape, a really sharp pair of scissors, and a container of silver sparkle.

45

Extra Support

Proper Nouns Explain that *Dribble* is the name of Peter's turtle and *Fudge* is the name of Peter's younger brother. The capital letters help the reader recognize *Fudge* and *Dribble* as names, not common nouns or verbs.

Math Link

Ask students how much time elapsed between the time the committee arrived at Peter's house and the time Sheila had to be home for dinner. Help students realize that two hours elapsed.

MINILESSON

Predicting Outcomes

TESTED SKILL

Teach/Model

Ask students what they do when they reach a suspenseful part of a story. Discuss how thinking about what might happen next in a story can help readers understand the story. Suggest that thinking about experiences students have had may help them make better predictions.

Think Aloud

On this page it seems that the committee has the project fairly well organized, but I don't think the boys like working with Sheila. Sheila doesn't seem too happy, either. I'll predict they are going to have disagreements that cause problems with the project.

Practice/Apply

- Ask students to locate and read aloud passages to this point in the story that might lead them to predict that the committee will have disagreements.
- After students have read the story, discuss how they periodically revised their predictions based on new information.

SKILL FINDER

Full lesson/Reteaching, pp. 59A–59B

Minilessons, p. 71 and Theme 5

Interact with Literature

Reading Strategies

Think About Words

Model how readers can combine the meanings of the base word *rail* and the prefix *mono-* to get the meaning of the word *monorail*.

Meeting Individual Needs: Guided Reading

Comprehension/Critical Thinking

1. What is the project topic? (transportation) How have the members divided the tasks? (Jimmy and Peter will each write five pages and make the poster; Sheila will write ten pages and copy all of the text.) Where are the poster and booklet kept? (under Peter's bed; with Sheila)
2. Do you think the group members will complete their project on time? Why or why not? (Answers may vary but should be supported by the text.)

Predicting/Purpose Setting

Ask students if any of their predictions have been accurate or their questions have been answered. Have them revise their questions or predictions and read to the bottom of page 51.

Informal Assessment

If students' responses indicate that they are understanding the selection, have them finish reading the selection independently or cooperatively.

Sheila carries our committee booklet back and forth with her. She doesn't trust us enough to leave it at my house! The posterboard fits under my bed, along with our supplies. We stack the library books on my desk. The reason I make sure we clean up good is that my mother told me if I left a mess we'd have to find some place else to work.

By our third meeting I told Jimmy and Sheila that I'd figured out the solution to New York City's traffic problems. "We have to get rid of the traffic," I said. "There shouldn't be any cars or buses or taxis allowed in the city. What we really need is a citywide monorail system."

"That's too expensive," Sheila said. "It sounds good but it's not practical."

"I disagree!" I told Sheila. "It's very practical. Besides getting rid of traffic it'll get rid of air pollution and it'll get people where they're going a lot faster."

"But it's not practical, Peter!" Sheila said again. "It costs too much."

I opened one of my books on transportation and read Sheila a quote. "'A monorail system is the hope of the future.'" I cleared my throat and looked up.

"But we can't write a report just about the monorail," Sheila said. "We'll never be able to fill twenty written pages with that."

"We can write big," Jimmy suggested.

46

Quick REFERENCE

Science Link

Transportation In an effort to clean up the air, developers are testing cars that run on electricity or hydrogen, which give off no exhaust. Some models use solar energy, reducing the need for pollution-generating power plants.

Background: FYI

Public Transportation According to the U.S. Bureau of the Census (1990), only 5.3% of the U.S. population travels to work using public transportation, such as buses, trains, and subways. This figure is down from 6.4% in 1980.

"No!" Sheila said. "I want a good mark on this project. Peter, you can write your five pages about the monorail system and how it works. Jimmy, you can write your five pages about pollution caused by transportation. And I'll write my ten pages on the history of transportation in the city." Sheila folded her arms and smiled.

"Can I write big?" Jimmy asked.

"I don't care how big you write as long as you put your name on your five pages!" Sheila told him.

"That's not fair!" Jimmy said. "This is supposed to be a group project. Why should I have to put my name on my five pages?"

"Then don't write BIG!" Sheila shouted.

"Okay. Okay . . . I'll write so small Mrs. Haver will need a microscope to see the letters."

"Very funny," Sheila said.

"Look," I told both of them, "I think all our written work should be in the same handwriting. That's the only fair way. Otherwise Mrs. Haver will know who did what. And it won't be a group project."

"Say, that's a good idea," Jimmy said. "Which one of us has the best handwriting?"

Me and Jimmy looked at Sheila.

"Well, I do have a nice even script," Sheila said. "But if I'm going to copy over your written work you better give it to me by next Tuesday. Otherwise, I won't have enough time to do the job. And you

47

M I N I L E S S O N

Genre
Realistic Fiction

Teach/Model

Ask students what they find appealing about the characters in the selection. Using the Think Aloud, help students understand that realistic fiction encompasses these characteristics:

- Its characters seem like people we know or might meet.
- The events seem like they could really happen.
- The author usually gives some information about the characters, but other information is revealed gradually over the course of the story.

Think Aloud

Peter, Sheila, and Jimmy seem like people I know, and their assignment is similar to assignments I've worked on. The way they work together in a group seems familiar too. I feel like I'm getting to know Peter as the story goes on. The story must be realistic fiction.

Practice/Apply

Ask students to point out additional realistic aspects of the selection.

Math Link

Ask students how many pages Sheila wrote. How many times more did she write than Peter or Jimmy? Have them write a number sentence to reflect this difference. (For example, 10 = 2 x 5, so Sheila wrote twice as many pages.)

Students Acquiring English

Assist students acquiring English in following the dialogue by having different students read the parts aloud.

Interact *with* Literature

Reading Strategies

Self-Question

Ask students to remember the questions they asked themselves before they began reading the selection. Discuss how well they feel they have answered those questions based on the story so far. Then encourage them to look at the illustrations in the rest of the story and to formulate new questions about the story.

two better get going on your poster." Sheila talked like she was the teacher and we were the kids.

Me and Jimmy designed the whole poster ourselves. We used the pros and cons of each kind of transportation. It was really clever. We divided a chart into land, sea, and air and we planned an illustration for each — with the airplane done in silver sparkle and the letters done in red and blue Magic Marker. We got halfway through the lettering that day. We also sketched in the ship, the plane, and the truck.

When Sheila saw it she asked, "Is that supposed to be a train?"

"No," I told her. "It's a truck."

"It doesn't look like one," she said.

"It will," Jimmy told her, "when it's finished."

"I hope so," Sheila said. "Because right now it looks like a flying train!"

"That's because the ground's not under it yet," Jimmy said.

"Yeah," I agreed. "See, we've got to make it look like it's on a street. Right now it does kind of look like it's up in space."

"So does the ship," Sheila said.

"We'll put some waterlines around it," I told her.

"And some clouds around the plane," Sheila said.

"Listen," Jimmy hollered, "did anybody ever tell you you're too bossy? This poster is ours! You do the booklet. Remember . . . that's the way you wanted it!"

"See . . . there you go again!" Sheila said. "You keep forgetting this is a committee. We're supposed to work together."

"Working together doesn't mean you give the orders and we carry them out," Jimmy said.

My feelings exactly! I thought.

Sheila didn't answer Jimmy. She picked up her things, got her coat, and left.

"I hope she never comes back," Jimmy said.

48

Quick**REFERENCE**

Multicultural Link

Encourage students who have lived in other places to describe the different means of transportation they have seen or used.

Meeting Individual Needs: Students Acquiring English

The expression *pros and cons* may be unfamiliar to some students. Point out that it refers to the arguments for and against something.

Art Link

Representing a three-dimensional object on a flat surface often creates problems for young artists. You may wish to show students how techniques such as overlapping and shading can create the illusion of depth or distance.

Social Studies Link

The earliest posters were called broadsides. They contained royal proclamations and political propaganda. By the 19th century, the popular broadside gave way to newspapers. Today posters are used for advertising or decoration.

MINILESSON

Study Skill

TESTED SKILL

Showing Information Graphically

Teach/Model

Ask students to name examples of graphic illustrations they have made or used. (Samples: graphs, story maps, word webs) Then help students design a graphic illustration, such as the table below, that displays the name of the committee members and their tasks.

Member	Role on Project
Sheila	
Peter	
Jimmy	

Discuss how graphic illustrations show a large amount of information in a small space and in a way that is easy to understand.

Practice/Apply

Challenge students to use what they know, as well as reference materials available in the classroom, to complete the chart below.

Type of Transportation	Pros	Cons
Land	1. 2.	1. 2.
Sea	1. 2.	1. 2.
Air	1. 2.	1. 2.

SKILL FINDER Full lesson, p. H2

Interact with Literature

Guided Reading

Comprehension/Critical Thinking

1. How did Peter feel about nearing the end of the project? (He looked forward to finishing the project.) Why? (He was tired of working with Sheila and of thinking about transportation.)
2. Based on your reading, what do you know about Fudge? (Sample: He is much younger than Peter; he tries to imitate what Peter does.)

Predicting/Purpose Setting

Ask students if their predictions were accurate or if their questions have been answered. After students read page 50, have them pose a question they think will be answered in the remainder of the selection, or have them predict the end of the story.

"She'll be back," I told him. "We're her committee."

Jimmy laughed. "Yeah . . . we're all one happy committee!"

I put our poster under the bed, said good-bye to Jimmy, then washed up for supper.

My mother was being pretty nice about our committee meetings. She arranged to have Fudge play at Ralph's apartment on Tuesdays and at Jennie's on Thursdays. Sam has the chicken pox, so he can't play at all.

I was glad that next week would be our last committee meeting after school. I was sick of Sheila and I was getting sick of Transportation. Besides, now that I knew a monorail system was the only way to save our city I was getting upset that the mayor and all the other guys that run things at City Hall weren't doing anything about installing one. If *I* know that's the best method of city transportation how come *they* don't know it?

The next day when I came home from school I went into my bedroom to see Dribble like I always do. Fudge was in there, sitting on my bed.

"Why are you in my room?" I asked him.

He smiled.

"You know you're not supposed to be in here. This is *my* room."

"Want to see?" Fudge said.

"See what?"

"Want to see?"

"What? What are you talking about?" I asked.

He jumped off my bed and crawled underneath it. He came out with our poster. He held it up. "See," he said. "Pretty!"

"What did you do?" I yelled. "What did you do to our poster?" It was covered all over with scribbles in every color Magic Marker. It was ruined! *It was a mess and it was ruined.* I was ready to kill Fudge. I grabbed my poster and ran into the kitchen to show it to my mother. I could hardly speak. "Look," I said, feeling a lump in my throat. "Just look at what he did to my poster." I felt tears come to

50

Self-Assessment

Encourage students to reflect on their reading with these questions:

- How well have I understood the selection so far?
- What reading strategies have I used to read hard parts?

QuickREFERENCE

Challenge

Despite their environmental benefits, few monorails exist in the world today. One of the reasons is the high cost of installation. Suggest that interested students research and briefly report to the class on monorails.

my eyes but I didn't care. "How could you let him?" I asked my mother. "How? Don't you care about me?"

I threw the poster down and ran into my room. I slammed the door, took off my shoe, and flung it at the wall. It made a black mark where it hit. Well, so what!

Soon I heard my mother hollering — and then, Fudge crying. After a while my mother knocked on my bedroom door and called, "Peter, may I come in?"

I didn't answer.

She opened the door and walked over to my bed. She sat down next to me. "I'm very sorry," she said.

I still didn't say anything.

51

MEETING INDIVIDUAL NEEDS

Extra Support

Idiom Students may be unfamiliar with the phrase *feeling a lump in my throat.* Model how to use context to figure out that this phrase refers to the feeling people have in their throat when they are about to cry.

MINILESSON

Making Inferences

REVIEW & MAINTAIN

Teach/Model

Imitate for students the actions of someone who has been waiting for a long time (cross your arms, tap your foot, look at your watch, sigh). Ask students to use the information you provide and their own experience to infer what is happening.

Read aloud the sentences on page 45 that refer to Dribble and Fudge. What can students infer about Dribble and Fudge? (Dribble is a pet and Fudge is a person.) Can they infer any additional information from the sentences? Have them fill in the chart below.

What Text Says	What I Infer

Practice/Apply

Ask students to look at the next references to Dribble and Fudge (page 50). What can they now infer about them? How does Peter's interaction with Fudge make clear that Fudge is his younger brother?

Students Acquiring English
Invite students acquiring English to show gestures used in their cultures by someone who has been waiting a long time.

SKILL FINDER

Full lesson/Reteaching, pp. 107A-107B

Minilessons, p. 95 and Themes 4 and 5

Interact *with* Literature

Reading Strategies

Predict/Infer

Model how to think about predictions and revise them if necessary, based on new information.

Think Aloud

Before I started to read, I predicted that there would be a problem with completing the project, because in some of the pictures Sheila, Peter, and Jimmy look unhappy as they work together. Now I see that Fudge's actions have created an even bigger problem. So now I predict that the committee will find a way to work out their differences. I'll evaluate my revised prediction when I've finished the story.

"Peter," she began.

I didn't look at her.

She touched my arm. "Peter . . . please listen . . . ."

"Don't you see, Mom? I can't even do my homework without him messing it up. It just isn't fair! I wish he was never born. Never! I hate him!"

"You don't hate him," my mother said. "You just think you do."

"Don't tell me," I said. "I mean it. I really can't stand that kid!"

"You're angry," my mother told me. "I know that and I don't blame you. Fudge had no right to touch your poster. I spanked him."

"You did?" I asked. Fudge never gets spanked. My parents don't believe in spanking. "You really spanked him?" I asked again.

"Yes," my mother said.

"Hard?" I asked.

"On his backside," she told me.

I thought that over.

"Peter . . . ." My mother put her arm around me. "I'll buy you a new posterboard tomorrow. It was really my fault. I should never have let him into your room."

"That's why I need a lock on my door," I said.

"I don't like locks on doors. We're a family. We don't have to lock each other out."

"If I had a lock Fudge wouldn't have gotten my poster!"

"It won't happen again," my mother promised.

I wanted to believe her, but really I didn't. Unless she tied him up I knew my brother would get into my room again.

The next day, while I was at school, my mother bought a new yellow posterboard. The hard part was explaining to Jimmy that we had to start all over again. He was a good sport about it. He said this time he'd make sure his truck didn't look like a flying train. And I said, this time I'd make pencil marks first so my letters didn't go uphill.

52

QuickREFERENCE

Students Acquiring English

Alert students to the statement "You don't hate him. You just think you do." Ask English-fluent students to explain what Peter's mother means.

Informal Assessment

Oral Reading Have one or two students read aloud pages 50–52 as a check of oral fluency. See the Oral Reading Checklist in the *Teacher's Assessment Handbook*.

Visual Literacy

Ask students to review the illustrations throughout the selection. Help students see that the characters' body language conveys what they're feeling.

MINILESSON

Fact and Opinion

REVIEW & MAINTAIN

Teach/Model

Review with students the difference between a fact and an opinion.

Fact	Opinion
• Can be proved • May describe something that has happened *(The teacher walked into the classroom.)* • May describe something that exists *(There is an oak tree on the playground.)*	• Cannot be proved • Describes what a person thinks or feels *(Summer is the nicest season; All students should learn to play a musical instrument.)*

Have volunteers read aloud the first two sentences of the last paragraph on page 52. Ask students to identify which of the sentences is a fact-statement (the first) and which is an opinion-statement (the second). Discuss how the first statement describes something that happened, while the second is an expression of opinion on the part of the narrator.

Practice/Apply

Have pairs of students review pages 44–52 to locate at least four examples of fact and opinion. Discuss with the entire class the examples found by each pair, and reinforce the difference between facts and opinions.

SKILL FINDER

Full lesson/Reteaching, Theme 2
Minilessons, Theme 2

Our committee met that afternoon. Sheila didn't mention the last time. Neither did we. Me and Jimmy worked on the poster while Sheila copied our written work into the booklet. We'd be ready to give our oral report to the class on Monday. Not like some committees who hadn't even started yet!

By five o'clock we had finished our poster and Sheila was almost done with the cover for our booklet. Jimmy walked over and stood behind her, watching her work.

After a minute he yelled, "What do you think you're doing, Sheila?"

I got up from the floor and joined them at my desk. I took a look at the cover. It was pretty nice. It said:

TRANSPORTATION IN THE CITY

Under that it said:

BY SHEILA TUBMAN, PETER HATCHER,
AND JAMES FARGO

And under that in small letters it said:

handwritten by miss sheila tubman

Now I knew why Jimmy was mad. "Oh no!" I said, holding my hand to my head. "How could you!"

Sheila didn't say anything.

"It's not fair," I told her. "We didn't put our names on the poster!"

"But the cover's all done," Sheila said. "Can't you see that? I'll never get the letters so straight again. It looks perfect!"

"Oh no!" Jimmy shouted. "We're not handing the booklet in like that. I'll rip it up before I let you!" He grabbed the booklet and threatened to tear it in half.

Sheila screamed. "You wouldn't! I'll kill you! Give it back to me, Jimmy Fargo!" She was ready to cry.

I knew Jimmy wouldn't tear it up but I didn't say so.

"Peter . . . make him give it back!"

"Will you take off that line about your handwriting?" I asked.

"I can't. It'll ruin the booklet."

"Then I think he should rip it up," I said.

Sheila stamped her foot. "Ooooh! I hate you both!"

"You don't really," I told her. "You just think you do."

"I know I do!" Sheila cried.

"That's because you're angry right now," I said. I couldn't help smiling.

Sheila jumped up and tried to get the booklet but Jimmy held it over his head and he's much taller than Sheila. She had no chance at all.

Finally she sat down and whispered, "I give up. You win. I'll take my name off."

"You promise?" Jimmy asked.

"I promise," Sheila said.

Jimmy set the booklet down on my desk in front of Sheila. "Okay," he said. "Start."

"I'm not going to make a whole new cover," Sheila said. "What I'll do is turn this bottom line into a decoration." She picked up a Magic Marker and made little flowers out of the words. Soon, *hand-written by miss sheila tubman* turned into sixteen small flowers. "There," Sheila said. "It's done."

"It looks pretty good," I told her.

MINILESSON

Writer's Craft
Humorous Dialogue

Teach/Model

Explain that *Tales of a Fourth Grade Nothing* is realistic fiction, a story that could happen in real life. The author, Judy Blume, made this story more realistic and enjoyable by adding humorous dialogue–lively, funny conversation between the characters.

Use the graphic organizer, as well as the dialogue in the story to this point, to discuss techniques for creating humorous dialogue.

Use of hyperbole, or exaggeration

"It looks perfect!" p. 55
"I'll kill you!" p. 55
"I hate you both!" p. 55

Use of the unexpected

Peter's dialogue on p. 55 that echoes what his mother said to him earlier in the story

Use of irony, or saying one thing when the opposite is meant

". . . we're all one happy committee!" p. 50

Practice/Apply

Have students locate and analyze other examples of humorous dialogue in this selection.

SKILL FINDER

Writing Activities: Write a Dialogue, p. 59D

Reading-Writing Workshop, p. 91A

Quick REFERENCE

MEETING INDIVIDUAL NEEDS

Students Acquiring English

Call students' attention to Peter's statement "You don't really. You just think you do." Help students realize that Peter is deliberately repeating what his mother has told him. Ask the class whether they think Peter is serious or trying to joke with Sheila.

Interact *with* Literature

Guided Reading

Comprehension/Critical Thinking

1. What problems did the committee overcome to complete the project? (Sheila's bossiness, the boys' trouble with drawing pictures on the poster, Fudge's messing up the poster, Sheila's trying to take most of the credit)
2. How would you describe the way the committee cooperated? The way Peter's family cooperated? (Answers will vary. Both the committee and the family worked through problems to reach a goal.)
3. What lessons about cooperation did you learn from reading this story? (Answers will vary. Students should recognize that communication and compromise are necessary for successful cooperation.)

"It would have looked better without those flowers," Jimmy said. "But at least it's fair now."

That night I showed my mother and father our new poster. They thought it was great. Especially our silver-sparkle airplane. My mother put the poster on top of the refrigerator so it would be safe until the next day, when I would take it to school.

Now I had nothing to worry about. Sheila had the booklet, the poster was safe, and our committee was finished before schedule. I went into my room to relax. Fudge was sitting on the floor, near my bed. My shoebox of supplies was in front of him. His face was a mess of Magic Marker colors and he was using my extra sharp scissors to snip away at his hair. And the hair he snipped was dropping into Dribble's bowl — which he had in front of him on the floor!

"See," he said. "See Fudge. Fudgie's a barber!"

That night I found out hair doesn't hurt my turtle. I picked off every strand from his shell. I cleaned out his bowl and washed off his rocks. He seemed happy.

Two things happened the next day. One was my mother had to take Fudge to the real barber to do something about his hair. He had plenty left in the back, but just about nothing in front and on top. The barber said there wasn't much he could do until the hair grew back. Between his fangs and his hair he was getting funnier looking every day.

The second was my father came home with a chain latch for my bedroom door. I could reach it when I stood on tip-toe, but that brother of mine couldn't reach it at all — no matter what!

Our committee was the first to give its report. Mrs. Haver said we did a super job. She liked our poster a lot. She thought the silver-sparkle airplane was the best. The only thing she asked us was, how come we included a picture of a flying train?

56

Self-Assessment

Ask students to evaluate how they did in reading this selection. Encourage them to ask themselves questions such as:

- Do the characters seem real?
- What parts of the story seemed most true to life?
- Were the predictions and self-questions I made at the start of the story helpful in understanding the selection? If so, how? If not, why not?

Quick REFERENCE

Home Connection

Encourage students to collect stories about school from older friends and relatives.

Social Studies Link

Have students read articles and books about transportation in the United States with their families. Provide class time for them to briefly report what they have learned and to recommend their favorite readings.

Extra Support

Rereading Reinforce students' understanding of the selection by rereading it. If desired, have volunteers read sections aloud. Also, pair students acquiring English with more proficient English readers to reread the selection.

Background: FYI

Guest Speaker Invite a guest speaker to share ideas about how people work together in organizations or businesses. Possible guests: the coach of a sports team or a medical professional who works in a hospital.

Interact *with* Literature

Responding Activities

Personal Response

Students can discuss realistic and unrealistic parts of the story or respond in another way.

Anthology Activities

Encourage students to choose from the activities on pages 58–59.

Literature Discussion

If you had been on the committee, would you have gotten along with the others? Why or why not?

Selection Connections

Have students complete the portion of the chart on *Literacy Activity Book* page 8 that refers to *Tales of a Fourth Grade Nothing.*

RESPONDING

More Super Ideas

Write a Description

What a Day!

Have you ever worked on a project on which everything seemed to go wrong? Maybe writing about your experience will help you recover from the disaster! First, explain what happened — you can be funny or serious. Then compare how you felt about your project with the way that Peter felt.

58

Informal Assessment

Students' responses should include support for their ideas and opinions.

Additional Support:

- Use Guided Reading questions to review.
- Have students create a selection summary.

QuickREFERENCE

Home Connection

Encourage students to retell the selection to members of their families. Students may wish to use drawings to illustrate their retellings.

MEETING INDIVIDUAL NEEDS

Challenge

Suggest that students analyze their disaster project for What a Day! and explain what they and others could have done to make the project turn out better.

Write an Advice Article

How to Live with Fudge . . .

It looks like living with a little brother — or sister — can be hazardous. Use Peter's experience to help you come up with a list of helpful hints for dealing with a younger sibling. Share your list with a partner. Then work together to turn your lists into a magazine advice article for older brothers and sisters.

Discuss Teamwork

All Together Now

With your partner or group, discuss how well you think Peter, Jimmy, and Sheila worked together. The teacher liked their project. Does that mean they were successful as a team? What advice about teamwork would you give them?

Draw a Comic Strip

Picture This!

Turn the story you have just read into a comic strip, and share it with classmates or your family. Draw and color the most important scenes and put the dialogue in speech balloons.

59

MEETING INDIVIDUAL NEEDS — Students Acquiring English

For the activity How to Live with Fudge . . ., have students read their advice articles aloud to small groups. Invite students acquiring English to give writers feedback about their articles and to suggest additional hints about living with a younger sibling.

Comprehension Check

To check comprehension, use these questions or *Literacy Activity Book* page 10.

1. What steps did the committee take to make sure their project was good? (Sample: divided up tasks, began right away)
2. How do the committee's experiences compare with your own experiences working in a group? (Answers should include references to the selection.)
3. If you could give Peter, Jimmy, and Sheila grades for cooperation, what would you give them? Why? (Answers should be supported by the story.)

Literacy Activity Book, p. 10

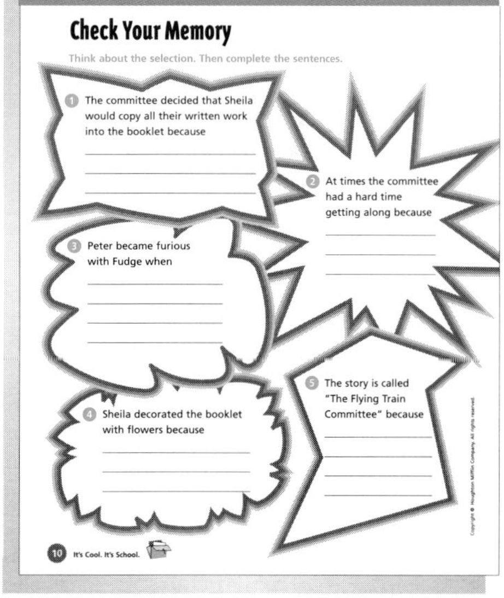
Check Your Memory

Think about the selection. Then complete the sentences.

1. The committee decided that Sheila would copy all their written work into the booklet because
2. At times the committee had a hard time getting along because
3. Peter became furious with Fudge when
4. Sheila decorated the booklet with flowers because
5. The story is called "The Flying Train Committee" because

10 It's Cool. It's School.

Portfolio Opportunity

- Comprehension Check: Save *Literacy Activity Book* p. 10.
- Save students' comic strips or written responses to the responding activities.

Instruct *and* Integrate

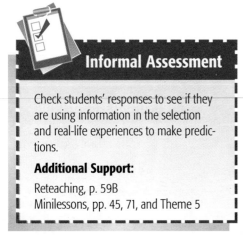

Comprehension

Transparency 1–3

Predicting Outcomes

When making predictions, remember to:
- use clues in the story,
- think about what has already happened in the story,
- think about what you know from real life.

WHAT I THINK WILL HAPPEN	WHY I THINK THIS WILL HAPPEN (clues in the story, what has already happened, real life)	WHAT REALLY HAPPENED
Sheila will be back.	Sheila promised to do ten pages. She wants a good mark. She cares about the project.	Sheila came back.

IT'S COOL. IT'S SCHOOL. Tales of a Fourth Grade Nothing COMPREHENSION SKILL Predicting Outcomes

TRANSPARENCY 1-3 TEACHER'S BOOK PAGE 59A

Literacy Activity Book, p. 11

Recess Racers

Read the story about some fourth graders. Then answer the questions.

Steve challenged Julie to a race at recess. Steve loved to race, and he usually won. Julie didn't like to lose races so she agreed to the contest on one condition. "I'll race with an apple on my head, and you have to balance an orange on yours."

"That's fine with me," said Steve. "I'll win no matter what."

"Here are the rules," Julie explained. "If the fruit falls off your head, you're allowed to pick it up and put it back. However, you have to continue racing from where it fell off. Mike can watch to make sure no one cheats."

On the call, "Ready, set, go!" Julie and Steve began walking as fast as they could. It wasn't easy. About every three steps or so, one racer lost his or her piece of fruit. Before they were halfway around the track, both racers were spending more time picking up their fruit than actually racing. It also didn't help when they started laughing.

"Hurry! The bell's going to ring!" Mike jumped up and down.

Just then, Julie and Steve noticed that someone else was watching the race. It was their teacher, Mrs. Wilson. She was laughing as hard as they were.

1. Why does Julie want the racers to balance fruit on their heads? ________
2. What happens when the school bell rings at the end of recess? ________
3. How do you think the race will end? ________

It's Cool. It's School. 11

Informal Assessment

Check students' responses to see if they are using information in the selection and real-life experiences to make predictions.

Additional Support:

Reteaching, p. 59B
Minilessons, pp. 45, 71, and Theme 5

INTERACTIVE LEARNING

TESTED SKILL

Predicting Outcomes

LAB, p. 11

Teach/Model

Ask students whether they try to figure out the ending of a movie as they are watching it. Help them realize that when they do this, whether while watching a movie or reading a story, they are predicting outcomes. Readers can predict outcomes by looking for clues in the story, thinking about what has already happened in the story, and thinking about what they know from their own experience.

Read the following passage from page 48:

> *Sheila didn't answer Jimmy. She picked up her things, got her coat, and left. "I hope she never comes back," Jimmy said.*

Ask students if, as they read, they thought that Sheila would quit the committee for good. Point out that they could make a prediction that she would be back. Model by using the chart on Transparency 1-3.

WHAT I THOUGHT WOULD HAPPEN	WHY I THOUGHT THIS WOULD HAPPEN (clues in the story, what has already happened, real life)	WHAT REALLY HAPPENED
Sheila will be back.	Sheila promised to do ten pages. She wants a good mark. She cares about the project.	Sheila came back.

Guide students in reviewing the steps for making predictions. Ask students what other predictions they made in this part of the story, and list their responses in the appropriate columns on the transparency.

Practice/Apply

- Have students make Predicting Outcomes charts to use for other episodes in the story.
- Have students use *Literacy Activity Book* page 11 to track their predictions about what will happen to the race.

SKILL FINDER Minilessons, pp. 45, 71, and Theme 5

Reteaching

Predicting Outcomes

MEETING INDIVIDUAL NEEDS

Read aloud a portion of the text that indicates a suspenseful moment. Then ask students what they thought would happen next. How did they think the story would end? Help students understand that when they guess what will happen next in a story, they are making a prediction.

Display Transparency 1–4, revealing only the passage in the first box. Ask a volunteer to read this passage aloud. Ask students questions about the passage to guide them to predict what will happen next in the story. Repeat with the remaining passages. Then discuss the predictions students made and the methods they used to guess the outcome of each part of the story. Finally, have students write an ending for the story based on what they know so far. Ask volunteers to share their writing with the class.

Transparency 1–4

IT'S COOL. IT'S SCHOOL.
Tales of a Fourth Grade Nothing
COMPREHENSION SKILL/RETEACHING Predicting Outcomes

Adventures in the Cafeteria Kitchen

"I think the gym is this way," Jenny said.
Jenny, Peter, and I had walked across town to see our team play Lincoln in the championships. By the time we got to Lincoln School, everyone had gone into the game.
"I'm not sure this is the right way. Mrs. Parkson will be worried if we don't get to the game soon." Peter was nervous.
"Come on, Peter, why don't we look around?" Jenny replied. "We've already missed half the game."
I pushed through a set of doors, and we stepped into the cafeteria.

The kitchen looked spooky. The only lights on were the red fire safety lights, and the machines looked big and dark.
"I told you it was neat," Jenny said as she moved closer.
"Really cool," I agreed.
Then Peter grabbed my arm. "What was that?" he whispered.
We all heard a strange noise. It came from inside the big walk-in refrigerator. We were too scared to move. The refrigerator door handle turned and the door creaked open.

Out of the dark refrigerator room stepped the school janitor.
"AAAGH!" he shouted, dropping an apple from his hand. "You kids surprised me. What are you doing back here?"
"I . . . uh, we were trying to get back to the gym, but we got lost," I told him. "What were you doing in the refrigerator?"
"That's where I keep my lunch," he replied. "Now you kids had better get going. The gym is this way." He led us down the long hall. "You really scared me," he said, and laughed.
"We know how you feel," Jenny said. Then she stopped. Mrs. Parkson was standing in the hallway ahead.
"Oh, *there* you are," she said, glaring at us.

TRANSPARENCY 1–4
TEACHER'S BOOK PAGE 59B

Adventures in the Cafeteria Kitchen

"I think the gym is this way," Jenny said.

Jenny, Peter, and I had walked across town to see our team play Lincoln in the championships. By the time we got to Lincoln School everyone had gone into the game.

"I'm not sure this is the right way. Mrs. Parkson will be worried if we don't get to the game soon." Peter was nervous.

"Come on, Peter, why don't we look around?" Jenny replied. "We've already missed half the game."

I pushed through a set of doors, and we stepped into the cafeteria.

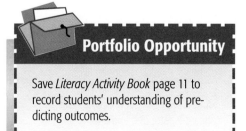

Portfolio Opportunity

Save *Literacy Activity Book* page 11 to record students' understanding of predicting outcomes.

Instruct *and* Integrate

Writing Skills and Activities

Transparency 1–5

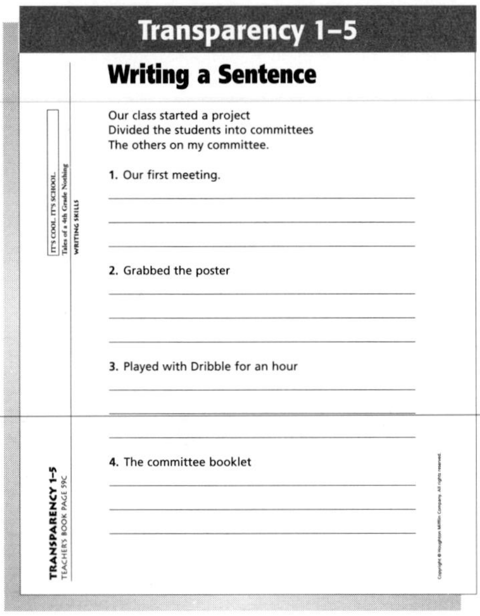
Writing a Sentence

Our class started a project
Divided the students into committees
The others on my committee.

1. Our first meeting.
2. Grabbed the poster
3. Played with Dribble for an hour
4. The committee booklet

IT'S COOL. IT'S SCHOOL. Tales of a 4th Grade Nothing WRITING SKILLS

TRANSPARENCY 1–5 TEACHER'S BOOK PAGE 59C

Literacy Activity Book, p. 12

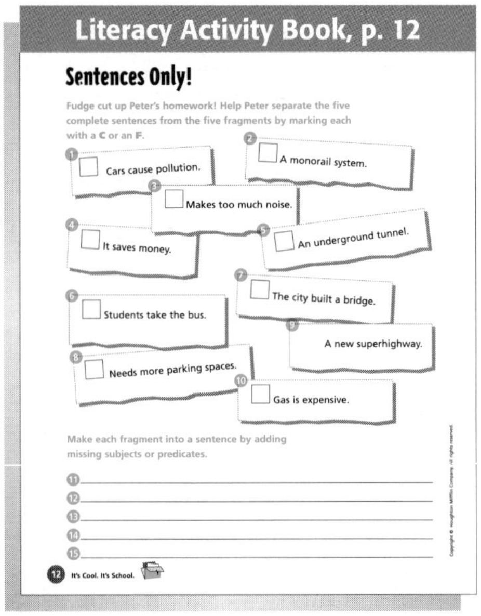
Sentences Only!

Fudge cut up Peter's homework! Help Peter separate the five complete sentences from the five fragments by marking each with a C or an F.

1. Cars cause pollution.
2. A monorail system.
3. Makes too much noise.
4. It saves money.
5. An underground tunnel.
6. Students take the bus.
7. The city built a bridge.
8. A new superhighway.
9. Needs more parking spaces.
10. Gas is expensive.

Make each fragment into a sentence by adding missing subjects or predicates.

11.
12.
13.
14.
15.

12 It's Cool. It's School.

Informal Assessment

Check students' writing for consistency as well as to make sure they have used complete sentences. Does the writing have a clear purpose and style? If students have worked cooperatively on a piece of writing, does it flow, or is it disjointed, especially in the places where one writer stopped and another began?

INTERACTIVE LEARNING

TESTED SKILL

Writing a Sentence

LAB, p. 12

Teach/Model Display Transparency 1–5. Have students read the three groups of words at the top of the transparency. Ask which group of words is a sentence. (the first) Remind students that a sentence is a group of words that tells a complete thought—it tells who or what the sentence is about and what that person or thing is or does. Ask students to explain why the second group of words is not a sentence. (It doesn't tell who divided the students.) Ask the same question about the third group. (It doesn't tell who the others are or what they did.) Have volunteers suggest ways of adding to the second and third groups to make them sentences.

Our class started a project.	complete sentence
Divided the students into committees.	no subject, doesn't tell who divided the students
The others on my committee	no verb, doesn't tell what the others did

Have students add to each of the other fragments on the transparency to create a complete sentence. They might want to write more than one sentence for each fragment. Ask volunteers to share their sentences by reading them aloud or writing them on the transparency.

Practice/Apply Assign the activity Social Studies: Transportation Project. Remind students to make sure that each of the sentences in their booklet is complete.

SKILL FINDER
Grammar, Theme 1, 59I–59J
Reading-Writing Workshop, pp. 90–91F

Writing Activities

Social Studies: Transportation Project

Cooperative Learning

Have students work in small groups, or committees, to do a project like the one Peter, Jimmy, and Sheila did in *Tales of a Fourth Grade Nothing.* Have each group choose a form of transportation and create a booklet and a poster. You might also have them do an oral report about their topic.

Shared Writing: Persuasive Paragraph

Remind students that Peter's solution to New York City's traffic problem was a citywide monorail. As a class, brainstorm transportation problems in your community and ways to address them. Use the following to prompt ideas:

- People should give up their cars and use public transportation.
- Bus routes should cover more or different parts of the community.
- The city or town should make a bike path.
- A new kind of public transportation is needed in the community.

Have the class choose one idea to write about. Work with students to write a persuasive paragraph stating the problem, and proposing an imaginative solution.

Write a Dialogue

Have students write a dialogue between two friends. They might choose two of the characters from *Tales of a Fourth Grade Nothing*, make up a dialogue between themselves and a real-life friend, or create two characters of their own. Before they begin to write, have students plan the topic of their dialogue and think about where it will take place. Will the friends be on the telephone? on the school bus? in the cafeteria?

Encourage students to use humor in their dialogues. *(See the Writer's Craft Minilesson on page 55.)*

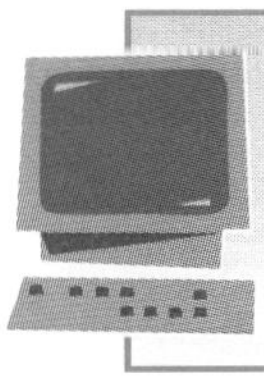

Students can use the Learning Company's new elementary writing center for all their writing activities.

Portfolio Opportunity

- Save *Literacy Activity Book* page 12 to record students' understanding of writing complete sentences.
- Save responses to activities on this page for writing samples.

Instruct *and* Integrate

Word Skills and Strategies

Literacy Activity Book, p. 13

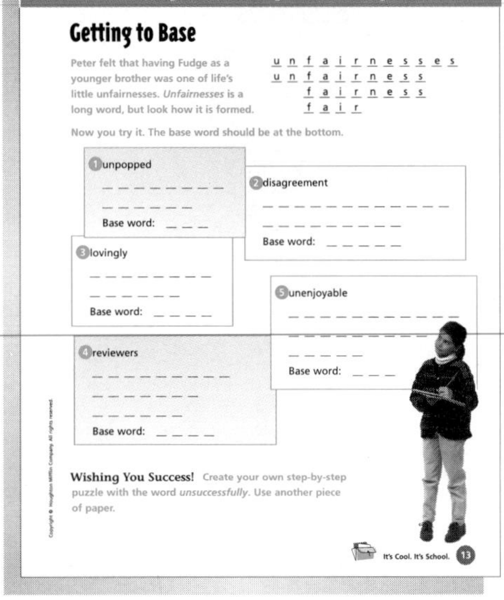

Getting to Base

Peter felt that having Fudge as a younger brother was one of life's little unfairnesses. *Unfairnesses* is a long word, but look how it is formed.

u n f a i r n e s s e s
u n f a i r n e s s
f a i r n e s s
f a i r

Now you try it. The base word should be at the bottom.

1 unpopped
Base word: ___

2 disagreement
Base word: _____

3 lovingly
Base word: ____

4 reviewers
Base word: ____

5 unenjoyable
Base word: ___

Wishing You Success! Create your own step-by-step puzzle with the word *unsuccessfully*. Use another piece of paper.

Copyright © Houghton Mifflin Company. All rights reserved.

It's Cool. It's School. 13

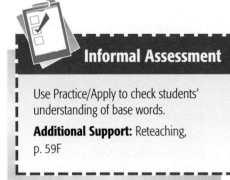

MEETING INDIVIDUAL NEEDS

Extra Support

Point out that the meaning of a base word is closely related to the meaning of the longer word. Make sure students understand that not every group of letters that happens to form a word within a longer word is a base word. For example, *top* is not the base word of *topic*.

Informal Assessment

Use Practice/Apply to check students' understanding of base words.

Additional Support: Reteaching, p. 59F

INTERACTIVE LEARNING

TESTED SKILL

Structural Analysis

Base Words

LAB, p. 13

Teach/Model Tell students that a long word that seems unfamiliar may actually contain a familiar base word. Write these sentences on the board.

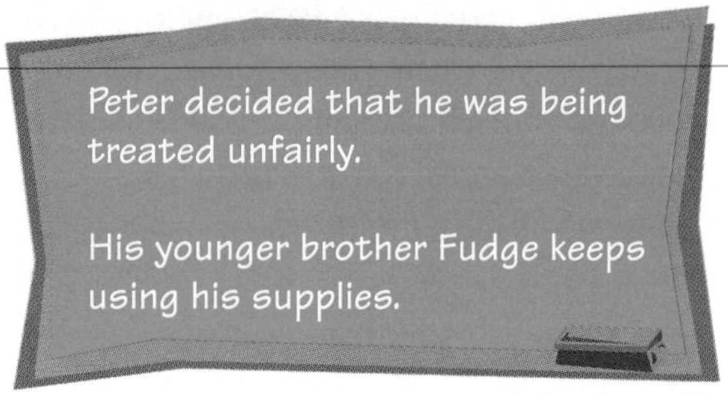

Peter decided that he was being treated unfairly.
His younger brother Fudge keeps using his supplies.

Remind students that a base word is a word to which beginnings and endings can be added. Read the sentences on the board aloud and have volunteers identify the words containing base words. As each word is identified, write the base word above it. *(decide, be, treat, fair, young, keep, use, supply).* Point out that a base word may be spelled differently when an ending is added to it. Use the words *using* and *supplies* as examples.

Practice/Apply Write each word below (except the base words) on an index card and give one card to each student. Have students determine the base word of their word and then find the other four students whose word has the same base word. Once students have found their "word-family members," have them write their base word on the board and their individual words beneath it. As a class, discuss how the words within each family are related in meaning.

live	divide	agree	sharp	real
lively	division	disagree	sharpest	realize
alive	divider	agreement	sharpening	reality
living	undivided	agreeable	sharply	realistic
relive	divisible	agreed	sharpness	really
livelihood	subdivide	agreeing	sharpener	unreal

Reteaching

Base Words

MEETING INDIVIDUAL NEEDS

Draw three houses and mailboxes on the board. Label the mailboxes *jump, hope,* and *copy*. Remind students that many words have a smaller base word and that words with the same base word are all part of the same word family. Write the words below on the board in random order. Have volunteers write each word in the appropriate house.

jumps	hoping	copies
jumping	hoped	copier
jumpy	hopeful	recopied
jumper	hopelessly	copying

MINILESSON

Think About Words

Teach/Model Review the Think About Words Strategy with students.

Then direct students to turn to page 46 in their anthologies and have them silently reread the argument between Peter and Sheila about the monorail. Use the Think Aloud below to model the Think About Words Strategy.

> **Think Aloud** Look at the last word in the second paragraph. This word comes up several times during Peter and Sheila's argument. If I didn't know this word I could try to pronounce it several ways. I might try SIE-stem or SEE-stem or SIH-stem. I'd recognize that *SIH-stem* is a word I know. Now look at the word *practical*. It looks like *practice*, but it doesn't seem to have much to do with doing something again and again. This word must be important because it's what the whole argument is about. Let's look it up in the dictionary.

Practice/Apply ***Cooperative Learning*** Have students work in pairs to find and discuss any unfamiliar words in *Tales of a Fourth Grade Nothing*. Then have the class compare their decisions about those words: Was the word important? What clues to meaning did they find in the word or in the text around it?

Think About Words Strategy

Ask yourself this question: Is this word important to your understanding of what you are reading?

If the answer is yes, follow these steps:

- Try to pronounce the word.
- Look for context clues.
- Think of other words that remind you of this one.
- Look for familiar prefixes, base words, roots, or suffixes.
- Use a dictionary.

Portfolio Opportunity

Save *Literacy Activity Book* page 13 to record students' understanding of base words.

Instruct *and* Integrate

Building Vocabulary

Literacy Activity Book, p. 14

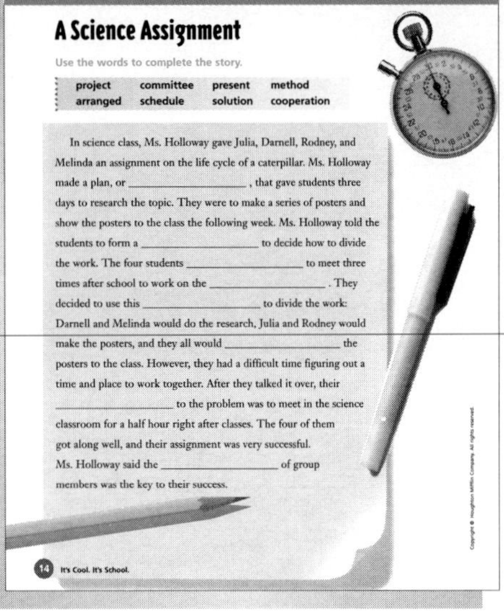

A Science Assignment

Use the words to complete the story.

project	committee	present	method
arranged	schedule	solution	cooperation

In science class, Ms. Holloway gave Julia, Darnell, Rodney, and Melinda an assignment on the life cycle of a caterpillar. Ms. Holloway made a plan, or ______________, that gave students three days to research the topic. They were to make a series of posters and show the posters to the class the following week. Ms. Holloway told the students to form a ______________ to decide how to divide the work. The four students ______________ to meet three times after school to work on the ______________. They decided to use this ______________ to divide the work: Darnell and Melinda would do the research, Julia and Rodney would make the posters, and they all would ______________ the posters to the class. However, they had a difficult time figuring out a time and place to work together. After they talked it over, their ______________ to the problem was to meet in the science classroom for a half hour right after classes. The four of them got along well, and their assignment was very successful. Ms. Holloway said the ______________ of group members was the key to their success.

14 It's Cool. It's School.

Use this page to review Selection Vocabulary.

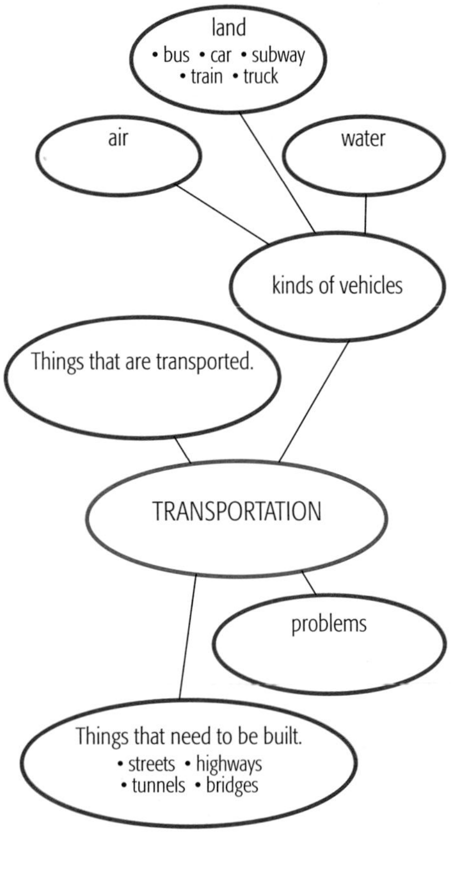

Vocabulary Activities

Synonym Concentration

Remind students that when the Flying Train Committee met, there was a lot of shouting, yelling, and hollering. Elict that those three words have the same meaning. Remind students that words with the same or nearly the same meaning are called *synonyms*.

Write each of the words shown on a card. You might want to make several sets. Have pairs of students play Synonym Concentration by following these directions.

dull	under	big	orders
boring	beneath	large	commands
ruin	snip	mad	small
destroy	cut	angry	little
flung	cheerful		
threw	happy		

Shuffle the cards. Place them in four rows, five cards to a row, with the words facing down. Player 1 turns over two cards. If the words on the cards are synonyms, Player 1 keeps the cards and takes another turn. If the words are not synonyms, Player 1 turns the cards over again, and Player 2 takes a turn. The player with the most cards wins.

Transportation Words

Work with students to brainstorm words related to transportation, organizing their ideas in a semantic map. Use the ideas from the partial map shown to start the brainstorming.

Vocabulary Notebook

Explain to students that readers and writers often keep track of new words they want to learn by recording them in a notebook. Suggest that students make vocabulary notebooks by stapling sheets of paper together or punching holes and fastening them with rings, paper fasteners, or yarn.

After students have assembled and decorated their Vocabulary Notebooks, have them write the letters of the alphabet in their notebooks, two or three per page, to help them order their vocabulary words. Remind them that recording a new word in the Vocabulary Notebook means writing it with correct spelling and explaining what it means in a way that will be remembered.

Spelling

FIVE-DAY PLAN

DAY 1	DAY 2	DAY 3	DAY 4	DAY 5
Pretest; Minilesson; Challenge Words/ Additional Words (opt.); Take-Home Word Lists (LAB)	First LAB page; Challenge Words Practice (opt.)	Check first LAB page; Second LAB page (except writing application)	Check second LAB page; writing application (LAB)	Test

Teaching CHOICES

MINILESSON

Spelling Words

*class
*plan
*desk
*still
*check
*dull
*cost
*trust
*snip
*knock

Challenge Words

*topic
*traffic
*sketch
*whisper
*script

Additional Spelling Words

odd
inch
past
crunch
kept

*Starred words or forms of the words appear in *Tales of a Fourth Grade Nothing.*

TESTED SKILL

Short Vowels

LAB, pp. 15–16

- Write *class, desk, still, cost,* and *dull* on the board. Have students listen for the vowel sound as you say each word.
- Ask students what vowel sound they hear in the word *class.* (/ă/) Then ask what letter spells the /ă/ sound. (a) Point out that the /ă/ sound is followed by the consonant sound /s/. Repeat this procedure with the remaining words. Explain that a short vowel sound spelled by a single vowel and followed by a consonant sound is the short vowel pattern.
- Write the Spelling Words on the board. Tell students that each Spelling Word has a short vowel sound. Say the Spelling Words and have students repeat them.

Spelling Assessment

Pretest

Say each underlined word, read the sentence, and then repeat the word. Have students write only the underlined words.

1. My class is learning about transportation.
2. Let's meet after school to plan the project.
3. I wish my desk was next to yours.
4. We're still working on our book report.
5. Ask the teacher to check your work.
6. That book was dull in some parts.
7. How much did your notebook cost?
8. Can I trust you with a big secret?
9. Use scissors to snip off uneven edges.
10. Please knock before coming in my room.

Test

Spelling Words Use the Pretest sentences.

Challenge Words

11. I need to practice writing in script.
12. The topic of my report is pollution.
13. The librarian told us to whisper.
14. Our bus got stuck in traffic.
15. I made a pencil sketch of my dog.

SKILL FINDER

Daily Language Practice, p. 59J
Reading-Writing Workshop, p. 91E

Literacy Activity Book, p. 15

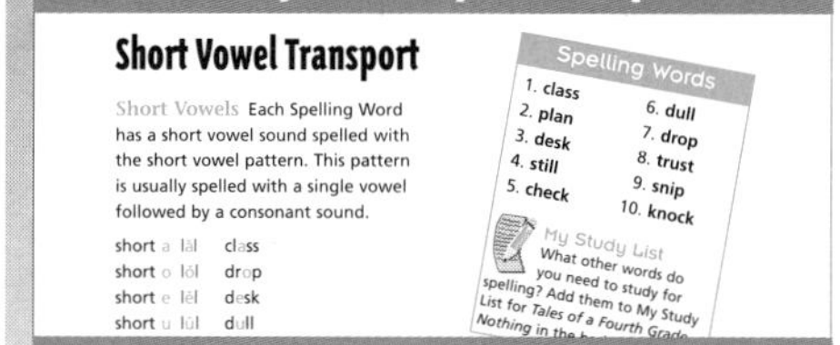
Short Vowel Transport

Short Vowels Each Spelling Word has a short vowel sound spelled with the short vowel pattern. This pattern is usually spelled with a single vowel followed by a consonant sound.

short a /ă/ class
short o /ŏ/ drop
short e /ĕ/ desk
short u /ŭ/ dull

Spelling Words
1. class 6. dull
2. plan 7. drop
3. desk 8. trust
4. still 9. snip
5. check 10. knock

My Study List
What other words do you need to study for spelling? Add them to My Study List for *Tales of a Fourth Grade Nothing* in the ...

Literacy Activity Book, p. 16

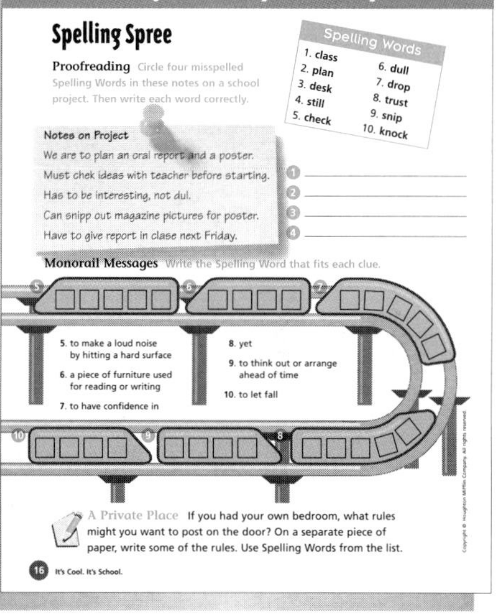
Spelling Spree

Proofreading Circle four misspelled Spelling Words in these notes on a school project. Then write each word correctly.

Spelling Words
1. class 6. dull
2. plan 7. drop
3. desk 8. trust
4. still 9. snip
5. check 10. knock

Notes on Project
We are to plan an oral report and a poster.
Must chek ideas with teacher before starting.
Has to be interesting, not dul.
Can snipp out magazine pictures for poster.
Have to give report in clase next Friday.

1 ____
2 ____
3 ____
4 ____

Monorail Messages Write the Spelling Word that fits each clue.

5. to make a loud noise by hitting a hard surface
6. a piece of furniture used for reading or writing
7. to have confidence in
8. yet
9. to think out or arrange ahead of time
10. to let fall

A Private Place If you had your own bedroom, what rules might you want to post on the door? On a separate piece of paper, write some of the rules. Use Spelling Words from the list.

16 It's Cool. It's School.

Copyright © Houghton Mifflin Company. All rights reserved.

Literacy Activity Book

Take-Home Word Lists: pp. 313–314

Spelling Vocabulary

Students can use the **Spelling Spree CD-ROM** for extra practice with the spelling principles taught in this selection.

MEETING INDIVIDUAL NEEDS

Challenge

Challenge Words Practice Have students write each Challenge Word. Then, for each word, have them write another word that they associate with it, and write a sentence using both words.

Example: topic–encyclopedia

I found lots of information about my topic in the encyclopedia.

Instruct *and* Integrate

Grammar

5-Day Planner FIVE-DAY PLAN

DAY 1	DAY 2	DAY 3	DAY 4	DAY 5
Daily Language Practice 1; Teach/Model; First LAB page	Daily Language Practice 2; Check first LAB page; Cooperative Learning	Daily Language Practice 3; Writing Application	Daily Language Practice 4; Reteaching (opt.); Second LAB page	Daily Language Practice 5; Check second LAB page; Students' Writing

Transparency 1–6

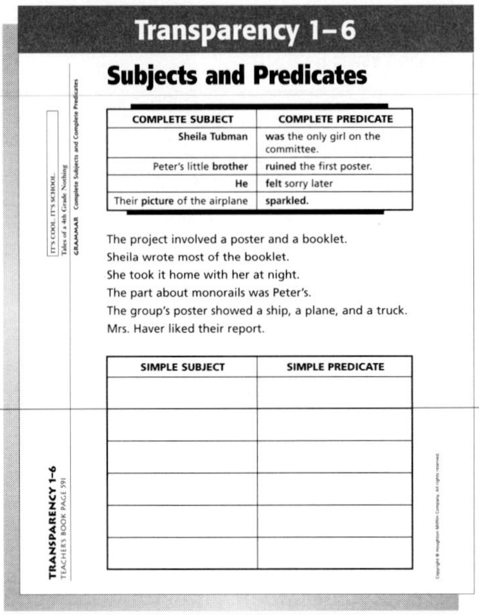

Subjects and Predicates

COMPLETE SUBJECT	COMPLETE PREDICATE
Sheila Tubman	was the only girl on the committee.
Peter's little **brother**	**ruined** the first poster.
He	**felt** sorry later
Their **picture** of the airplane	**sparkled.**

The project involved a poster and a booklet.
Sheila wrote most of the booklet.
She took it home with her at night.
The part about monorails was Peter's.
The group's poster showed a ship, a plane, and a truck.
Mrs. Haver liked their report.

SIMPLE SUBJECT	SIMPLE PREDICATE

Literacy Activity Book, p. 18

Literacy Activity Book, p. 17

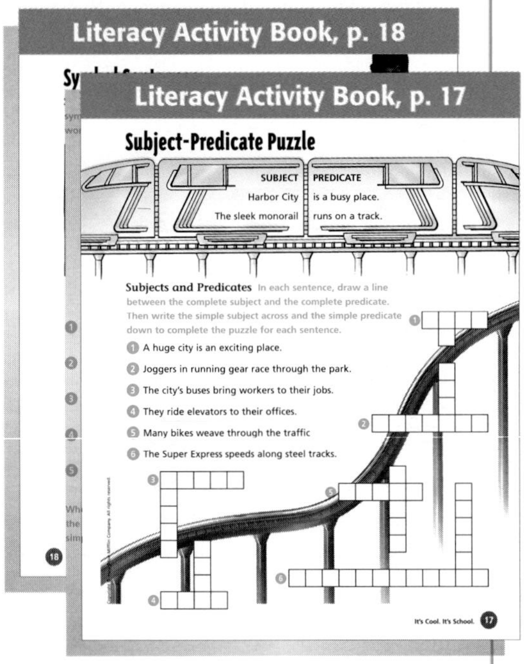

Subject-Predicate Puzzle

SUBJECT	PREDICATE
Harbor City	is a busy place.
The sleek monorail	runs on a track.

Subjects and Predicates In each sentence, draw a line between the complete subject and the complete predicate. Then write the simple subject across and the simple predicate down to complete the puzzle for each sentence.

1. A huge city is an exciting place.
2. Joggers in running gear race through the park.
3. The city's buses bring workers to their jobs.
4. They ride elevators to their offices.
5. Many bikes weave through the traffic
6. The Super Express speeds along steel tracks.

It's Cool. It's School. 17

INTERACTIVE LEARNING

TESTED SKILL

Subjects and Predicates

LAB, pp. 17–18

Every sentence has a **subject** and a **predicate**.

- The **complete subject** includes all the words that tell whom or what the sentence is about. The main word in the complete subject is the **simple subject**.
- The **complete predicate** includes all the words that tell what the subject does or is. The main word in the complete predicate is the **simple predicate**.

Teach/Model Invite volunteers to draw pictures of kinds of transportation at the chalkboard. Ask other students to suggest sentences about the activity. (Write each sentence so that it has only one subject and one verb.) Example:

The three students drew pictures of a bus, a train, and a plane.

Ask students to tell whom or what each sentence is about and what the subject is or does. Introduce *complete subject* and *complete predicate*. Explain that every sentence has these two parts. Ask students to find the main word in the subject and the main word in the predicate. Introduce *simple subject* and *simple predicate*.

Display Transparency 1–6. Elicit that the simple subject may be more than one word if it is a name. Help students understand why *picture*, not *airplane*, is the subject of the last sentence. Elicit that the simple and complete subjects may be the same as may be the simple and complete predicates. Ask volunteers to divide the subjects from the predicates in the other sentences and to find the simple subjects and the simple predicates.

SKILL FINDER Reading-Writing Workshop, p. 91E

Informal Assessment

Responses to the activities should indicate general understanding of subjects and predicates.

Additional Support:
Reteaching, p. 59J

INTERACTIVE LEARNING *(continued)*

Practice/Apply

***Cooperative Learning:* Sentence Construction** Form Construction Crews of four to six students. Half of the students in each crew form the Subject Team and half form the Predicate Team. Ask each crew member to write a short sentence consisting only of a simple subject and a simple predicate. The Subject Team builds the simple subjects into complete subjects. The Predicate Team builds the simple predicates into complete predicates. Tell the teams to join their subjects and predicates, and invite them to share their favorite constructions.

Writing Application: Transportation Proposal If students could arrive at school any way they like, how would they come? by parachute? by motorcycle? by helicopter? Invite them to write a paragraph explaining their choice. Remind them to check that each sentence has a subject and a predicate.

Students' Writing To help students eliminate sentence fragments, encourage them to check works in process to be sure that all sentences have subjects and predicates.

Reteaching

Subjects and Predicates

MEETING INDIVIDUAL NEEDS

Write simple sentences on strips of paper, and then cut them apart between the complete subject and the complete predicate. (Be sure there is at least one half of a sentence for each student.) Put the strips in a box. Draw two columns on chart paper. Label them *Subjects* and *Predicates*.

Review the definitions of subjects and predicates. Then invite each student to draw a strip from the box. Ask the student if the strip tells who or what or if it tells what someone or something is or does. Direct the student to tape the strip in the appropriate column on the chart and to underline or highlight with a marker the simple subject or the simple predicate. When finished, invite students to match the subjects and the predicates.

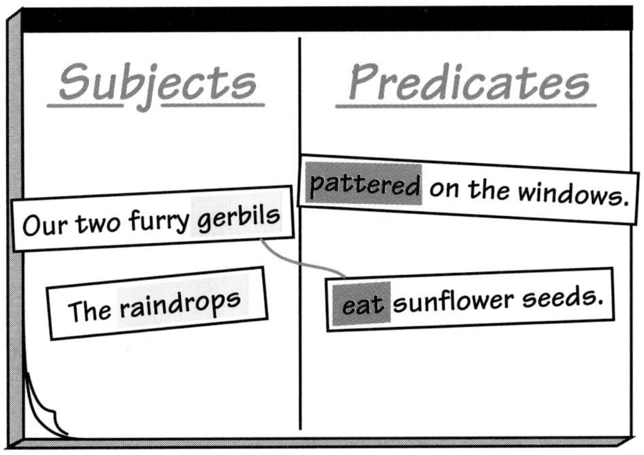

Students Acquiring English Be sure these students read or practice the sentences orally before they do the activity.

More Practice

Houghton Mifflin English Level 4
Workbook Plus, pp. 7–8, 9–10, 11–12
Reteaching Workbook, pp. 4–6

Writers Express
Writers Express SourceBook, pp. 69–70

Daily Language Practice

Focus Skills

Grammar: Subjects and Predicates
Spelling: Short Vowels

Every day write one sentence fragment on the chalkboard. Have each student write the sentence fragment correctly on a sheet of paper. Tell students to add a subject or a predicate to complete the sentence and to correct any misspelled words. Have students correct their own paper as a volunteer corrects the sentence on the chalkboard.

Students Acquiring English Have these students work with fluent English-speaking students.

Sample responses:

1. The whole clas.
   The whole **class chose the project**.
2. Our part of the plann.
   Our part of the **plan is clear**.
3. Is so dul.
   That poster is so **dull**.
4. Still works every night at his dask.
   Jimmy still works every night at his **desk**.
5. Hear a nock at the door.
   I hear a **knock** at the door.

Instruct *and* Integrate

Communication Activities

Listening and Speaking

Committee Report

Cooperative Learning

Divide the class into committees of three or four (heterogeneous groups will benefit students acquiring English). Provide each committee with a section of a daily newspaper. Have each group choose one story from the newspaper to be the topic for a brief oral report. Set a reasonable time limit for committees to complete their work, and ask the groups to deliver the report for the rest of the class.

Review Transparency 1–1 (see page 41C) with students, and ask them to use information from the transparency and their own committee experience to suggest guidelines for working in a group. Post the guidelines in a prominent location.

How to Work in a Group

- Members should stay focused on the goal of the group.
- Members should allow others to express their opinions.
- Each member should fulfill his or her responsibility.
- Members should settle their differences in such a way that all members get a part of what they wanted.

Audio Tape
for It's Cool. It's School.:
Tales of a Fourth Grade Nothing

Students Acquiring English will benefit from several listenings.

Informal Assessment

For the activity Committee Report, use the how to list to evaluate students' understanding of working in groups.

Campaign Speech

MEETING INDIVIDUAL NEEDS

Challenge Propose that Peter, Jimmy, and Sheila are each running for class president. Ask students to choose the character they feel is most qualified to be class president and give a brief speech in which they try to persuade their classmates to vote for their candidate.

Students Acquiring English may want to prepare a campaign poster for their candidate instead of a speech.

Viewing

Creating Posters

Review with students the features included on the poster that Peter and Jimmy created. Lead a discussion about what makes an effective poster, and create a list of criteria on the chalkboard.

Have students make posters advertising the book *Tales of a Fourth Grade Nothing.* The posters can focus on any aspect of the book, from the excitement of its plot to the quality of the author's writing. Display the posters in the classroom and have students evaluate their effectiveness based on the criteria from the class discussion.

Students Acquiring English In preparation for the activity, have students acquiring English work together to list all of the information they can find in the story describing the poster.

The drawing and words catch and hold the viewer's attention.

The poster communicates a clear message.

The message is simple and direct.

The drawings and words are well placed on the poster.

Working Together Collage

MEETING INDIVIDUAL NEEDS

Students Acquiring English Provide students with a variety of magazines and newspapers and a large sheet of posterboard. Have them title the posterboard "Working Together," and suggest that they create a collage, using the following steps. Display the finished collage on the bulletin board or in a common area.

1 Cut out drawings or photographs showing people working or playing in pairs or groups.

2 Cut out pictures of offices, schools, or other surroundings that provide an environmental context for the groups of people.

3 Arrange each type of group within its context in the collage, and glue the pictures to the posterboard.

Materials
- magazines
- newspapers
- posterboard
- crayon or marker
- safety scissors
- white glue

Portfolio Opportunity
- Save students' posters to record students' understanding of effective poster techniques.
- Save the collage in a class portfolio.

Instruct *and* Integrate

Cross-Curricular Activities

Book List

Science

Wings, Wheels, and Snails
by Tom Stacy

From Cycle to Spaceship: The Story of Transport
by Michael Pollard

Social Studies

State and Local Government
by Laurence Santrey

Local Government
by Barbara Feinberg

Choices for Social Studies

A Scavenger Hunt

Cooperative Learning

Have teams of students find representations of a wide variety of modes of transportation through many different time periods and across many different cultures. Encourage them to search picture books or movies as well as standard references and then to make models or drawings of what they find. Teams can challenge each other for the number and variety of transportation modes. Hint: Don't forget walking and swimming.

Students Acquiring English Encourage students acquiring English to ask parents or family members about modes of transportation in their home countries during specific time periods.

Researching Local Government

Challenge Challenge students to learn how people work together in local government to make decisions. Suggest that they interview community officials, attend meetings, or accompany officials through a workday. Have them summarize their findings on a poster and present the poster to the class.

Students might observe a city council committee meeting.

Art

A Unique Design

Show clippings and tell students about madcap races staged by groups or communities—hospital bed races or makeshift regattas in which anything that floats can compete. Then assign teams to design an unusual vehicle. Encourage them to use any appropriate means for their designs (pencil drawings, construction paper, frozen dessert stick models, and so on). Teams can unveil their drawings and models on a special presentation day.

Math

Way Back Then

Challenge Help students understand what common transportation was like before the automobile was invented. Have pairs of students research how fast stagecoaches once traveled. Then have them think of a trip they take frequently by car and use a map or atlas to determine the distance. Ask students to figure out the length of time the same trip would have taken by stagecoach. Then ask them to determine how many times they could make the trip by car in the time it would have taken by stagecoach.

Students Acquiring English In preparation, show students acquiring English what stagecoaches looked like and describe how they operated.

42 miles ÷ 10.5 hours = 4 miles per hour
42 miles ÷ 1 hour = 42 miles per hour

Introduce the Literature

Activating Prior Knowledge

Use the following ideas to stimulate students' curiosity about each poem.

"I'm in Another Dimension"

- Ask students to think of one characteristic that is common to their favorite teachers.

"Last Night"

- Ask students if they have ever been called upon in class when they could not remember the answer. What happened ?

"Ten Minutes Till the Bus"

- Ask students to describe a typical morning before school at their house.

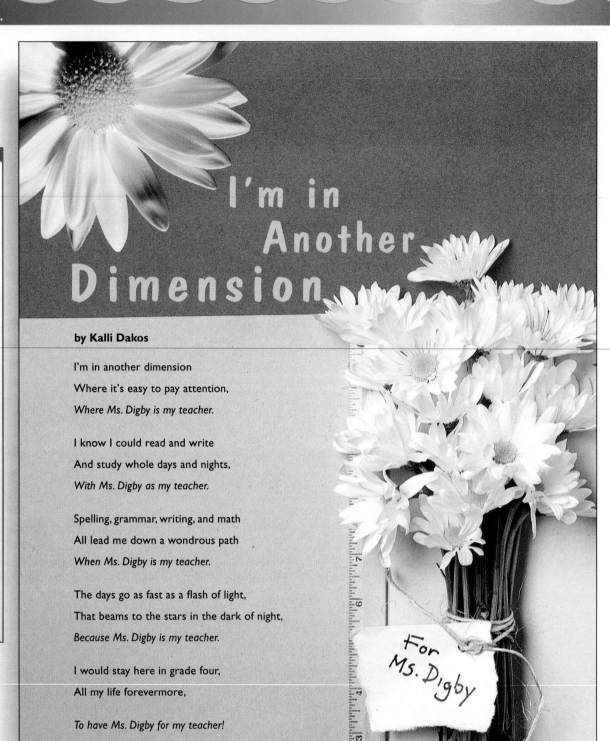

I'm in Another Dimension

by Kalli Dakos

I'm in another dimension
Where it's easy to pay attention,
Where Ms. Digby is my teacher.

I know I could read and write
And study whole days and nights,
With Ms. Digby as my teacher.

Spelling, grammar, writing, and math
All lead me down a wondrous path
When Ms. Digby is my teacher.

The days go as fast as a flash of light,
That beams to the stars in the dark of night,
Because Ms. Digby is my teacher.

I would stay here in grade four,
All my life forevermore,

To have Ms. Digby for my teacher!

60

Interact with Literature

Reading the Poetry

- After students have read the poems, encourage them to reread critically by asking themselves what each line means.
- Ask pairs of students to rewrite "Ten Minutes Till The Bus" in paragraph form, using at least five sentences from the speaker's viewpoint.

Ten Minutes Till the Bus

by David L. Harrison

Ten whole minutes
Till the bus,
Scads of time,
What's the fuss?
Two to dress,
One to flush,
Two to eat,
One to brush,
That leaves four
To catch the bus,
Scads of time,
What's the fuss?

Last Night

by David L. Harrison

Last night I knew the answers.
Last night I had them pat.
Last night I could have told you
Every answer, just like that!
Last night my brain was cooking.
Last night I got them right.
Last night I was a genius.
So where were you last night!

61

Interact *with* Literature

Predict/Infer

Assign one poem to each of three groups. Ask each group to identify where the poem takes place, to describe the situation, and to identify who is speaking. Ask groups to identify the words or lines in the poem that led them to make these inferences. (Sample: For "I'm in Another Dimension," have students tell which words suggest that the author is daydreaming about his or her teacher.)

Instruct *and* Integrate

Music

Challenge If one of the poems on these pages were to be set to music, what should the music sound like? Challenge students to think about the types of instruments (violins or trumpets, for example) and percussion (such as drums or cymbals) that would enhance the mood of the poem.

Students Acquiring English In preparation for the above activity, have students acquiring English make a word web for musical instruments, including some specific to their primary cultures.

Math

Number Sentences Ask students to write a number sentence that describes the speaker's thoughts in "Ten Minutes Till The Bus."
[10 - 2 - 1 - 2 -1 = 4 *or*
10 - (2 + 1 + 2 +1) = 4]

Writing

Write a Poem Ask students to write a paragraph about their most unusual preparing-for-school experience. Then, challenge them to write a poem using some or all of this information. Suggest that they use the poems on pages 60–61 as models or that they experiment with other forms of poetry.

Introduce the Literature

Activating Prior Knowledge

Discuss comic strips using the following questions:

- What is your favorite comic strip?
- What do you like best about that comic strip? (For example, the illustrations, a particular character, the humor, etc.)

Students Acquiring English For the above activity, pair students acquiring English with English-proficient speakers to talk about the humor in the comic strips. You might also bring in comic strips for students to read.

About the Cartoonist

Students might be interested to know that Charles Schulz created his cartoon strip "Peanuts" in 1950 and is now one of the most widely syndicated cartoonists ever; the strip appears daily in more than 2000 newspapers worldwide. Schulz bases the strip on semiautobiographical experiences, including his experiences in the army.

Interact with Literature

Reading Comic Strips

Encourage students to find all of the comics in a newspaper. Discuss the differences between the comic strips. Then discuss the comics that appear on the editorial pages. Point out that these comics are used to persuade readers to adopt a particular opinion.

Instruct and Integrate

MINILESSON

Genre

Comic Strip

Teach/Model

Discuss with students the comic strip features that Charles M. Schulz uses. Elicit the following characteristics from discussion:

- *Frames* are the individual boxes of a comic strip.
- *Illustrations* are the pictures in a comic strip. The pictures are often *caricatures* in which characters' appearances are exaggerated.
- *Speech* or *thought bubbles* contain the words a character says or thinks.
- *Characters* are the people, animals, or objects in a comic strip.

Practice/Apply

Feature	Example
Frames	
Illustrations	
Speech bubbles	
Characters	

Create this chart on the chalkboard. Ask volunteers to write in examples of each feature using "Classroom Peanuts." For *Frames*, have a volunteer write the number of frames in one of the comic strips. For *Illustrations*, have the volunteer write a feature done in caricature, such as Sally's hair.

Interact with Literature

Ask students to think back to a humorous aspect or event on the first day of the school year. Students can create a story map such as the one shown here and then use it to create a comic strip about the humorous event. Display students' comic strips in the classroom.

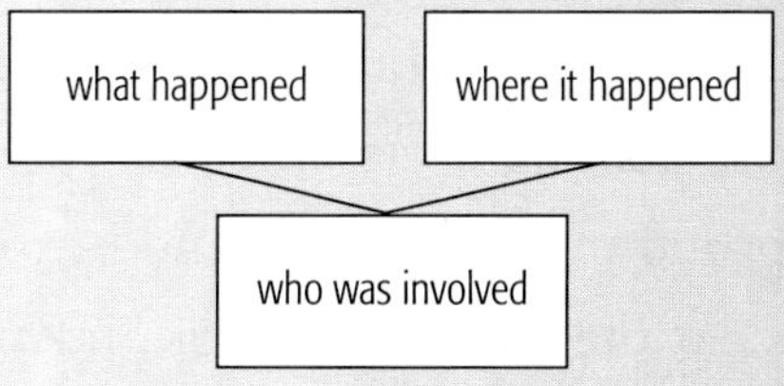

SELECTION: I'm New Here

by Bud Howlett

- American Bookseller Pick of the List
- Reading Rainbow Review Book

Selection Summary

Jazmin Escalante, a young girl whose family has moved to the U.S. from El Salvador, is nervous about going to school. On the first day, Jazmin is lonely and embarrassed. She doesn't know English, she is placed in the fourth grade when she should be in fifth, her teacher mispronounces her name, and some rude children call her "Taco." But the next few days of school are better: In an ESL class Jazmin meets other children who speak Spanish and a teacher who can pronounce her name; and in soccer she scores her team's two winning goals. At the end of the week, Jazmin is moved up to a fifth grade class. There she meets Allison, who becomes her friend, and she doesn't feel new anymore.

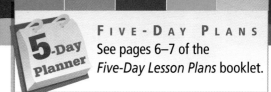

FIVE-DAY PLANS
See pages 6–7 of the *Five-Day Lesson Plans* booklet.

Lesson Planning Guide

	Skill/Strategy Instruction	Meeting Individual Needs	Lesson Resources
1 **Introduce the Literature** *Pacing: 1 day*	**Preparing to Read and Write** Prior Knowledge/Building Background, 63C **Selection Vocabulary,** 63D • register • papers • customs **Spelling Pretest,** 81H • grade • meet • seem • neat • wait • away • safe • afraid • least • crayon	**Support in Advance,** 63C **Students Acquiring English,** 63C **Other Choices for Building Background,** 63C **Spelling Challenge Words:** 81H • playground • repeat • United States • squeeze • Wednesday	***Literacy Activity Book,*** Vocabulary, 19 **Transparencies:** Building Background, 1–7; Vocabulary, 1–8 **Great Start** CD-ROM software, "It's Cool. It's School." CD
2 **Interact with Literature** *Pacing: 1–3 days*	**Reading Strategies** Monitor, 64, 70, 74 Predict/Infer, 64, 76 Think About Words, 68, 70, 74 Evaluate, 76 **Minilessons** ✓ Sequence of Events, 65 Writer's Craft: Varying Sentence Types, 67 Problem Solving/Decision Making, 69 Predicting Outcomes, 71 Genre: Narrative Nonfiction, 77	**Choices for Reading,** 64 **Guided Reading,** 64, 66, 72, 78 **Students Acquiring English,** 67, 70, 72, 77, 78, 81 **Extra Support,** 79 **Challenge,** 73	**Reading-Writing Workshop:** Personal Narrative, 90–91F ***Literacy Activity Book,*** Selection Connections, 7–8; Comprehension Check, 20 **Study Skills:** Parts of a Book, 81N, H3 **Audio Tape** for It's Cool. It's School.: *I'm New Here* The Learning Company's Ultimate Writing & Creativity Center software
3 **Instruct and Integrate** *Pacing: 1–3 days*	✓ **Comprehension:** Sequence of Events, 81A **Writing:** Journal Writing, 81C ✓ **Word Skills and Strategies:** Structural Analysis: Inflected Forms, 81E **Building Vocabulary:** Vocabulary Activities, 81G ✓ **Spelling:** Spelling Long *a* and Long *e*, 81H ✓ **Grammar:** Kinds of Sentences, 81I **Communication Activities:** Listening and Speaking, 81K; Viewing 81L **Cross-Curricular Activities:** Social Studies, 81M–81N; Art, 81N	**Reteaching:** Sequence of Events, 81B **Activity Choices:** Journal, Personal Narrative, Description, Welcome, 81D **Reteaching:** Structural Analysis: Inflected Forms, 81F **Activity Choices:** Multiple-Meaning Words, Bilingual Dictionary, Word History: *soccer,* 81G **Challenge Words Practice:** 81H **Reteaching:** Kinds of Sentences, 81J **Activity Choices:** Listening and Speaking, 81K; Viewing 81L **Activity Choices:** Social Studies, 81M–81N; Art, 81N	**Reading-Writing Workshop:** Personal Narrative, 90–91F **Transparencies:** Comprehension, 1–9; Writing, 1–10; Word Skills, 1–11; Grammar, 1–12 ***Literacy Activity Book,*** Comprehension, 21; Writing, 22; Word Skills, 23; Building Vocabulary, 24; Spelling, 25–26; Grammar, 27–28 **Audio Tape** for It's Cool. It's School.: *I'm New Here* **Spelling Spree** CD-ROM **Channel R.E.A.D.** videodisc: "Suspended in Space" The Learning Company's Ultimate Writing & Creativity Center software

✓ ***Indicates Tested Skills.*** *See page 40F for assessment options.*

Introduce *the* Literature

Preparing to Read and Write

Support in Advance

Use these activities for students who need extra support before participating in the whole-class activity.

Picture Walk Have students describe the illustrations in the selection. Can they predict what the story is about? Why might the girl in the cover photograph be smiling?

Management Tip
Students not needing support in advance can write in their journals.

Students Acquiring English
Encourage students acquiring English to share experiences similar to those of the girl in the story.

INTERACTIVE LEARNING

Prior Knowledge/Building Background

Key Concept Being in a new situation

New Situations Ask students to think about new situations they have been in. Display Transparency 1–7. Encourage volunteers to name one of the situations and the feelings associated with it. Record students' responses on the transparency. When feelings such as fear, discomfort, and shyness are named, ask students to tell if and how they overcame these feelings.

How Does It Feel to Be New?

New Situation	How It Feels
Going to the dentist for the first time	Scary, uncomfortable

Transparency 1–7

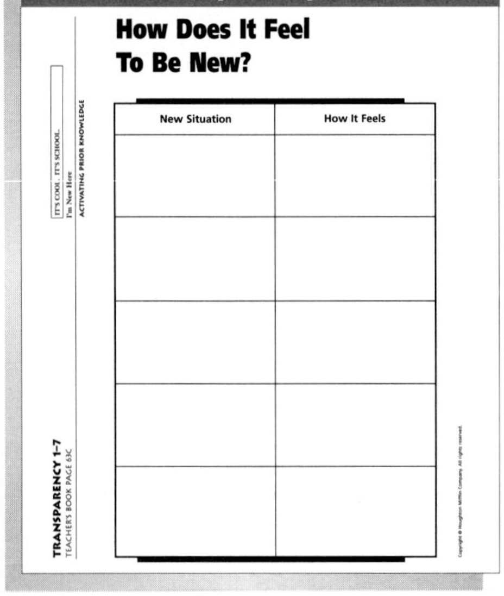
How Does It Feel To Be New?

New Situation	How It Feels

IT'S COOL. IT'S SCHOOL. I'm New Here ACTIVATING PRIOR KNOWLEDGE
TRANSPARENCY 1–7 TEACHER'S BOOK PAGE 63C

Great Start
For students needing extra support with key concepts and vocabulary, use the "It's Cool. It's School." CD.

Other Choices for Building Background

Understanding Each Other

Students Acquiring English Ask students to name places, people, and objects that have been important in new experiences they have had. Ask groups of students to illustrate each item and to write the appropriate English word below their illustration. Students not familiar with English might wish to add the corresponding word in their primary language. Assemble the finished products to create a newcomer's dictionary.

Welcome Poster

Extra Support Divide students into small groups and have each group create a poster to welcome non-English-speaking students from other countries to their school.

Spelling You may want to give the Spelling Pretest on page 81H before students read the selection.

Daily Language Practice Use the sentences on page 81J as daily practice of the spelling and grammar skills taught in this theme.

INTERACTIVE LEARNING

Selection Vocabulary

Key Words

- customs
- papers
- register

Display Transparency 1–8. Ask a volunteer to read Sentence 1 aloud. Encourage students to use the context of the sentence to determine what they think the word *customs* means. Write their thoughts in the space provided. Then, have students use dictionaries to find the meaning closest to the one they have proposed. Repeat the activity for Sentences 2 and 3.

Figuring Out Word Meanings

Word in Context	We Think It Means	Dictionary Meaning
When my family went to Venezuela last year, we had to take our luggage through *customs* before we could leave the airport.	Answers should reflect an understanding of the context of the sentence.	The inspection of a person's baggage when traveling between countries.

Vocabulary Practice Have students work independently or in pairs to complete page 19 of the *Literacy Activity Book.*

Transparency 1–8

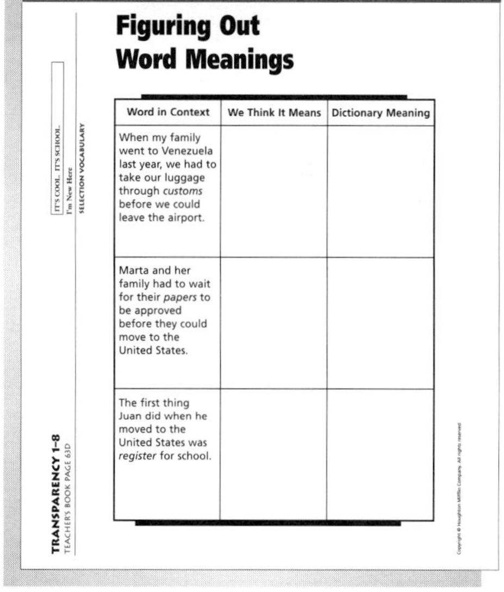

IT'S COOL. IT'S SCHOOL.
I'm New Here
SELECTION VOCABULARY

Figuring Out Word Meanings

Word in Context	We Think It Means	Dictionary Meaning
When my family went to Venezuela last year, we had to take our luggage through *customs* before we could leave the airport.		
Marta and her family had to wait for their *papers* to be approved before they could move to the United States.		
The first thing Juan did when he moved to the United States was *register* for school.		

TRANSPARENCY 1–8
TEACHER'S BOOK PAGE 63D

Social Studies

Teacher FactFile

El Salvador

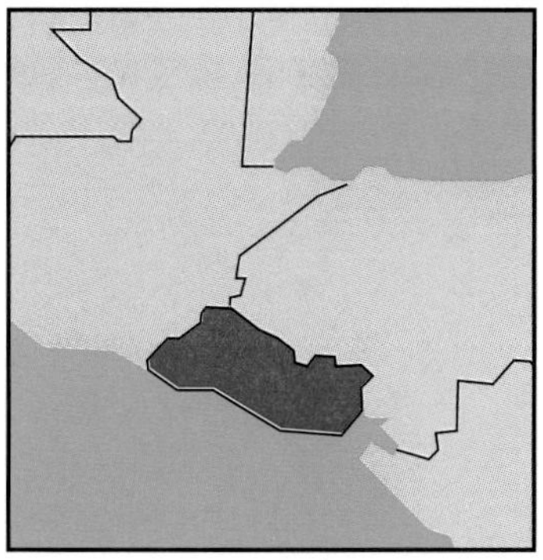

- Before the Spanish arrived in Salvadoran territory in the sixteenth century, the area was occupied by five Native American tribes. The oldest–the Pocomam, Chortî, and Lenca–were related to the Maya. The civilization of the predominant tribe–the Pipil–resembled that of the Aztecs in Mexico.
- The Spanish arrived in 1524; later Spain divided El Salvador into two jurisdictions: San Salvador and Sonsonate.
- El Salvador obtained its independence in 1821.
- El Salvador endured decades of military dictatorships and political violence. Then a new constitution was adopted in 1983, and presidential elections were held in 1984.

Literacy Activity Book, p. 19

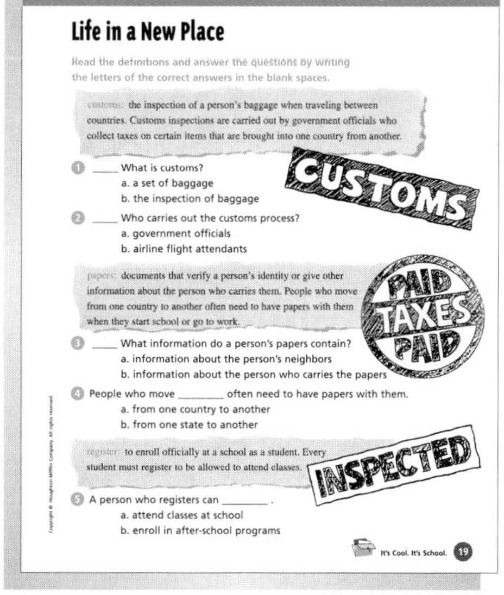

Life in a New Place

Read the definitions and answer the questions by writing the letters of the correct answers in the blank spaces.

customs: the inspection of a person's baggage when traveling between countries. Customs inspections are carried out by government officials who collect taxes on certain items that are brought into one country from another.

1. _____ What is customs?
   a. a set of baggage
   b. the inspection of baggage
2. _____ Who carries out the customs process?
   a. government officials
   b. airline flight attendants

papers: documents that verify a person's identity or give other information about the person who carries them. People who move from one country to another often need to have papers with them when they start school or go to work.

3. _____ What information do a person's papers contain?
   a. information about the person's neighbors
   b. information about the person who carries the papers
4. People who move ________ often need to have papers with them.
   a. from one country to another
   b. from one state to another

register: to enroll officially at a school as a student. Every student must register to be allowed to attend classes.

5. A person who registers can ________ .
   a. attend classes at school
   b. enroll in after-school programs

It's Cool. It's School. 19

Interact *with* Literature

Reading Strategies

▶ **Monitor**
Predict/Infer

Discussion Suggest that students will increase their understanding and enjoyment of the selection by monitoring their reading and predicting what will happen next in the story. Discuss how they might apply these strategies to the selection.

Predicting/Purpose Setting Encourage students to volunteer questions they have about this page (for example, Who is this girl? Where has she moved from?), or to make predictions, and to look for answers to their questions as they read.

Choices for Reading

Independent Reading	**Cooperative Reading**
Guided Reading	**Teacher Read Aloud**

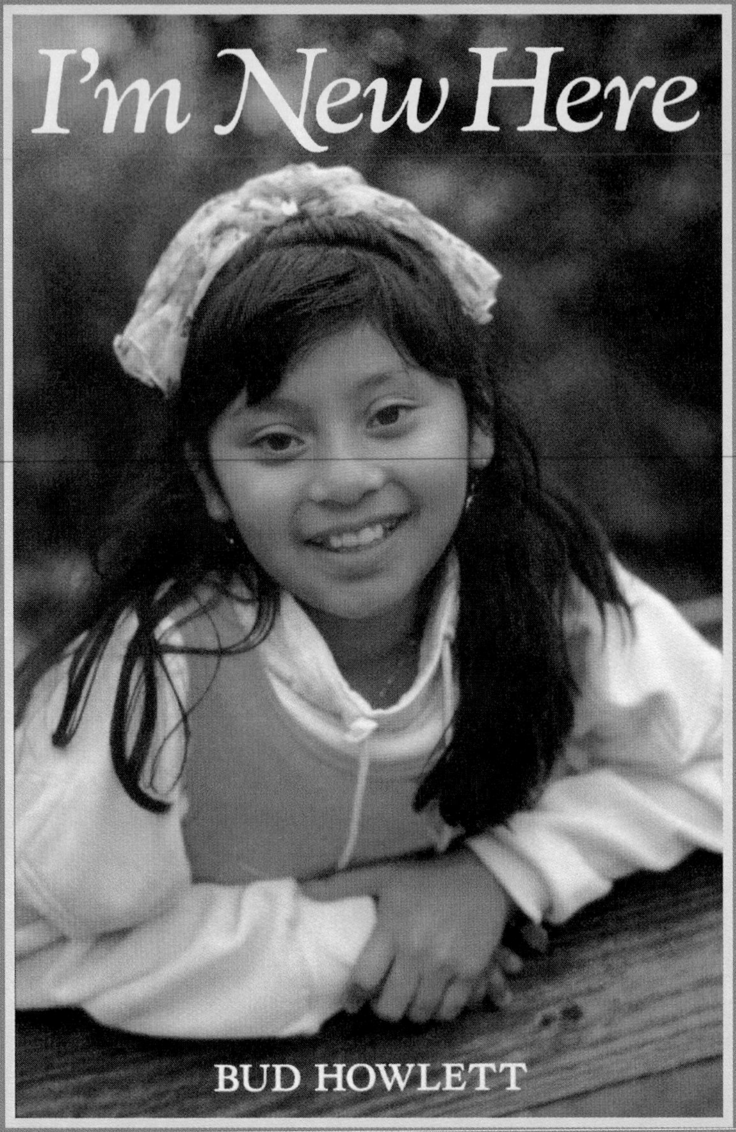

64

Meeting Individual Needs: Guided Reading

Have students who are using the Guided Reading option read to the end of page 66. Ask them if they have found answers to their purpose-setting questions. Use the questions on page 66 to check students' comprehension.

Quick REFERENCE

Journal
Encourage students to record their questions and predictions about the selection in their journals.

I was so afraid. It was my first day of school in the United States and I didn't speak English.

My name is Jazmin Escalante (Haz-meen Es-ka-lan-teh). I came to America from El Salvador. I'm new here.

The day before school started I said to my mother, "Mami, I'm scared! I won't know what to do at school. I won't know where to go."

"Don't worry, Jazmin," answered my mother. "It will be all right. We'll walk to school together today so you'll know where everything is. No one will know we went ahead of time. It will be our secret."

I thought it was a great idea to go to school before all the other kids arrived. But I was still worried about speaking only Spanish in an American school.

"But Mami, I don't even speak English. I won't know what to do. I won't know what they're talking about."

Mami didn't speak very much English either. She always spoke Spanish to my father, my brother, Juanito, and me.

"We'll all learn together, won't we, Jazmin? Get Juanito and we'll go. Remember, your little brother will start school as soon as he gets all of his shots. You can help him when he starts school next week."

65

MINILESSON

Sequence of Events

TESTED SKILL

Teach/Model

Ask a volunteer to define *sequence* (order of events), and write the definition on the chalkboard. Then draw the chart below. Using the Think Aloud, encourage students to fill in the chart by following clue words in the story. The chart should cover the sequence of the story through Jazmin's first day at school in the United States.

Sequence of Events

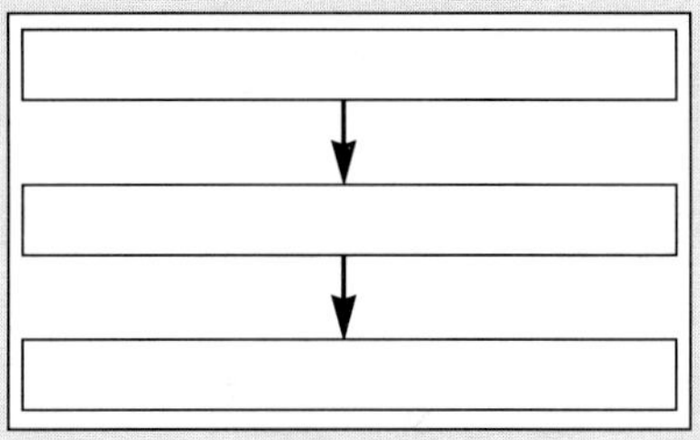

Think Aloud

I can use clue words and this chart to trace the sequence of the story. If I write "Jazmin came to the United States" in the first box, I can then list the events of the story in the order that they happen. Looking for words like *before*, *tomorrow*, *then*, and *finally* will help me place events in the correct order.

Practice/Apply

Ask students to add and fill in cells on their charts that reflect the remainder of the story.

SKILL FINDER

Full lesson/Reteaching, pp. 81A–81B

Minilessons, p. 101 and Theme 5

Social Studies Link

El Salvador El Salvador is located on the Pacific coast of Central America, south of Guatemala and Honduras. It is the most densely populated country in Central America and the only one that does not have a Caribbean coastline.

Vocabulary

Pronunciation In Spanish, the letter *J* is pronounced like the English letter *H*. (Invite a Spanish-speaking student to pronounce Jazmin's name correctly.) Understanding this will help students follow events in the story.

Interact *with* Literature

Guided Reading

Comprehension/Critical Thinking

1. Who is the main character in this story? How do you know? (Jazmin is the main character. I know because she is the narrator of the story and she tells about her experiences.)
2. How does Jazmin feel about starting school in a new place? (She is worried that she won't know where to go; since she speaks only Spanish, she is afraid she won't understand anyone.)
3. Jazmin and her mother visited school the day before classes began. Why did her mother tell Jazmin that the visit would be their secret? (Answers will vary. Students should indicate an understanding that Jazmin might feel embarrassed if others knew she had visited school before classes began.)

Predicting/Purpose Setting

Discuss with students whether any of their predictions have come to pass or their purpose-setting questions have been answered. Encourage students to list new predictions or questions. Then ask them to read halfway through page 73 to see what events develop and what answers they find to their questions.

It was almost two miles to Elmwood School from our apartment. We walked up to the front of the school and between two buildings. The school was more modern than the school in El Salvador where I went to third grade. I never went to fourth grade. Because of the fighting it wasn't safe on the streets. I stayed home and took care of my brother. Mami said we would be safe going to school here in the United States.

She pointed to a sign. "That says 'Office.' That's where we'll go tomorrow to register, Jazmin. I'll be with you."

Together, Mami, Juanito, and I walked past the office. All the classrooms opened onto an outside covered walk. There were no children, no teachers, only us. It was very quiet. As we went down the walk our feet echoed loudly on the hard concrete. I wanted

66

Informal Assessment

If students' responses indicate that they are understanding the selection, have them finish reading the selection independently or cooperatively.

QuickREFERENCE

Social Studies Link

History Civil unrest and political upheaval have plagued El Salvador since the late 1940s, when workers began to demand economic and social reforms. The workers met with little response from large landowners and the right-wing government. Tensions escalated, and in the period 1979–1983, more than 35,000 civilians were killed. Jazmin's inability to attend school is an example of how normal life was interrupted by the fighting.

to look in a classroom, but the window in the door was too high.

"Let's walk around to the other side of the building," Mami said. "Maybe we can see in a window there."

The other windows were lower. Juanito and I ran up to the first one. I could see but Juanito couldn't, so I held him up while we looked in. The classroom was very large. It was clean and neat and the chairs and desks were all in rows. I counted. There were twenty-eight chairs. A teacher's desk with books on top of it was at the front of the room.

On the chalkboard were some neatly written words. I didn't know what they said; I only knew Spanish. I wanted so much to learn English! Butterflies danced in my stomach. What would my first day of school be like? How would I feel when those empty desks had kids in them?

Juanito was getting heavy so I put him down. We walked over to the playground.

"In the corner of the room by the door I saw some balls," said Juanito. "Do you think they play soccer here?"

"Oh, I hope so," I said. "I can play soccer well even if I can't speak English."

I wondered if they played the same games we had played in El Salvador.

67

MINILESSON

Writer's Craft
Varying Sentence Types

Teach/Model

Ask students what they find interesting about writing they like. (Answers might include realistic dialogue, vivid descriptive details, and development of interesting characters.) Then ask students to name the kinds of sentences they see in the third full paragraph on page 67. (declarative, interrogative, exclamatory) What is it about exclamations and questions that enlivens the writing?

Practice/Apply

Ask students to write a short paragraph describing their first day at school. Urge them to include at least one exclamation and one question in their writing.

Students Acquiring English

Some students may need help with English punctuation. For example, in Spanish, exclamation points and question marks appear upside down before these sentence types. (End punctuation—periods, exclamation points, and question marks—is also used.) Help students understand that these beginning marks are not used when writing in English.

SKILL FINDER
Writing Activities: Write a Personal Narrative, p. 81D
Reading-Writing Workshop, p. 91A

Multicultural Link

Soccer In most Latin American countries, soccer is a hugely popular sport, and children grow up playing the game at school and in their neighborhoods. (People in most countries of the world, including Latin America, refer to the game as "football.") Soccer has become increasingly popular in the United States, and today many communities have youth soccer leagues.

Interact *with* Literature

Reading Strategies

Think About Words

Some students may be unfamiliar with the meaning of a "dry throat." Discuss with them how they can use context to figure out that it is a feeling a person experiences when frightened or nervous. Ask students why Jazmin is nervous.

Reading Strategies

Think About Words

Students who do not speak Spanish may need help understanding the phrase "Ay, buenos días, Señora," which means "Good day, ma'am." Help them understand that this is a common form of address in Spanish. You may want to have a Spanish-speaking student read aloud the Spanish words and phrases in the selection so that other students can hear how the words sound.

Mami didn't need to get me up the next morning. I was already awake when she came into my room. I wanted to go to school but I was afraid. My throat was dry and I swallowed hard lots of times while I was getting dressed.

I wanted to look my best. I decided to wear the flowered dress I had worn to church when we first came here to San Rafael.

Usually I had breakfast, but today I couldn't eat anything and Mami didn't make me. She took my hand. "Come, Jazmin," she said. "This will be a new and wonderful adventure."

The walk didn't take long, but now the school looked different. There were buses and cars in the parking lot. The flag was up and there were people everywhere. We walked to the office. I felt better because I knew where it was. We went inside and lots of people were in line at the counter. They were all speaking English. Mami said they were filling out their papers. I hoped we had all of ours. Once, at customs, we hadn't had all the right papers and they made us go back home. Mami was holding my hand and I could feel her shaking a little. I thought it was all right for me to be scared if Mami was.

When it was our turn, the lady behind the counter spoke to us in English. I could tell Mami didn't understand. The lady called to someone in the next room and another lady came out. "*Ay, buenos días, Señora.* I am Sofia Rodriguez," she said. She spoke to Mami in Spanish and told her she would help us fill out the

68

QuickREFERENCE

Multicultural Link

Guest Speaker Invite parents or other volunteers who have come from another country; have learned English as a second language; or have worked with non-English speakers in your school or community to tell the class about their experiences.

69

MINILESSON

Problem Solving/ Decision Making

REVIEW & MAINTAIN

Teach/Model

Ask students to identify the problems Jazmin has faced so far in the selection and to tell how she has begun to solve these problems. Present the following chart on the chalkboard, and fill in the first three boxes as shown.

Practice/Apply

Work with students as they complete the chart using information from the story. Then help them use the information to generate problem-solving ideas (for example, the idea that one might go to an unfamiliar place the day before an important event to ease nervousness).

Problem Solving		
Character: Jazmin		
Problem: knows nothing about new school	**Decision:** goes the day before anyone else	**Solution:** knows her way around on the first day
Problem:	**Decision:**	**Solution:**
Problem:	**Decision:**	**Solution:**
What I learned about problem solving:		

SKILL FINDER

Full lesson/Reteaching, Theme 3

Minilessons, Theme 3

Home Connection

Family Stories Children may enjoy hearing family members tell about how they felt on their first day in school or, if they were new to this country, how they felt upon arriving.

Interact *with* Literature

Reading Strategies

Think About Words

Students who do not speak Spanish may need help understanding that the word *niña* means *young girl* or, in this usage, *little one*. Discuss with them how they can use the context to see that *niña* is used here as an affectionate term of address.

Reading Strategies

Monitor

Discuss with students how the last paragraph on page 71 can be misleading unless they recognize that the teacher is pronouncing Jazmin's name incorrectly. The spelling "Jazz-min" is used to emphasize the mispronunciation.

papers. She was a parent who helped other Spanish-speaking families.

She took us outside and told me a little about the school. She showed me the papers we had to fill out. She seemed to know that I was afraid. She put a large, warm hand on my shoulder. It was very steady and strong. "Don't worry, Jazmin," she said. "I will see that you get to your classroom. They will like you here, *niña*, and you will like them."

Mami finished with my papers and I knew it was time to go to my classroom. I was so afraid that I was afraid to say I was afraid!

"Jazmin," said Señora Rodriguez, "they are putting you in fourth grade since you didn't attend fourth grade in El Salvador."

"Fourth grade," I thought. "I should be in fifth grade. I didn't know they would do that." Now I was afraid I would be bigger than the other children. Things were not starting out well for me.

70

QuickREFERENCE

Vocabulary

Pronunciation In Spanish, when a *tilde* (~) appears over the letter *n*, the *n* is pronounced NYAH, as in *niña* (NEEN-yah). When a double *l* appears, it is pronounced as a *y*, as in *bella* (BAY-ya).

MEETING INDIVIDUAL NEEDS — Students Acquiring English

Find out if any of your students acquiring English have adopted common English names. Discuss why and then have those students help others pronounce their original names exactly as they should be.

Mami put her arm around me as we started toward my new classroom. We went the same way we had gone the day before. We passed the room I had looked into and stopped at a door that had the number 7 on it. Mami kissed me and gave me a very strong hug. "Good-bye, *bella* (bay-ya)," she said. She called me *bella* when she wanted me to know that I was special. In Spanish it means "pretty one." As she walked away, I felt very empty inside.

Señora Rodriguez took me over to the teacher. "This is Jazmin Escalante," she said. "She is new here. She's from El Salvador." I recognized my name and the words "El Salvador." "This is your teacher, Jazmin," she said to me in Spanish. "Her name is Mrs. Edwards." Señora Rodriguez left and I was alone with my new teacher and my new class.

Mrs. Edwards walked me to the front of the class. She turned me to face the boys and girls. Looking at my registration card, she said, "This is 'Jazz-min' Escalante. She has come from El Salvador. She's new here."

MINILESSON

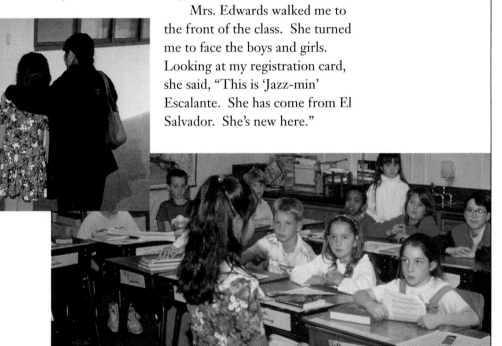

Predicting Outcomes

REVIEW & MAINTAIN

Teach/Model

Ask students what information they use to predict outcomes. Then ask why it is helpful to make predictions. Volunteers may share predictions they made at the beginning of the story, discussing whether any of the predictions need additions or revisions. Then read aloud the last two paragraphs on page 70. Ask students if this information might cause them to change predictions they made earlier and, if so, how.

Practice/Apply

- Ask students to locate passages from the story to this point that helped them develop or revise their predictions.
- Have students note details in the story after this point that caused them to further revise or make additions to their predictions.

SKILL FINDER
Full lesson/Reteaching, pp. 59A–59B

Minilessons, p. 45 and Theme 5

Multicultural Link

Salvadoran Culture El Salvador, like most Central American countries, is a cultural blend of Spanish and Indian traditions. Traditional folk festivals are held in city squares lined with Spanish-inspired architecture. Art, music, literature, and food exemplify the preservation of both lines of ancestral heritage.

Interact *with* Literature

Guided Reading

Comprehension/Critical Thinking

1. What did Jazmin do to prepare for her first day at school? (She visited the school with her mother and little brother the day before.)
2. What kind of day is Jazmin having so far? What details from the selection make you think so? (Not good. She's in a lower grade than she expected, she cannot join in with the class, and she feels left out and lonely.)
3. If you were Jazmin, what would you want to tell your teacher? (Answers might include Jazmin's unhappiness at having her name mispronounced and being left out of activities.)

Predicting/Purpose Setting

Ask students either to pose a question that they think will be answered in the remainder of the selection or to predict the end of the story.

"Oh, no! Not 'Jazz-min'!" I thought. "Can't the teacher say my name right? Now all the other children will say it wrong, too." First I was mad at my teacher. Then I was mad at my name. "Why couldn't I have a name that was easy to say, like Maria?"

I didn't have much time to worry because Mrs. Edwards took me to a seat on one side of the room. I sat down and looked around. All of the children were looking at me. I wanted to smile but I couldn't, so I pretended to read a book I found on my desk.

Mrs. Edwards brought me some papers. She put them on my desk with a box of crayons.

"Color?" she asked. She opened the crayons and showed me that she wanted me to color the pictures. I began to color very carefully. If this was all I could do, I was going to do it well.

As I was coloring, I listened to the rest of the class. I didn't understand what they were saying, but I knew they were doing math. I could do some of the problems on the board, but no one asked me to do anything but color.

I had never felt so alone. I didn't know anyone and no one knew me. I didn't even know how to say hello. When I looked around the room I saw two other children whose skin was almost as dark as mine. Did they speak Spanish? I wondered how long it

72

Self-Assessment

Ask students to reflect on their reading with questions such as:

- How well have I understood the story so far?
- How well has monitoring worked as a strategy for me?

Quick REFERENCE

Journal

Ask students to use their journals to record how well they think their purpose-setting questions have helped them understand and remember the story.

Students Acquiring English

Encourage students acquiring English to share their own experiences as newcomers to the United States or to their school.

would be before I found out if there was anyone for me to talk to.

The children soon finished doing their math and took out other books, which looked like readers. They moved into small groups but I stayed in my seat. The teacher brought me more papers to color. I picked up the reading book on my desk. At least I could look at the pictures. The reading period seemed very long.

Finally a bell rang and everyone lined up at the door to go outside. I didn't know whether to line up or stay in my seat, so I stayed.

"Jazz-min," said the teacher as she motioned to me with her hand. She took my hand and we walked outside. She called to another girl, who came over to us. I heard Mrs. Edwards say "Jazz-min" and "El Salvador" and "Spanish" to her. The two of us stood together during the recess and watched the other kids playing. The girl pointed to them and said something in English but I didn't understand what she said.

At lunchtime the teacher brought the same girl over to me. Mrs. Edwards pointed at her and said "Emily."

I repeated "Emily." Emily pointed to where the cafeteria was and showed me how to get lunch. We sat together on a bench. Several children from my class walked by and said "Hi, Jazz-min."

73

MEETING INDIVIDUAL NEEDS

Challenge

Syntax Native Spanish speakers sometimes arrange words in English sentences in a way that seems unfamiliar to native English speakers. Ask a student who is fluent in both Spanish and English to explain to the class why this might happen.

Interact *with* Literature

Reading Strategies

Monitor

Students may misread the dialogue on page 74. Help them understand that Jazmin's mother is saying that Jazmin cannot change where she was born. The sentence could be misread to mean that people in El Salvador (where Jazmin was born) cannot change.

Reading Strategies

Think About Words

If students do not understand the acronym *ESL*, ask them how they can use the context of the first full paragraph on page 75 to figure out that it stands for *English as a second language*. Invite students acquiring English to tell classmates what ESL is and what they do in their ESL classes.

Then one boy shouted, "Hey, Taco!" Several others did, too. "Taco, Taco, Taco!" they yelled. They were pointing at me. Why were they being so mean?

A lady in the cafeteria made them stop, but when I looked for Emily, she was gone. I was alone. I didn't have anyone to sit with. I walked outside and sat on a bench by myself.

When the first day was over, I ran all the way home. Mami was waiting at the door and I hugged her and cried. I told her that no one at school cared about me and I didn't have any friends. "I don't want to go back to school, Mami. They made fun of me because I don't speak English and I look different. They called me 'Taco'!"

"Change out of your good dress, *bella*, and dry your eyes," said Mami. "Let's talk with your father." Mami and Papi and Juanito all sat down with me.

"You will learn English, Jazmin, before you know it. So that will change. Where you were born, you can't change," said Mami.

"Be proud of where you come from, *bella*," said my father. He swelled out his chest. "Blood flows in your veins from the great Mayan civilization. You are a special person."

Juanito squeezed in between my father and me. He took my hand. "You are special to me, too, Jazmin," he said.

On the second day of school, I was watching the other students do their math, but I didn't have a book.

74

Informal Assessment

Oral Reading Have one or two students read aloud pages 74–75 as a check of oral reading fluency. See the Oral Reading Checklist in the *Teacher's Assessment Handbook*.

QuickREFERENCE

Social Studies Link

History The Mayan civilization flourished in southern Mexico and Central America from before 1000 B.C. until about A.D. 1500. Notable Mayan accomplishments include a 365-day calendar thought to be more accurate than the Gregorian calendar; an original system of writing; refined sculpture and architecture; and a system of mathematics that preceded that of Europeans by centuries.

While I was wondering how to get one, the classroom door opened and a lady spoke to my teacher. "Haz-meen Es-ka-lan-teh, please," she said.

The new lady was Señora Diaz. She said my name the right way and spoke to me in Spanish. She was a teacher who would help me learn English in a special class. She was called an ESL teacher. She walked me down the hall to her room and I met several other kids who spoke Spanish. I was going to come to Señora Diaz every day for an hour and a half.

The next day, Señora Diaz gave me books in Spanish to read. She said I would get a math book and could start using it with the other students.

On Thursday, Mrs. Edwards's class went outside to play soccer. They picked teams and I was the last one chosen. I didn't know that our class played soccer on Thursdays and I had worn a dress. But when the soccer game started, I felt good for the first time since I started school, because I could play. For once I could do what everyone else did.

Math Link

Time How much time did Jazmin spend with Señora Diaz each week? Students can calculate the total using mental math and then describe their thinking. (Possible answers: Add the whole hours for a total of 5 hours, and then add the halves; every 2 days is another whole hour, so 4 days makes 2 hours, and the half-hour from Friday is left over. So, $5 + 2 = 7 + \frac{1}{2} = 7\frac{1}{2}$ hours.)

Interact *with* Literature

Reading Strategies

Predict/Infer

Ask students what they can tell, or infer, about Jazmin's classmates' attitudes by their behavior toward Jazmin after the soccer game. Discuss with them how making inferences helps them understand as they read.

Reading Strategies

Evaluate

Ask students how, on a scale of 1 to 10, they would rate Jazmin's experience in Mrs. Edwards's class. Encourage students to discuss their reasons for their responses. Help them understand that the strategy they are using is called evaluating.

76

QuickREFERENCE

Vocabulary

Students unfamiliar with sports terms may not understand the words *dribble* and *goalie*. In soccer, *dribble* refers to moving the ball down the field using a rapid succession of short kicks. The word *goalie* refers to the player who stands at the goal and tries to keep the opponents' ball from being kicked into the goal net. Ask students if the meanings of these words differ in other sports.

When the ball came to me, I dribbled it down the field and kicked it past the goalie. My team cheered, "Yeah, Jazz-min! Yeah, Jazz-min!" A few kids patted me on the back. Before the game was over, I scored another goal. We won 2 to 1 and I scored both goals. Kids talked to me all the way back to the classroom. I didn't know what they were saying, but I was happy.

At the end of my first week, Señora Diaz and El Director (the principal) called me into the library. They said that I read very well in Spanish, and my math was excellent, so they had decided to move me into fifth grade. I knew I would have to work very hard but it would be better to be with kids my age. I knew I would have to meet all new kids, but I thought I could do it.

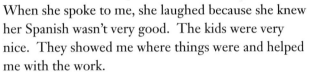

My new class was not bad. The teacher, Mrs. Robertson, was very nice and knew a few Spanish words. When she spoke to me, she laughed because she knew her Spanish wasn't very good. The kids were very nice. They showed me where things were and helped me with the work.

A blond girl from my class went out to recess with me on my first day in fifth grade. She took my hand and we walked around the playground. She pointed at things and gave their names in English. "Tree," she said. I said it, too. "Playground," she said, pointing at the ground.

I said, "Playground."

She named more words than I could ever remember in one day. I said them all back to her. When the

77

Students Acquiring English

Have students familiar with soccer compare the names for positions in their primary languages.

MINILESSON

Genre

Narrative Nonfiction

Teach/Model

Ask students how they can tell whether a story describes real events and real characters. Using the Think Aloud, help students understand the characteristics that narrative nonfiction encompasses:

- It tells a story.
- It describes real people and real events.
- It includes facts (which can be verified) and opinions (the author's personal beliefs).
- It includes a main idea about the topic and supporting details that give more information.

Think Aloud

The pictures of Jazmin, her family, and her teachers make me think that the characters are real and that the events of the story really happened. The author presents the main idea of Jazmin's first week at school and gives details (in the form of facts) to support this main idea. I think this story is narrative nonfiction.

Practice/Apply

Ask students to point out other features of the selection that lead them to conclude that it belongs to the narrative nonfiction genre.

Interact with Literature

Guided Reading

Comprehension/Critical Thinking

1. Why does Jazmin consider Allison to be her friend? (Allison teaches Jazmin English words, stays with her, and defends them both when a boy calls them names.)
2. How have Jazmin's feelings changed since the beginning of the selection? (At first she is scared but excited; then she is sad and lonely; finally she is happy and hopeful.)
3. If Jazmin were a new student in your class, how would you act toward her? What might you do to make her feel welcome? (Responses should indicate students' awareness that new students often feel lonely and left out of the group.)

bell rang, she looked at me and said slowly, "My name is Allison."

I understood what she said. "My name is Haz-meen." She gave my hand a squeeze and we ran into class.

Allison walked up to Mrs. Robertson and said, "The new girl's name is 'Haz-meen,' not 'Jazz-min.' "

At lunchtime, Allison was waiting for me. When she took my hand I saw how light her skin was. We must have looked funny together. As we walked toward the cafeteria a boy who was walking behind us yelled, "Salt and pepper! Salt and pepper!" Allison dropped my hand and turned around. She grabbed the boy by the shoulders and shook him. She was yelling something at him. He turned and ran down the hall and didn't say anything.

I don't know what Allison said but she had to be the best kind of friend you could ever have. When she took my hand again I said, "*Mi amiga*" (my friend).

"*Mi amiga*," repeated Allison.

I had made a friend. A real friend.

I didn't feel like I was new here anymore.

Self-Assessment

Encourage students to ask themselves questions such as:

- Did the questions I asked or the predictions I made at the start of the selection help me understand the selection? What other questions or predictions might have been more helpful?
- Which reading strategy was most helpful to me in understanding this story?

QuickREFERENCE

Students Acquiring English

Do students have a friend or family member like Allison who has been helpful in learning English? Ask students to list ways or explain how friends and classmates can help a new student learn English.

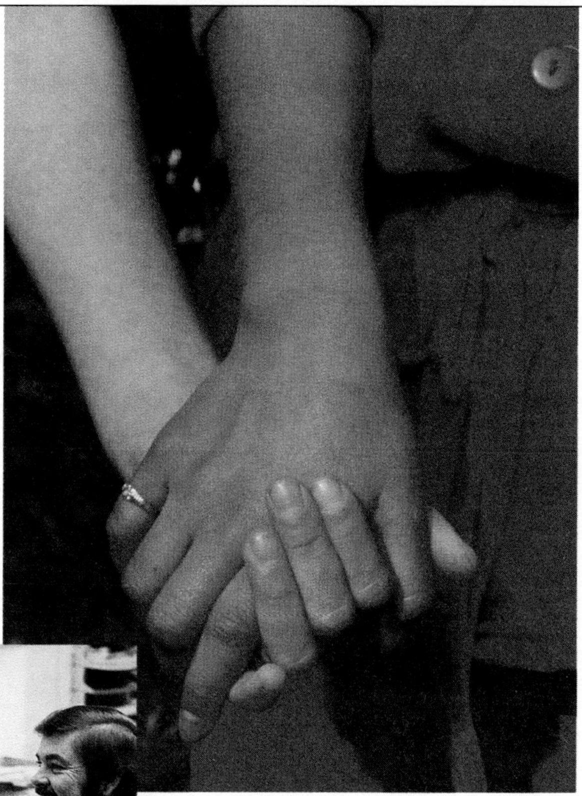

Meet the Author

BUD HOWLETT

Bud Howlett, seen here talking to a student from Haiti, is a California native who spent a lot of time in school. He started as a student, became a teacher, and ended up as an elementary school principal, a job he held for nearly twenty-four years. In between, he worked as a custodian, coached, refereed, supervised the playground, and even drove the schoolbus! When Howlett worked at the San Rafael City Schools, he knew many children like Jazmin Escalante. In his job he helped children from other countries learn English and become more comfortable in American schools. He saw close-up what it's like to be the "new kid" in class. Now Bud Howlett is a writer and a photographer. He took the photographs in *I'm New Here* to go with Jazmin's story.

79

Extra Support

Rereading Reread the story with students who need extra support. Encourage students to read sections aloud.

More About the Author

Bud Howlett

Bud Howlett has been called "one of the most knowledgeable, successful, and articulate educators in America." In what has proved to be a long and varied career, he taught elementary school for ten years, served as an elementary school principal for nearly twenty-four years, and was the coordinator for bilingual education for the San Rafael (California) City Schools. Howlett was born in Detroit, Michigan, graduated from Antioch College, and received a master's degree from Claremont Graduate School. Howlett says that his motivation to work with children came from his early work as a professional clown.

In 1986 Bud Howlett was named Outstanding Elementary Administrator in Marin County, California. He was recognized for exemplary service to children by the California State Assembly. His first book, *How to Choose the Best School for Your Child*, was awarded the Parents' Choice Award in 1991. Currently Howlett is a writer and photographer who also gives workshop presentations nationwide.

Interact *with* Literature

Responding Activities

Personal Response

Students may draw a picture of a favorite event from the story or choose their own way of responding.

Anthology Activities

Encourage students to choose from the activities on pages 80–81.

Literature Discussion

What could Mrs. Edwards have done differently to make Jazmin feel more welcome?

Selection Connections

Invite students to complete the part of the chart on *Literacy Activity Book* page 8 that refers to *I'm New Here.*

RESPONDING

New Ideas Welcome!

Write a Letter

Dear Jazmin . . .

Write a letter to Jazmin and tell her how you felt about her first day at school. You could offer her encouragement, support, or advice. Let her know whether her experience was similar to any of your experiences at school.

Draw a Picture

Classy Art . . .

Draw a picture of your classroom. Then study the pictures and reread the descriptions of Jazmin's classroom. Use your drawing to explain to a friend or family member how your classroom is similar to or different from Jazmin's.

80

Informal Assessment

Students' responses should indicate general understanding of the selection.

Additional Support:

- Use Guided Reading questions to review and, if necessary, reread.
- Ask students to write a summary of the selection in their journals.

Nuevas ideas ¡Adelante!

Comparing School Stories

Problems, Problems, Problems . . .

In *I'm New Here* and in *Tales of a Fourth Grade Nothing*, the main characters have to solve problems in school situations. Jazmin wants to fit in at a new school. Peter wants to get a project done in a new work group. Discuss with a partner how they each solve their problems.

Write a Diary Entry

New in Town?

It sure can be tough being new in town. Think of a time when you were new at school, or in your neighborhood, or in some other situation. Did any difficult, funny, or unusual things happen to you? Pick one of those episodes and write an entry in your diary telling what happened.

81

QuickREFERENCE

Home Connection

Students and their families may enjoy learning more about El Salvador by borrowing materials from the library or talking with families who have immigrated to the United States from El Salvador.

Students Acquiring English

MEETING INDIVIDUAL NEEDS

For the New in Town? activity, you may wish to ask students acquiring English and other interested students to act out an episode as well as, or instead of, writing a diary entry about it.

Teaching CHOICES

Comprehension Check

To check selection comprehension, use the following questions and/or *Literacy Activity Book* page 20.

1. Who made Jazmin feel the most welcome? How? (Students should provide details from the story to support their choice.)

2. Compare and contrast Jazmin's experiences with your own first week at a new school or at the beginning of a new school year. (Answers will vary but should include both comparisons and contrasts.)

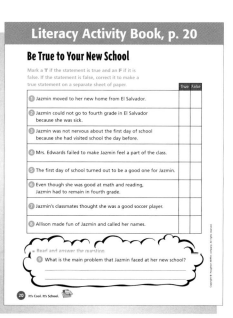

Literacy Activity Book, p. 20

Be True to Your New School

Mark a T if the statement is true and an F if it is false. If the statement is false, correct it to make a true statement on a separate sheet of paper.

	True	False
1 Jazmin moved to her new home from El Salvador.		
2 Jazmin could not go to fourth grade in El Salvador because she was sick.		
3 Jazmin was not nervous about the first day of school because she had visited school the day before.		
4 Mrs. Edwards failed to make Jazmin feel a part of the class.		
5 The first day of school turned out to be a good one for Jazmin.		
6 Even though she was good at math and reading, Jazmin had to remain in fourth grade.		
7 Jazmin's classmates thought she was a good soccer player.		
8 Allison made fun of Jazmin and called her names.		

Read and answer the question.

9 What is the main problem that Jazmin faced at her new school?

20 It's Cool. It's School.

Portfolio Opportunity

- Comprehension Check: Save *Literacy Activity Book* page 20.
- Include students' drawings and written work from the responding activities.

Instruct *and* Integrate

Comprehension

Transparency 1–9

Sequence

	Jazmin was put in a fifth-grade class.
	Some students were mean to Jazmin in the cafeteria.
	The fourth-grade teacher had Jazmin color during class.
	Jazmin made a new friend at school.
	Jazmin went with her mother and brother to look at the school.
	Jazmin told her mother that she didn't want to go back to school.
	In the soccer game, Jazmin scored the winning goals.
	Jazmin was afraid of the first day of school.

IT'S COOL. IT'S SCHOOL. I'm New Here COMPREHENSION SKILL

TRANSPARENCY 1-9 TEACHER'S BOOK PAGE 81A

INTERACTIVE LEARNING

TESTED SKILL

Sequence of Events

LAB, p. 21

Teach/Model Ask students how they signal the order of events when they tell a story to a friend. Help them understand that the specific words they use to tell the story (such as *first, next, then, before, after that,* and *finally*) indicate the sequence of the story, or the order in which events take place.

Ask students why paying attention to the sequence of events in the selection is important. Help them see that understanding the sequence lets them note Jazmin's changing feelings during the story. Display Transparency 1–9. Invite students to number the events in the correct sequence, and write the correct answer on the transparency. You may wish to model sentence number 1 for students and discuss the clue words.

Sequence of Events	
7	Jazmin was put in a fifth grade class.
4	Some students were mean to Jazmin in the cafeteria.
3	The fourth grade teacher had Jazmin color during class.
8	Jazmin made a new friend at school.
2	Jazmin went with her mother and brother to look at the school.
5	Jazmin told her mother that she didn't want to go back to school.
6	In the soccer game, Jazmin scored the winning goals.
1	Jazmin was afraid of the first day of school.

Informal Assessment

Check students' responses to see whether they understand the correct sequence of events in the selection.

Additional Support:

Reteaching, p. 81B
Minilessons, pp. 65, 101, and Theme 5

SKILL FINDER Minilessons, pp. 65, 101; Theme 5

INTERACTIVE LEARNING (CONT.)

Practice/Apply

- Have students use *Literacy Activity Book* page 21 for further practice in tracking the sequence of events.
- Review some of the clue words that signal sequence of events. Have students work in pairs to find clue words such as these in the selection.

Students can use the **Channel R.E.A.D.** videodisc "Suspended in Space" for additional support with Sequence of Events.

Reteaching

MEETING INDIVIDUAL NEEDS

Sequence of Events

Ask students why it is important to keep track of the sequence of events in a story. On the chalkboard, write the questions that appear below. (Sequence words in the questions are underscored to emphasize their importance.) Encourage students to use their books to answer the questions. Then have students work in small groups to create a time line of the story events.

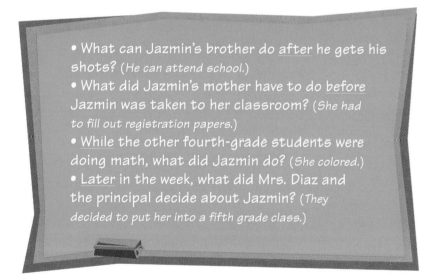

- What can Jazmin's brother do <u>after</u> he gets his shots? *(He can attend school.)*
- What did Jazmin's mother have to do <u>before</u> Jazmin was taken to her classroom? *(She had to fill out registration papers.)*
- <u>While</u> the other fourth-grade students were doing math, what did Jazmin do? *(She colored.)*
- <u>Later</u> in the week, what did Mrs. Diaz and the principal decide about Jazmin? *(They decided to put her into a fifth grade class.)*

Literacy Activity Book, p. 21

What a Nightmare!

Write different Clue Words to complete the sentences.

At the same time
After that
Next
Finally
Then
First

My Bad Day

________. I burned my toast. ________. I spilled my glass of juice. ________. I missed the school bus. ________. I stepped in a mud puddle. ________. I found that I had lost my homework. ________. I woke up and realized that it was all a bad dream.

Write about a good or a bad day you once had. Use as many of the Clue Words as you can.

Copyright © Houghton Mifflin Company. All rights reserved.

It's Cool. It's School. 21

Portfolio Opportunity

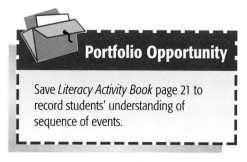

Save *Literacy Activity Book* page 21 to record students' understanding of sequence of events.

Instruct *and* Integrate

Writing Skills and Activities

Transparency 1–10

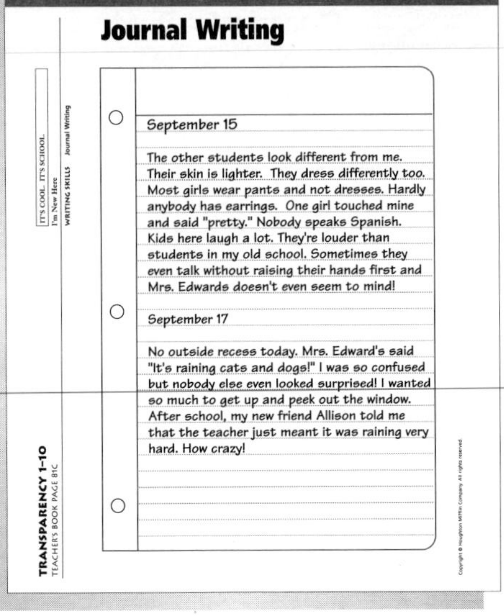
Journal Writing

September 15

The other students look different from me. Their skin is lighter. They dress differently too. Most girls wear pants and not dresses. Hardly anybody has earrings. One girl touched mine and said "pretty." Nobody speaks Spanish. Kids here laugh a lot. They're louder than students in my old school. Sometimes they even talk without raising their hands first and Mrs. Edwards doesn't even seem to mind!

September 17

No outside recess today. Mrs. Edward's said "It's raining cats and dogs!" I was so confused but nobody else even looked surprised! I wanted so much to get up and peek out the window. After school, my new friend Allison told me that the teacher just meant it was raining very hard. How crazy!

TRANSPARENCY 1-10

Literacy Activity Book, p. 22

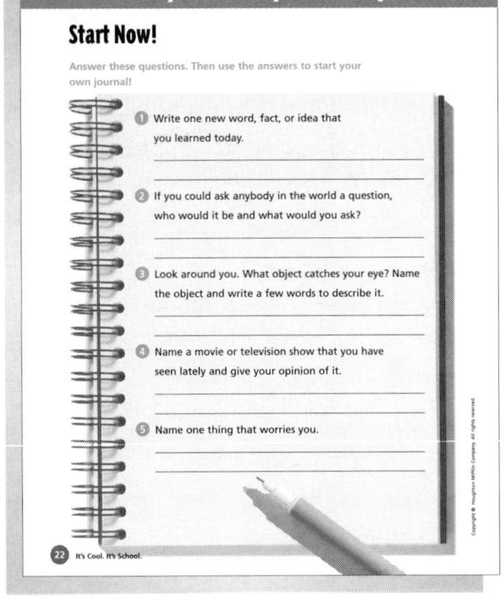
Start Now!

Answer these questions. Then use the answers to start your own journal!

1. Write one new word, fact, or idea that you learned today.
2. If you could ask anybody in the world a question, who would it be and what would you ask?
3. Look around you. What object catches your eye? Name the object and write a few words to describe it.
4. Name a movie or television show that you have seen lately and give your opinion of it.
5. Name one thing that worries you.

22 It's Cool. It's School.

Informal Assessment

Check students' journals for frequency and variety of entries. You might have students keep dialogue journals to share with one another or with you, or if journals are to be kept private, discuss with students the kinds of entries they are making and how they feel about keeping a journal.

INTERACTIVE LEARNING

Journal Writing

LAB, p.22

Teach/Model Tell students that keeping a journal can serve many purposes. It can be a place to store information they don't want to forget, a place to record observations, or a place to explore private thoughts and feelings.

Assure students that there is no right or wrong in journal writing. Stress that journal entries are unfinished pieces of writing, so students shouldn't worry about correct spelling or grammar.

Display Transparency 1–10. Tell students that these are entries Jazmin might have made if she were keeping a journal. Discuss the sample entries. Then work with the class to brainstorm other possible topics for journal entries. No ideas should be excluded.

Journal Topics

- interesting dreams you've had
- anything that has been worrying or bothering you
- reactions to and questions about things you've seen, read, or listened to (TV, movies, books, music)
- quotes or conversation you've overheard
- lists of interesting or unfamiliar words and expressions
- story ideas
- facts, ideas, information that you've learned
- long and short-term goals
- drawings
- clippings from newspapers, magazines, brochures, programs

Practice/Apply Assign the activity Keep a Journal.

Writing Activities

Keep a Journal

Have students keep a writing journal for a week. Encourage them to carry it to and from school and to include a variety of thoughts and observations. At the end of the week, discuss with students what they did or did not like about keeping a journal. Suggest that they continue making entries and that they refer to the journal for writing ideas.

Students Acquiring English Remind students that they can write in their primary language, in English, or in a combination of both languages.

Plan a Welcome

Cooperative Learning

Ask students to imagine that they are part of a welcoming committee for new students. Have them work in groups to plan a way to make new students feel more comfortable during their first week of school. Ask each group to prepare a plan in the form of a paragraph or two or a set of guidelines.

Shared Writing: Description

Students Acquiring English Ask students what Jazmin would see if she looked in the window of your classroom. Work with students to write a description of the classroom and the objects in it, from Jazmin's point of view at the window.

Students can use The Learning Company's new elementary writing center for all their writing activities.

Write a Personal Narrative

Invite students to write a personal narrative about a time when they were in a new situation or when they felt different from others around them. Remind students to include details and dialogue to bring the experience to life for the reader and to vary the types of their sentences to make the writing more interesting. *(See the Writer's Craft Minilesson on page 67.)*

Portfolio Opportunity

Save responses to activities on this page for writing samples.

Instruct *and* Integrate

Word Skills and Strategies

Literacy Activity Book, p. 23

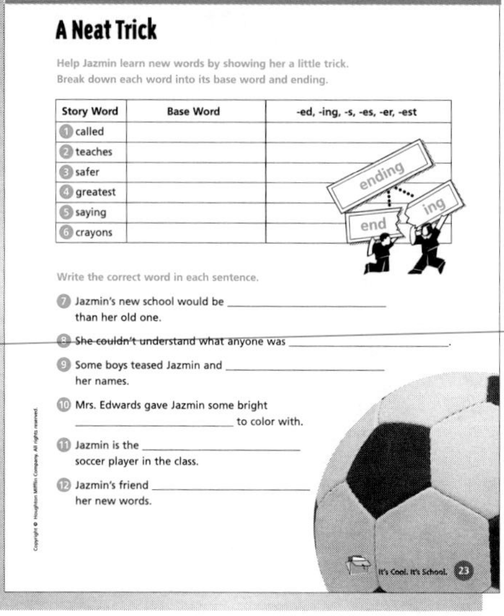
A Neat Trick

Help Jazmin learn new words by showing her a little trick. Break down each word into its base word and ending.

Story Word	Base Word	-ed, -ing, -s, -es, -er, -est
1 called		
2 teaches		
3 safer		
4 greatest		
5 saying		
6 crayons		

Write the correct word in each sentence.

7 Jazmin's new school would be ______ than her old one.

8 She couldn't understand what anyone was ______.

9 Some boys teased Jazmin and ______ her names.

10 Mrs. Edwards gave Jazmin some bright ______ to color with.

11 Jazmin is the ______ soccer player in the class.

12 Jazmin's friend ______ her new words.

It's Cool. It's School. 23

MEETING INDIVIDUAL NEEDS — Extra Support

Point out that in some words, such as *teacher,* the ending *-er* is a suffix that means "someone who." In other words, such as *thing* and *number, s, ed, ing, er,* and *est* are part of the base word and are not endings or suffixes.

Students Acquiring English Review the difference between nouns and verbs and brainstorm examples with students to help them differentiate between the two functions of the inflected form *-s* or *-es.*

Informal Assessment

Use Practice/Apply to check students' understanding of inflected forms.

Additional Support:

Reteaching, p. 81F

INTERACTIVE LEARNING

TESTED SKILL

Structural Analysis
Inflected Forms

LAB, p. 23

Teach/Model Write the following sentences and word endings on the board.

> The school was putting Jazmin in fourth grade. She worried that she would be bigger than the other students, maybe the biggest!

-s or *-es*   *-ed*   *-ing*   *-er*   *-est*

Ask students to find each word in the sentences that is made up of a base word and one of the five endings. (putting, worried, bigger, students, biggest) Have volunteers write each word under the ending it contains. Have others write the base word for each word. Remind students that the spelling of a base word sometimes changes when an ending is added.

Tell students that being able to recognize word endings can help them figure out the meaning of unfamiliar words. Explain that the *-s* or *-es* ending can be added to a noun to mean "more than one" or to a verb. The *-ed* and *-ing* can signal verbs; *-er* is added to a word when comparing two things; and *-est* is added to compare three or more things.

Practice/Apply ***Cooperative Learning*** Have students work in pairs to examine one page from *I'm New Here* and fill out a chart like the one shown.

Words Found on Page 70

Word	Base Word	Ending
papers	paper	s
helped	help	ed
families	family	es
showed	show	ed
seemed	seem	ed
finished	finish	ed
putting	put	ing
bigger	big	er
starting	start	ing
things	thing	s

Reteaching

Inflected Forms

Write these words on the board.

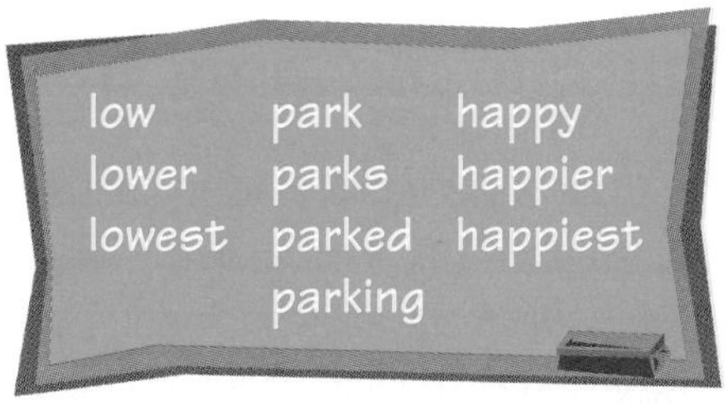
low lower lowest
park parks parked parking
happy happier happiest

Work with students to identify the endings added to the base word in each group. Have students tell or demonstrate the difference in meaning between the base word and the words with an ending. Point out the two meanings of *parks* (noun and verb). Also point out the spelling change in *happy* when an ending is added.

MINILESSON

Dictionary

Alphabetical Order/Guide Words

Teach/Model Write each word below on a piece of cardboard or paper and distribute them among ten students.

scatter	sheet	school	sharp	shame
shelf	science	shadow	same	shelter

Have the students arrange themselves so that their words are in alphabetical order. Then have them explain why they positioned themselves the way they did (starting with the first letter of the word and progressing to the second, third, and so on).

Using Transparency 1–11, remind students that the two words at the top of a dictionary page, called guidewords, tell the first word and the last word found on that page. Explain that all of the other words on the page come between the guidewords in alphabetical order. Ask a volunteer to explain how to use guidewords to find a word in the dictionary.

Practice/Apply Write the guidewords *beef/beginning* on the board. Under them write the words below. Have students circle the words that would be found on a page with those guidewords.

beggar	before	beech	beetle	behind
begun	beehive	bedroom	began	been

Transparency 1–11

Word Skills

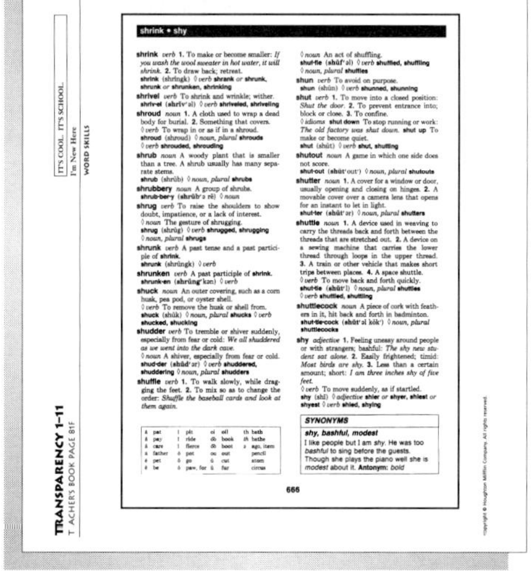

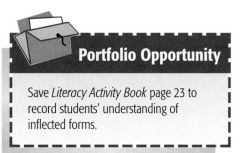

Portfolio Opportunity

Save *Literacy Activity Book* page 23 to record students' understanding of inflected forms.

Instruct *and* Integrate

Building Vocabulary

Literacy Activity Book, p. 24

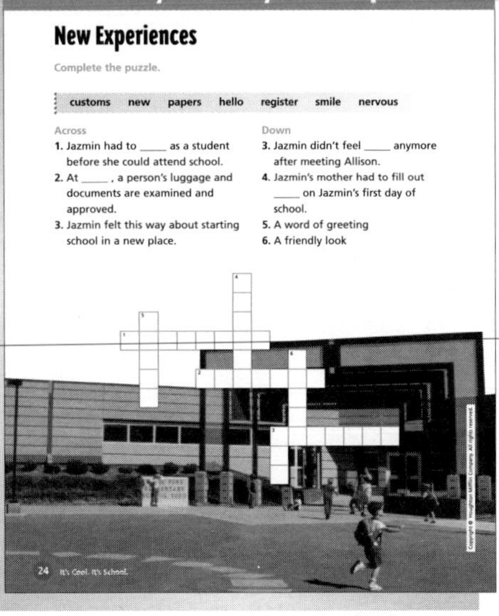

New Experiences

Complete the puzzle.

customs new papers hello register smile nervous

Across
1. Jazmin had to _____ as a student before she could attend school.
2. At _____, a person's luggage and documents are examined and approved.
3. Jazmin felt this way about starting school in a new place.

Down
3. Jazmin didn't feel _____ anymore after meeting Allison.
4. Jazmin's mother had to fill out _____ on Jazmin's first day of school.
5. A word of greeting
6. A friendly look

24 It's Cool. It's School.

Use this page to review Selection Vocabulary.

Vocabulary Activities

Multiple-Meaning Words

Ask students this riddle: How is a hospital patient like a photographer? (They both get shots.) Tell students that many jokes and riddles are plays on words, such as *shots*, that have more than one meaning.

Have students make up their own riddles or draw captioned cartoons based on multiple-meaning words. This list of words from *I'm New Here* may provide inspiration: *grade, row, felt, lot, counter, customs, right, box, rest, board, watch, change, chest, dribbled, light, play, worn.*

Bilingual Dictionary

MEETING INDIVIDUAL NEEDS

Students Acquiring English Display a sample phrase book or bilingual dictionary. Ask students why such reference books are made and who might use them. Have students who are acquiring English work with native English speakers to develop a bilingual dictionary they can all use. Suggest that they start by defining and illustrating nouns.

Word History: *soccer*

Share this word history with students, writing *association, assoc., soc,* and *soccer* on the board as you do so.

The word *soccer* has nothing to do with "socking" a ball. Originally the game was known in England as *association football*—or simply *association.* Players shortened this to the abbreviation *assoc.* and then shortened it again to *soc.* Meanwhile, at the Rugby School in England, a game called Rugby football was being played—and that name was shortened to *rugger.* A similar *-er* ending was added to the shortened word *soc,* and it became the name we use today—*soccer.*

Spelling

FIVE-DAY PLAN

DAY 1	DAY 2	DAY 3	DAY 4	DAY 5
Pretest; Minilesson; Challenge Words/ Additional Words (opt.); Take-Home Word Lists (LAB)	First LAB page; Challenge Words Practice (opt.)	Check first LAB page; Second LAB page (except writing application)	Check second LAB page; writing application (LAB)	Test

MINILESSON

Spelling Words
*grade
*meet
*seem
*neat
*wait
*away
*safe
*afraid
*least
*crayon

Challenge Words
*playground
*repeat
*United States
*squeeze
Wednesday

Additional Spelling Words
dream
spray
reach
gain
steep

*Starred words or forms of the words appear in *I'm New Here.*

TESTED SKILL

Spelling Long *a* and Long *e*

LAB, pp. 25, 26

- Write the word *grade* on the board. Say the word aloud and have students repeat it. Ask them what vowel sound they hear in *grade*. (/ā/) Write the words *wait* and *away* on the board, and say each word. Elicit that /ā/ can be spelled *a*-consonant-*e*, *ai*, or *ay*. Underline these patterns in the words on the board.
- Introduce the /ē/ sound in the same way, using the words *seem* and *neat*.
- Write the Spelling Words on the board. Tell students that each Spelling Word has the /ā/ sound or the /ē/ sound. Say the Spelling Words and have students repeat them.

Spelling Assessment

Pretest

Say each underlined word, read the sentence, and then repeat the word. Have students write only the underlined words.

1. What grade are you in?
2. I hope I meet new friends at school.
3. The other students seem friendly.
4. Keep your desks neat and clean.
5. I can't wait for the first day of school.
6. Please put away your books.
7. Put your lunch money in a safe place.
8. Don't be afraid to ask questions.
9. I like soccer best and tennis least.
10. My purple crayon is broken.

Test

Spelling Words Use the Pretest sentences.

Challenge Words

11. Who is the President of the United States?
12. We go to the playground for recess.
13. Music class is every Wednesday afternoon.
14. Can you please repeat the question?
15. If you squeeze the toy, it squeaks.

SKILL FINDER
Daily Language Practice, p. 81J
Reading-Writing Workshop, p. 91E

Literacy Activity Book, p. 25

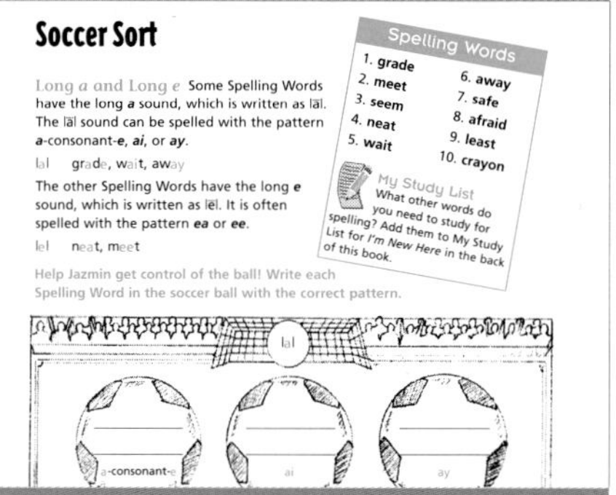
Soccer Sort

Long *a* and Long *e* Some Spelling Words have the long *a* sound, which is written as /ā/. The /ā/ sound can be spelled with the pattern *a*-consonant-*e*, *ai*, or *ay*.

/ā/ grade, wait, away

The other Spelling Words have the long *e* sound, which is written as /ē/. It is often spelled with the pattern *ea* or *ee*.

/ē/ neat, meet

Spelling Words: 1. grade 2. meet 3. seem 4. neat 5. wait 6. away 7. safe 8. afraid 9. least 10. crayon

My Study List: What other words do you need to study for spelling? Add them to My Study List for *I'm New Here* in the back of this book.

Help Jazmin get control of the ball! Write each Spelling Word in the soccer ball with the correct pattern.

Literacy Activity Book, p. 26

Spelling Spree

New-School Blues Complete this story by writing the Spelling Words that fit the blanks.

I don't _ _ _ _ like the nervous type, but on my first day at my new school, I shook like a leaf. I wanted to _ _ _ _ new kids, but I didn't know how to go about it.

Just as I was thinking how _ _ _ _ and clean the room was, I stepped on a _ _ _ _ _ _. My feet flew out from under me, and I landed with a thud in another boy's lap. "Well!" he said, startled. "Welcome to fourth _ _ _ _ _!" With that, we both began to laugh. What on earth had I been _ _ _ _ _ _ of?

Spelling Words: 1. grade 2. meet 3. seem 4. neat 5. wait 6. away 7. safe 8. afraid 9. least 10. crayon

Proofreading Circle four misspelled Spelling Words. Then write each word correctly.

Dear Berta,
I'm glad you have come to our town from so far awey. It is saif here, so you'll never have to be afraid again. I can hardly wate until summer, when we will have a lot of fun. It will be here before we know it. (At leest I hope so!)

1 ___
2 ___
3 ___
4 ___

Welcoming Words On a separate piece of paper, write a dialogue in which you welcome a new student from another country. Remember to capitalize and punctuate your dialogue correctly. Use Spelling Words from the list.

26 It's Cool. It's School.

Copyright © Houghton Mifflin Company. All rights reserved.

Literacy Activity Book

Take-Home Word Lists: pp. 313–314

Students can use the **Spelling Spree CD-ROM** for extra practice with the spelling principles taught in this selection.

MEETING INDIVIDUAL NEEDS

Challenge

Challenge Words Practice Have students use the Challenge Words to write school rules or customs that new students would need to know.

Instruct *and* **Integrate**

Grammar

5-Day Planner FIVE-DAY PLAN

DAY 1	DAY 2	DAY 3	DAY 4	DAY 5
Daily Language Practice 1; Teach/Model; First LAB page	Daily Language Practice 2; Check first LAB page; Cooperative Learning	Daily Language Practice 3; Writing Application	Daily Language Practice 4; Reteaching (opt.); Second LAB page	Daily Language Practice 5; Check second LAB page; Students' Writing

Transparency 1–12

Kinds of Sentences

STATEMENT	Jazmin walked two miles to see her school.
QUESTION	Did it seem far?
COMMAND	Try to imagine how she felt.
EXCLAMATION	The next day she would be there!

The first day finally came

What a hard day it was

Jazmin sat at the edge of the room

Why did she have to color

Show Jazmin to her desk

Who finally said her name correctly

She loved soccer

Do not forget Jazmin's story

IT'S COOL. IT'S SCHOOL. I'm New Here GRAMMAR Kinds of Sentences

TRANSPARENCY 1–12 TEACHER'S BOOK PAGE 81I

Literacy Activity Book, p. 28

Literacy Activity Book, p. 27

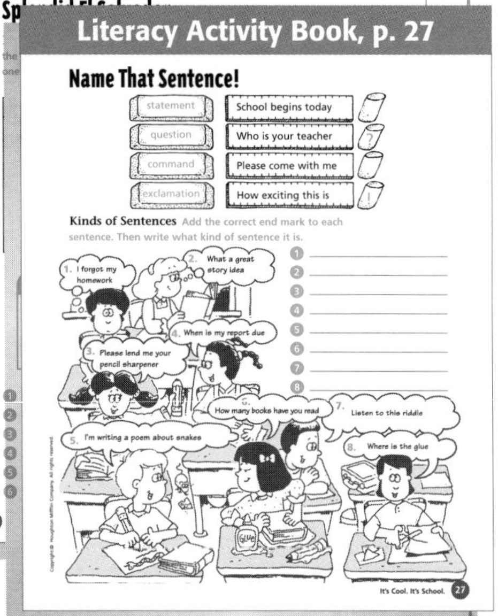

Informal Assessment

Responses to activities should indicate a general understanding of types of sentences.

Additional Support:
Reteaching, p. 81J

INTERACTIVE LEARNING

TESTED SKILL

Kinds of Sentences

LAB, pp. 27–28

- A **statement** tells something. It ends with a **period**.
- A **question** asks something. It ends with a **question mark**.
- A **command** tells someone to do something. It ends with a **period**.
- An **exclamation** shows strong feeling, such as surprise, excitement, or fear. It ends with an **exclamation point**.

Teach/Model Write these sentences from *I'm New Here* on the chalkboard.

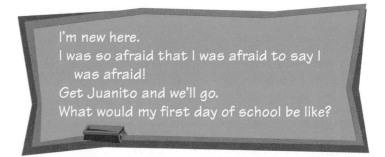

> I'm new here.
> I was so afraid that I was afraid to say I was afraid!
> Get Juanito and we'll go.
> What would my first day of school be like?

Then, write the purposes of the four kinds of sentences: tell something, ask a question, tell someone to do something, and show strong feeling.

Divide students into four groups. Ask each group to identify the purpose of one of the sentences and to read it aloud in a way that conveys the purpose. Invite groups to share their responses. Discuss with students how each kind of sentence is punctuated.

Display Transparency 1–12. Introduce the terms *statement, question, command*, and *exclamation*. Then ask volunteers to add end marks to the remaining sentences and to label them.

Encourage students to generate their own statements, questions, commands, and exclamations. Record their sentences on the chalkboard.

SKILL FINDER Reading-Writing Workshop, p. 91E

INTERACTIVE LEARNING *(continued)*

Practice/Apply

***Cooperative Learning:* Quotations** Have students work in small groups with one person as the recorder. The group role-plays entering a school where nobody speaks their language. What might they say? What might they think? As students suggest responses, the recorder writes them down. After ten sentences, the group checks to see how many kinds of sentences they have generated. Have them label each one and make up others for any missing types. Remind them to check for correct end marks.

Writing Application: Personal Profile Invite students to prepare personal profiles to share with the class. Each student should write (1) two statements that tell something about themselves, (2) two questions that they dislike being asked, (3) two commands that they dislike being given, and (4) two exclamations that express something they feel strongly about.

Students' Writing Suggest that students check their work in process to see whether they have used correct end punctuation.

More Practice

Houghton Mifflin English Level 4
Workbook Plus, pp. 3–4, 5–6, 87–88
Reteaching Workbook, pp. 2, 3, 57

Writers Express
Writers Express SourceBook,
pp. 3–4, 5–6, 73–74, 116

Reteaching

Kinds of Sentences

MEETING INDIVIDUAL NEEDS

Review the differences among the four types of sentences by demonstrating how a statement can be turned into a question, an exclamation, or a command by changes in wording and punctuation.

I like pizza.	Pizza is fantastic!	Do you like pizza?	Please pass the pizza.
statement	*exclamation*	*question*	*command*

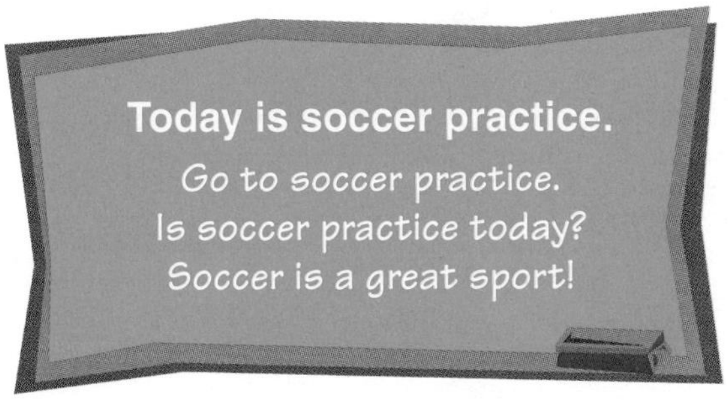

Today is soccer practice.
Go to soccer practice.
Is soccer practice today?
Soccer is a great sport!

Then write a short statement at the top of the chalkboard. Divide students into teams of three. One student from each team comes forward and writes a question, an exclamation, or a command based on the statement. The next student chooses another type, and the third student must write a sentence of the remaining type. Have the teams compare their sentences when finished. Play additional rounds, starting with a question, an exclamation, or a command.

Daily Language Practice

Focus Skills

Grammar: Kinds of Sentences
Spelling: Long *a* and Long *e*

Every day write one sentence on the chalkboard. Have each student write the sentence correctly on a sheet of paper. Tell students to correct any incorrect end marks as well as any misspelled words. Have students correct their own paper as a volunteer corrects the sentence on the chalkboard.

1. Are you ever afrade to start a new grade?
   Are you ever **afraid** to start a new grade**?**
2. Please mete me at lunch.
   Please **meet** me at lunch.
3. I will wate at the door?
   I will **wait** at the door**.**
4. Your desk looks so neet and clean?
   Your desk looks so **neat** and clean**!**
5. Does this crayone seem too dark!
   Does this **crayon** seem too dark**?**

Instruct *and* Integrate

Communication Activities

Listening and Speaking

Introducing Yourself

Pose the following situation for students: You have been placed in a new classroom where you don't know anyone. The teacher has given the class a five-minute break for students to get to know one another. What would be a good way to meet your fellow students? (introduce yourself)

Divide students into groups. Have each group list at least three pieces of information that are important to include when introducing yourself. (Sample: your name, where you are from, your interests) Then give students index cards, and have them write information about themselves using the group's list as a guide. Finally, have each student introduce herself or himself to the group.

Audio Tape
for It's Cool. It's School.: *I'm New Here*

Words from Other Languages

Cooperative Learning

Divide the class into four groups. Assign each group a foreign language. Provide the groups with appropriate sources of words in their assigned language (for example, foreign-language dictionaries or guidebooks for tourists). Have each group find five foreign words and their English translations. Ask a volunteer from each group to present the words to the class. If possible, invite a fluent speaker of each language to be on hand to help with pronunciation.

Students can select a "Word of the Day" from those presented and focus on pronunciation and meaning of the word throughout the day.

Viewing

What We Don't See

Ask students how our way of seeing things can also depend on how familiar those things are to us. To help them think about their responses, have students either draw or write about the front of their house (or the front of the school, or any other familiar building or room) from memory, recalling as many details as possible. Then have them compare their drawings or written descriptions with the actual place. Discuss any differences between how they remembered a familiar place and how it really appears.

Watching a Video

Students Acquiring English Show a video about improving students' success at school, such as *Skills for Classroom Survival* (National Geographic), or one that tells a school-related story, such as *Crow Boy* (Weston Woods). Ask students what they think about the main ideas or characters.

Portfolio Opportunity

- Use a video camera to record students' introductions.
- Include students' drawings and written descriptions in their portfolios.

Cross-Curricular Activities

Choices for Social Studies

El Salvador Quiz Show

Divide the class into three teams: two teams will compete to answer questions; the third team will be the questioners. Have each team research and write questions (and answers) about the geography, history, and climate of El Salvador. (Sample question: Does the number of daylight hours vary greatly from season to season? Give the reason for your answer.) Develop a method for scoring, and rotate the roles of questioning and answering teams.

Travel Poster

El Salvador is a beautiful country with glorious natural attractions. Have students make travel posters that highlight one or more of El Salvador's natural wonders. Students may add a phrase or slogan to enhance the message of their pictures.

Materials

- posterboard
- construction paper
- safety scissors
- pencils, crayons, markers
- glue
- magazine photographs

Choices for Social Studies *(continued)*

An Informational Interview

1. Have students identify people in the school or neighborhood who use more than one language in their jobs. (Possibilities include a bilingual or ESL teacher or a merchant in an ethnic neighborhood.)
2. Ask students what they would like to learn from these people about their bilingual jobs. Help students list interview questions, and arrange a time for a guest to come to class.
3. Have students conduct the interview and, later, share what they learn.

Art

Tell a Story

Oral tradition is strong among Salvadorans; many folktales and myths have been passed from generation to generation. Have students continue the tradition by researching ancient Mayan or modern Salvadoran myths or folktales and retelling them to the class. Make sure that storytelling guidelines, practice time, and a storytelling area—perhaps in a circle on the floor—are all established before the first student performs.

MINILESSON

Study Skill

Parts of a Book

Teach/Model

Ask students how they use a book to research a topic. In discussion, highlight the following parts of a book:

- title page—lists the title of the book, the author's name, and often the name of the publisher
- copyright page—includes the copyright symbol (the small circle with a *c* in it) and the year the book was published
- table of contents—lists the chapters of the book and the page number on which each begins
- glossary—defines words related to the subject
- index—refers the reader to pages where important names, places, and topics appear

Practice/Apply

For the quiz show on page 81M (or other activities for this selection that require research), have students identify the parts of the books they are using. How would their work be affected if the books did not contain these parts?

SKILL FINDER Full lesson, p. H3

Introduce the Literature

Building Background

This selection describes unusual schools. Ask students to describe the most unusual school they have attended or the most unusual school activity in which they have participated.

Interact with Literature

Predict/Infer

Draw the following chart on the chalkboard and encourage students to make inferences about each school based on the pictures and descriptions.

School	Inference	What Leads Me to Make the Inference
Children of the Rainbow	They travel.	The circus goes to lots of cities to perform. It came to our city for two nights last summer.

This Is School? Cool!
If you think all schools are alike, think again
THE GREATEST SHOW ON EARTH
Circus School
For some people, school is a circus. The Children of the Rainbow spin, twirl, leap, and go to school as they tour with the famous Ringling Brothers and Barnum & Bailey Circus.
82

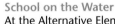

Ballet School
At the New Ballet School in New York City, students dance their way through school. Talented children from all over the city study dance as well as regular school subjects.

School by Satellite
This fifth grader in Washington, D.C., is talking to a diver on a coral reef in Belize, in Central America. How does she do it? The Jason Project allows students at participating schools to go on field trips via satellite TV.

School on the Water
At the Alternative Elementary School Number 1, in Seattle, Washington, students use their math skills to build sailboats. They even have their own boat club!

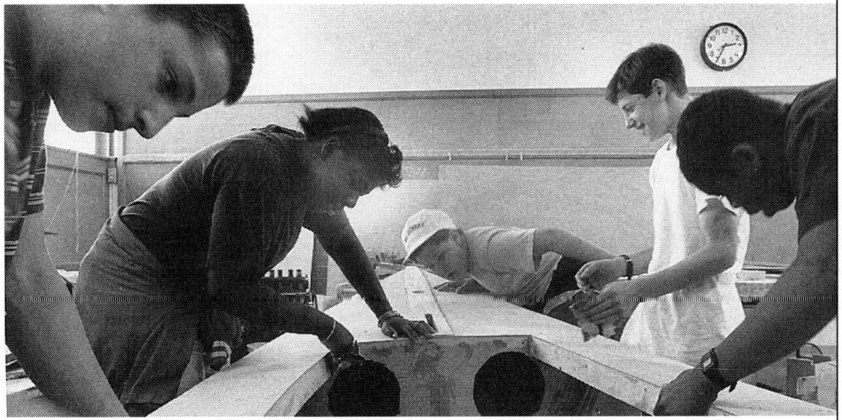

Instruct *and* Integrate

Math

Reading a Map Ask students to locate Seattle, Washington; New York, New York; and Washington, D.C., on a map. Then tell them that the Ringling Brothers and Barnum & Bailey Circus is currently performing in Seattle and must plan next month's schedule. The circus has been asked to perform in New York City and Washington, D.C. Using the scale on the map, ask students to find the shortest route for the circus to take to do all three shows. Approximately how far will the circus travel?

Writing

Some special schools require an application in which the prospective student explains reasons for wanting to attend that school. Ask students to choose one of the schools described in the selection and write two or three paragraphs listing reasons they are interested in the school and what they hope to learn there.

Students Acquiring English As an alternate approach to the above activity, less-proficient students acquiring English may draw a picture of what they would like to learn and write captions for the picture.

Introduce the Literature

Building Background

Ask students to describe unusual ways they have learned concepts in math or other subjects. What made the method unusual? Did the method help them remember the concept being taught? Alert students to notice as they read that the selection focuses on an unusual method for learning arithmetic.

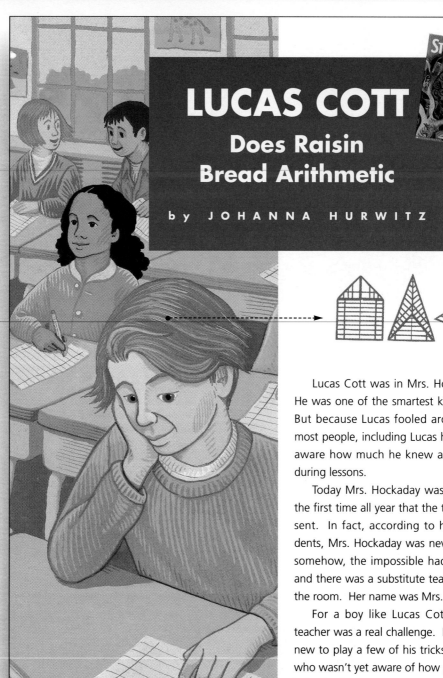

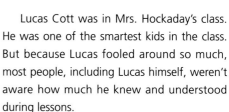

LUCAS COTT Does Raisin Bread Arithmetic

by JOHANNA HURWITZ

Paper airplane figure 1

Lucas Cott was in Mrs. Hockaday's class. He was one of the smartest kids in the class. But because Lucas fooled around so much, most people, including Lucas himself, weren't aware how much he knew and understood during lessons.

Today Mrs. Hockaday was out ill. It was the first time all year that the teacher was absent. In fact, according to her former students, Mrs. Hockaday was never absent. Yet somehow, the impossible had come to pass and there was a substitute teacher in front of the room. Her name was Mrs. Lindenbaum.

For a boy like Lucas Cott, a substitute teacher was a real challenge. It was someone new to play a few of his tricks on. Someone who wasn't yet aware of how good he was at being bad.

Interact with Literature

Draw a Venn diagram on the chalkboard as shown. Ask students to think of words and phrases to describe Lucas and Cricket. Discuss whether the words and phrases describe just Lucas, just Cricket, or both Lucas and Cricket. Then write the words and phrases in the appropriate place on the diagram.

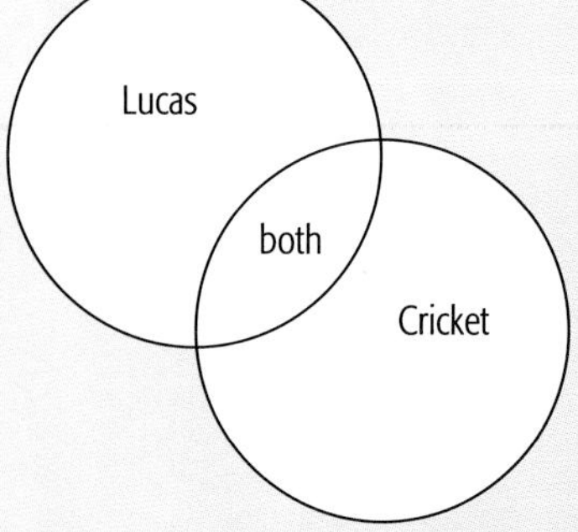

During arithmetic, Mrs. Lindenbaum surprised everyone. Instead of telling them to take out their arithmetic workbooks, she handed out sheets of blank paper.

"Mrs. Lindenbaum, Mrs. Lindenbaum," called out Cricket Kaufman as she waved her hand in the air. "For arithmetic we never use these pieces of paper. We write in our workbooks."

"Thank you for that information," said the substitute. "Nevertheless, as Mrs. Hockaday didn't leave any lesson plans for me today, I have a special assignment for you to do."

Lucas looked over at Cricket. She seemed miserable. He knew she loved writing answers into her arithmetic workbook. Unlike Lucas's workbook or the workbook of most of the other students, there was no crossing out and very little erasing or smudging in Cricket's book. She worked very hard at perfection and sometimes she almost achieved it.

Mrs. Lindenbaum pulled a brown paper grocery bag out from under Mrs. Hockaday's desk. From it she removed what looked very much like a large loaf of bread. Lucas looked with amazement. It was bread!

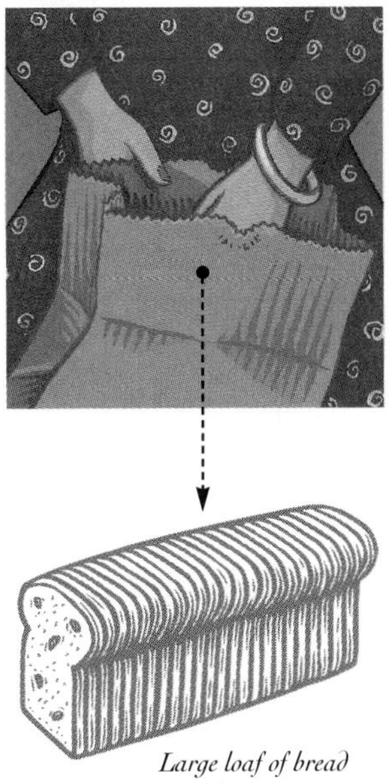

Large loaf of bread
figure 2

Mrs. Lindenbaum walked up and down the aisles and gave a slice of bread to each of the surprised students. When she was finished, every one of the 24 students in Lucas's class had a slice and the bag was empty.

"It's raisin bread," said Julio Sanchez aloud. "I love raisin bread. Why don't we study about bread every day?"

"Are you sure this is arithmetic?" asked Cricket, looking very puzzled. Usually Cricket knew everything. She certainly knew a slice of raisin bread when she saw it. It did not look at all like arithmetic.

Lucas didn't stop to worry about whether their substitute was confused about subjects. He just picked up his slice of bread and took a large bite. It tasted great.

"Do you have any cream cheese in that bag?" he called out with his mouth full.

"Stop eating that bread," Mrs. Lindenbaum instructed. "First we have to do our lesson. The raisin bread can teach us about fractions. We will also practice the scientific method of observation."

Mrs. Lindenbaum told the students to trace the slice of bread onto the sheet of paper. Then they had to mark the location

Interact with Literature

Predict/Infer

Ask students to predict how the teacher plans to use the loaf of raisin bread to teach arithmetic. Discuss with students how and why they made their predictions. During the discussion, help students see that making predictions helps readers think about what they are reading and that thinking about previous experiences may help them make better predictions. Then ask students to finish reading the selection to check their predictions.

Interact with Literature

Sequence of Events

After students have read the selection, write the following sentences on the chalkboard. Ask the students to renumber them in the correct sequence. Then discuss with students how sequencing helps readers better understand and remember the selection.

3 1. Lucas ate 2/128 of the raisins.

1 2. Twenty-four students each received a slice of bread.

4 3. Lucas weighed his slice of bread.

6 4. Lucas laughed because he knew what was in his lunch bag.

5 5. Lucas discovered tiny ridges in the bread.

2 6. Lucas took a large bite out of his slice of bread.

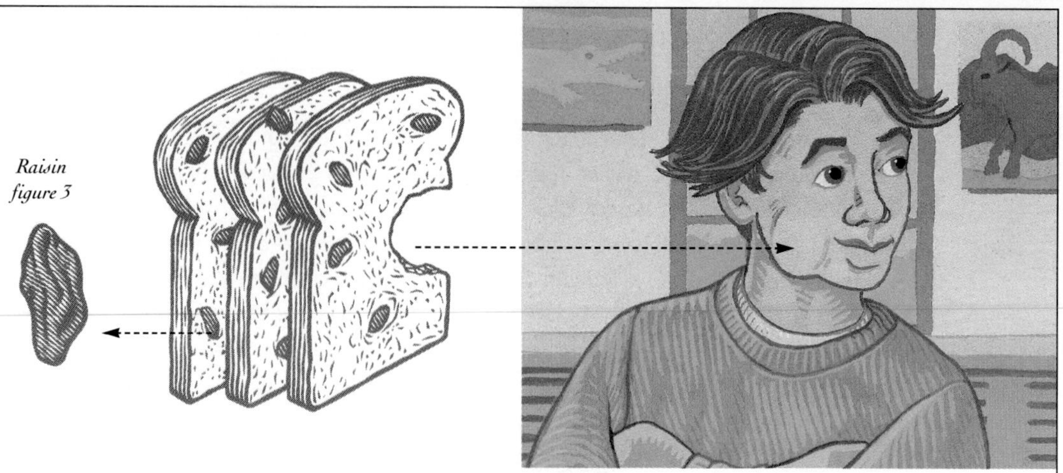

of the raisins. Two of Lucas's raisins were moving through his digestive system so he didn't know how to mark that on his paper.

Mrs. Lindenbaum wrote some questions on the chalkboard:

1. How many slices of bread are in the loaf?
2. What fraction of the loaf is your slice?
3. How many raisins are in your slice?
4. How many raisins in the whole loaf?
5. What fraction of raisins are in your slice?
6. How much does your slice of bread weigh?
7. Look at your slice of bread with a magnifying glass. Describe what you see, smell, feel, and taste!

Mrs. Lindenbaum removed a small scale from the brown paper bag. Lucas wondered what else was in the bag. Maybe there was something else to eat. The one bite of raisin bread had whetted his appetite. Lunch time wasn't for another hour and a half.

The students took turns weighing their bread. Lucas's slice weighed the least because part was missing. But it was interesting to see that none of the slices were exactly the same. Some weighed a bit more than others. And although there were still four raisins in his remaining portion of bread plus two in his stomach, Lucas could see that some students only had a total of four or five raisins in their full slice. Julio had eight raisins.

"Hey, neat-o," said Julio when he realized he hit the raisin jackpot. When all the raisins were added together, there were 128!

"Can I eat the bread now?" Julio asked.

"Not yet," said Mrs. Lindenbaum. "Continue studying your bread and answer question number five." From her brown paper bag she removed half a dozen magnifying glasses.

Lucas picked off another tiny bit of his bread and stuck it in his mouth when no one was looking. He couldn't help it. But it wasn't fun to nibble at bread like a mouse. He wanted to chew down on a real big piece of bread.

When it was his turn with the magnifying glass, Lucas pretended he was a detective.

86

Interact with Literature

MEETING INDIVIDUAL NEEDS

Students Acquiring English

Role Playing Have students work in mixed groups of three to role play the responses that Lucas, Cricket, and Julio might give to parents who asked, "What did you do in math today?"

He'd seen an old Sherlock Holmes movie once. Sherlock Holmes would have looked for fingerprints and teeth marks and things like that. Lucas was surprised to discover the tiny ridges in the bread. Never in his life had he thought about the texture of bread. If he were an ant, he thought, it would be hard to walk across the surface of the bread. Then he rested his head on the desk, next to the bread, and inhaled deeply. There was a nice bready smell.

Little ant
figure 4

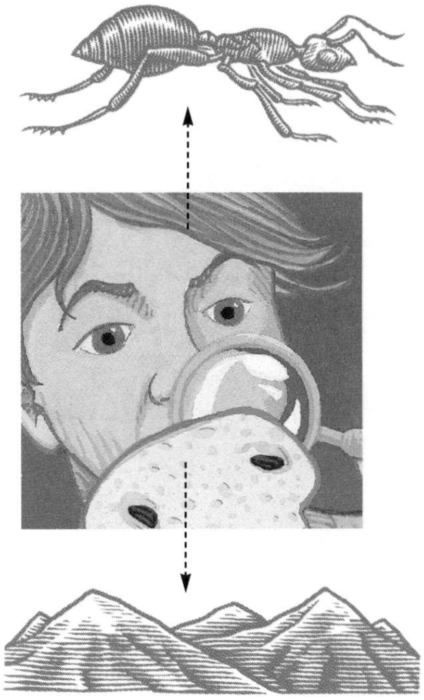

Really-hard-to-climb mountain
figure 5

Lucas couldn't bear it any longer. He grabbed the slice of bread and folded it in half. In two bites, it was all in his mouth: chewy and delicious.

"What are we going to study tomorrow?" he asked the substitute after he swallowed the bread. "How about pepperoni pizza?"

"I second the motion," said Julio Sanchez. He looked forward to eating $\frac{8}{128}$ or $\frac{1}{16}$ of the total pieces of pepperoni on a pizza.

"Don't worry about tomorrow. There is plenty to learn today," said Mrs. Lindenbaum. She looked into the brown paper bag again.

Lucas hoped Mrs. Hockaday wasn't too sick. Maybe just a mild case of yellow fever or smallpox. (Those were diseases he had read about in a library book. He was, after all, a pretty smart kid and knew all sorts of things one wouldn't have suspected.) He liked eating $\frac{1}{24}$ of a loaf of bread. If Mrs. Lindenbaum and her brown paper bag were around, there would be a lot of other things Lucas might learn from the sub and her unusual teaching methods.

"School is like a slice of raisin bread," pointed out Mrs. Lindenbaum. "Some of it may seem plain and a bit dull. You can't expect raisins all the time. But when you least expect it there can be a surprise, like a raisin in the midst of a piece of boring white bread."

Lucas laughed to himself. Mrs. Lindenbaum didn't know that inside his lunch bag, his mother had put a whole box of raisins.

87

Instruct and Integrate

Math

Invite students to create other fun math activities that use food.

Writing

Ask students to write a summary for Mrs. Hockaday describing the concept their substitute teacher taught the class and how she taught that concept.

Instruct and Integrate

MINILESSON

Study Skill
Graphs

Teach/Model

On the chalkboard, draw a bar graph as shown below. Help students understand that the bar on the graph represents the number of raisins in Julio's piece of bread. Ask students how many raisins are in Lucas's piece of bread, and have a volunteer plot the number in a bar on the graph.

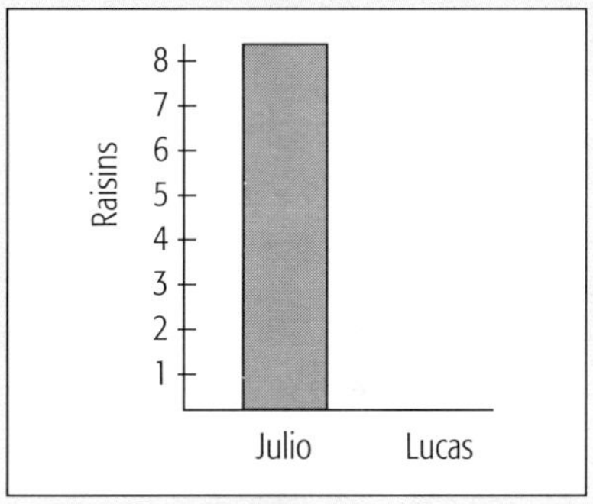

Then draw a pictograph as shown below. Ask students to describe how the pictograph is similar to the bar graph. How is it different?

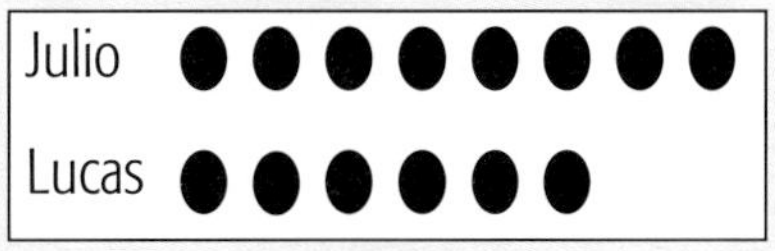

Practice/Apply

Ask students to assume that Cricket has five raisins in her piece of bread. Have a volunteer plot Cricket's raisins on the bar graph and the pictograph.

SKILL FINDER Full lesson, p. H4

Introduce the Literature

Activating Prior Knowledge

Invite students to think of times when they were asked or assigned to do something they particularly did not want to do. What happened? Did the experience turn out better or worse than expected? Ask volunteers to share their experiences with the class.

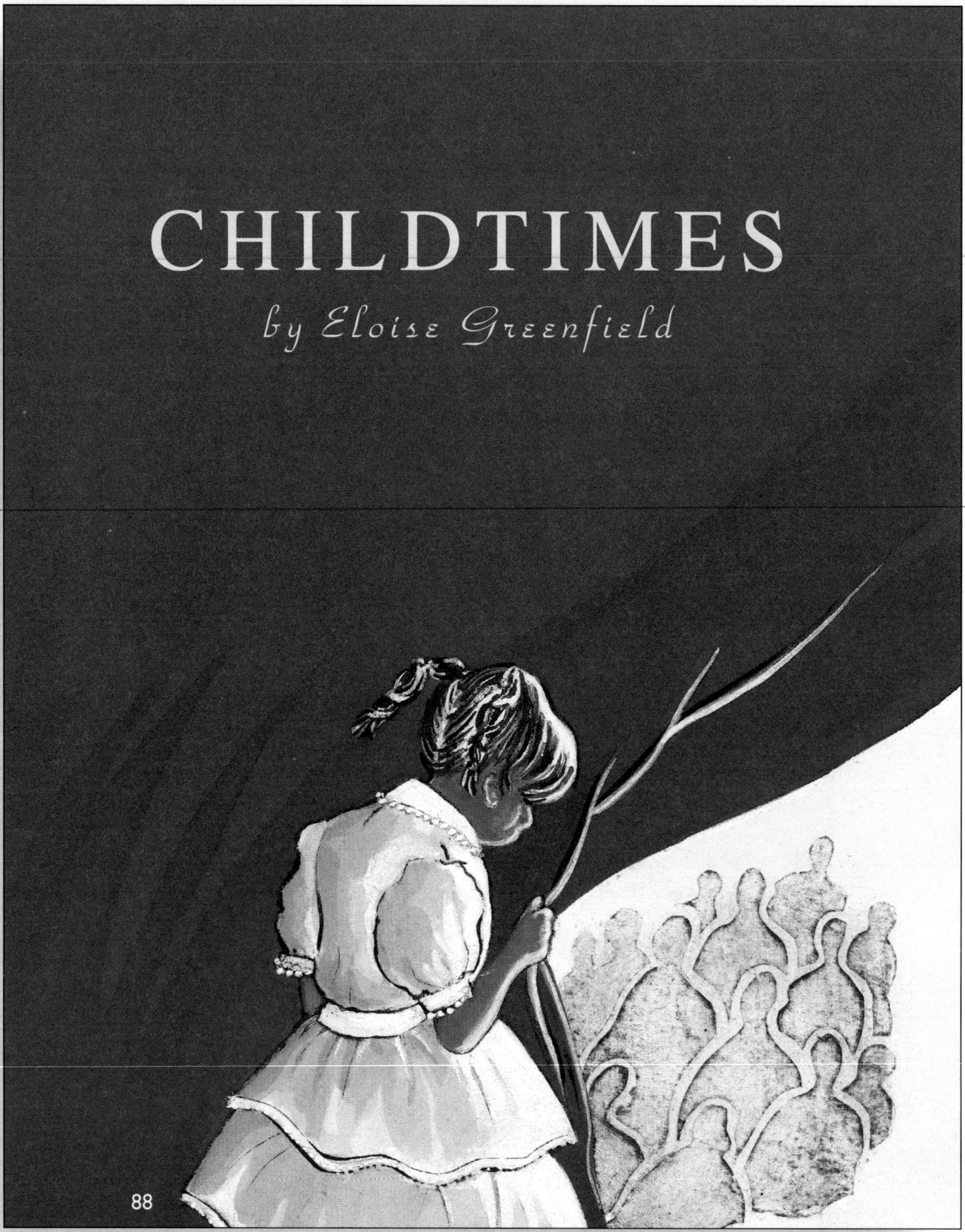

Interact with Literature

Thinking Critically

Cooperative Learning

Ask pairs of students to discuss and list possible reasons that the speaker wanted to be part of a group rather than have a big part in the play. You might also invite students to write a letter to the drama teacher stating which type of role they would choose for themselves and why. Students can share their letters in small groups.

Expanding Literacy
Memoir

A Play

When I was in the fifth grade, I was famous for a whole day, and all because of a play. The teacher had given me a big part, and I didn't want it. I liked to be in plays where I could be part of a group, like being one of the talking trees, or dancing, or singing in the glee club. But having to talk by myself — *uh uh!*

I used to slide down in my chair and stare at my desk while the teacher was giving out the parts, so she wouldn't pay any attention to me, but this time it didn't work. She called on me anyway. I told her I didn't want to do it, but she said I had to. I guess she thought it would be good for me.

On the day of the play, I didn't make any mistakes. I remembered all of my lines. Only — nobody in the audience heard me. I couldn't make my voice come out loud.

For the rest of the day, I was famous. Children passing by my classroom door, children on the playground at lunchtime, kept pointing at me saying, "That's that girl! That's the one who didn't talk loud enough!"

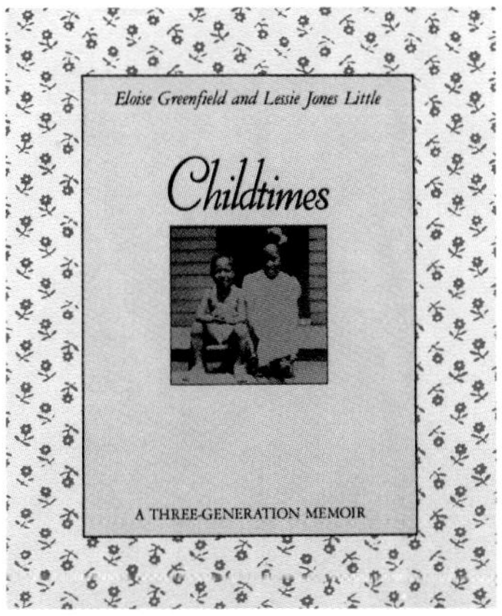

I felt so bad, I wanted to go home. But one good thing came out of it all. The teacher was so angry, so upset, she told me that as long as I was in that school, I'd never have another chance to ruin one of her plays. And that was such good news, I could stand being famous for a day.

89

Interact with Literature

Vocabulary

Have students look up *famous* and *infamous* in the dictionary. Discuss with students the differences in meaning. Then ask whether this writer could be called infamous rather than famous.

Instruct and Integrate

Writing

Emphasizing Strategies Ask a volunteer to read the first paragraph aloud. Discuss with students why the author chose to italicize the words *uh uh!* Demonstrate ways to use dashes, italics, and exclamation points for emphasis. Ask students to identify other words and phrases in the selection that the author has emphasized. Then have students practice reading the paragraphs aloud, placing emphasis where appropriate. Finally, invite students to use these strategies themselves as they write brief accounts of the experiences they described in Activating Prior Knowledge.

Theater

Putting on a Play Students may enjoy turning this selection into a short play. Ask volunteers to play the roles of the teacher, the narrator/author, other students in the class, and audience members. Encourage students to improvise their roles where the selection does not provide specific lines.

Students Acquiring English Encourage students acquiring English to act alongside English-proficient speakers.

Reading-Writing Workshop

A Personal Narrative

About the Workshop

This workshop includes suggestions and ideas to help you guide students through the process of writing a personal narrative. Workshop minilessons focus on writing good beginnings, supplying details, and creating dialogue. These skills are included in the assessment criteria at the end of the workshop.

Keep these considerations in mind:

- Because students are working with familiar content, this mode provides students with a unique opportunity to focus on organizing and shaping material.
- Some students may consider writing about painful experiences. Help them to decide whether to explore these topics in the classroom setting and, if so, whether their writing will be private or shared.

Connecting to *Childtimes*

This brief account can familiarize students with the form and type of content appropriate for a personal narrative.

Introducing the Student Model

Tell students that they are going to read a true story written by another fourth grader, Anthony Yengo. Have students read Anthony's story. Then discuss the questions on page 91.

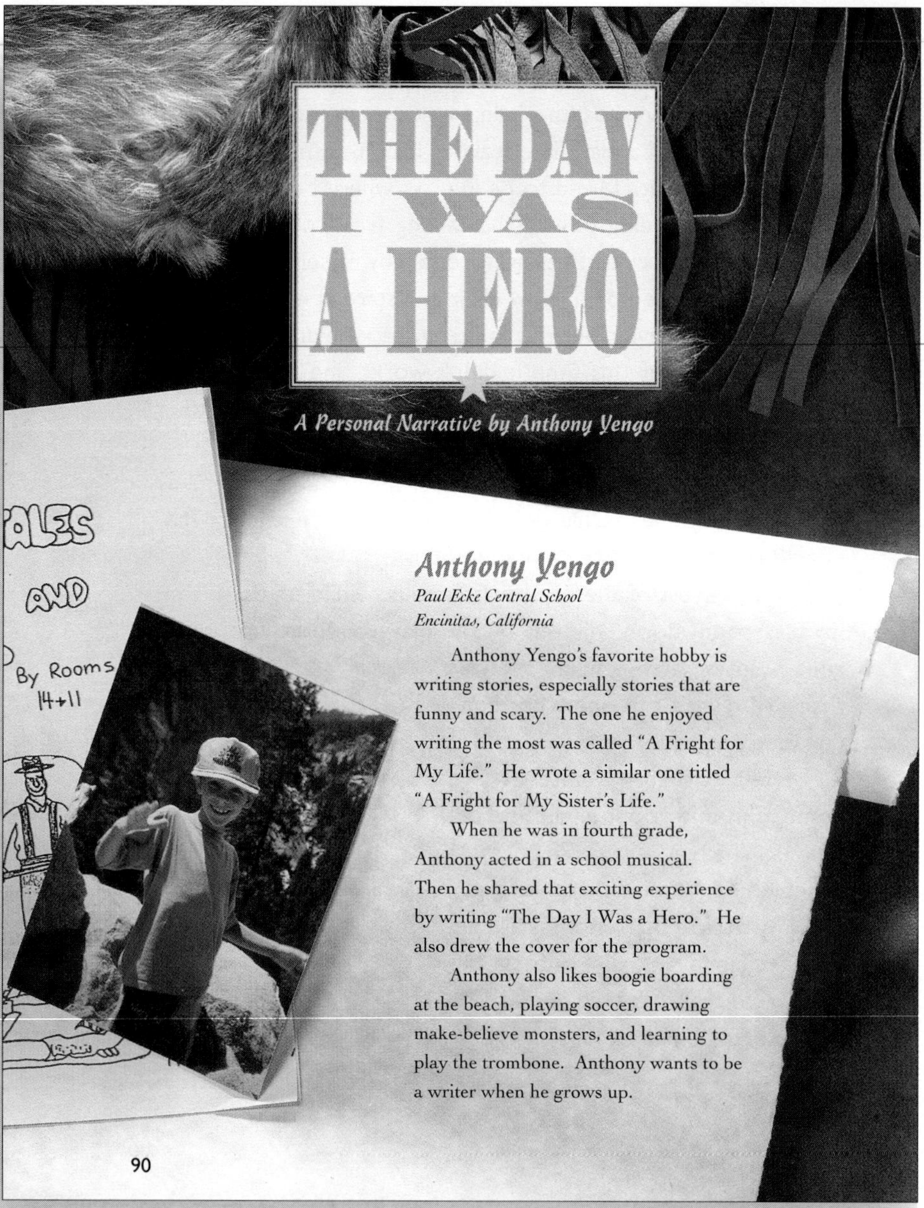

THE DAY I WAS A HERO

A Personal Narrative by Anthony Yengo

Anthony Yengo
Paul Ecke Central School
Encinitas, California

Anthony Yengo's favorite hobby is writing stories, especially stories that are funny and scary. The one he enjoyed writing the most was called "A Fright for My Life." He wrote a similar one titled "A Fright for My Sister's Life."

When he was in fourth grade, Anthony acted in a school musical. Then he shared that exciting experience by writing "The Day I Was a Hero." He also drew the cover for the program.

Anthony also likes boogie boarding at the beach, playing soccer, drawing make-believe monsters, and learning to play the trombone. Anthony wants to be a writer when he grows up.

90

SKILL FINDER

PREWRITING/DRAFTING

Workshop Minilessons
- Good Beginnings, p. 91A
- Supplying Details, p. 91B
- Dialogue, p. 91C

Theme Resources
- Sequence, pp. 81A–81B

Writing
- Writing a Sentence, p. 59C
- Varying Sentence Types, p. 67
- Thoughts vs. Dialogue, p. 99

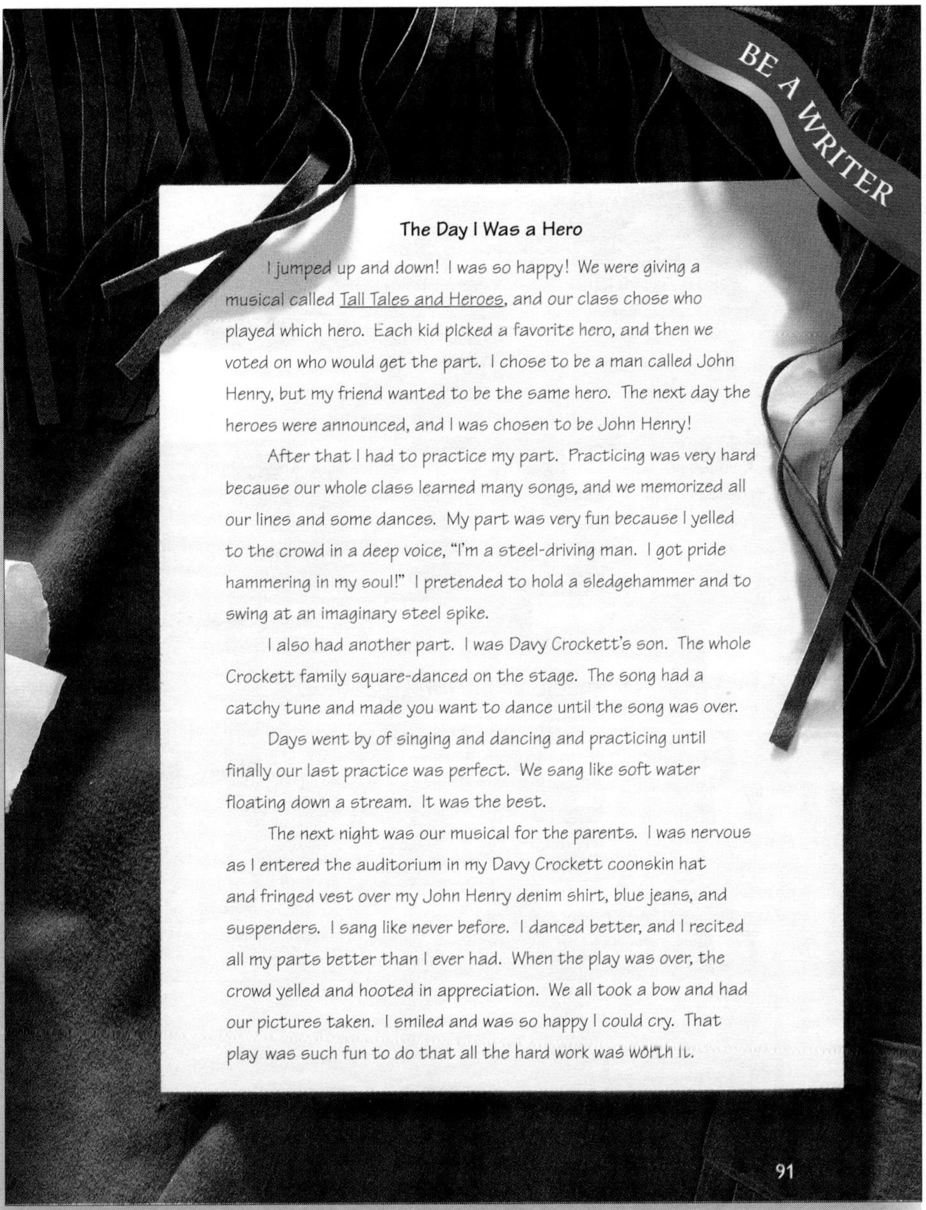

The Day I Was a Hero

I jumped up and down! I was so happy! We were giving a musical called Tall Tales and Heroes, and our class chose who played which hero. Each kid picked a favorite hero, and then we voted on who would get the part. I chose to be a man called John Henry, but my friend wanted to be the same hero. The next day the heroes were announced, and I was chosen to be John Henry!

After that I had to practice my part. Practicing was very hard because our whole class learned many songs, and we memorized all our lines and some dances. My part was very fun because I yelled to the crowd in a deep voice, "I'm a steel-driving man. I got pride hammering in my soul!" I pretended to hold a sledgehammer and to swing at an imaginary steel spike.

I also had another part. I was Davy Crockett's son. The whole Crockett family square-danced on the stage. The song had a catchy tune and made you want to dance until the song was over.

Days went by of singing and dancing and practicing until finally our last practice was perfect. We sang like soft water floating down a stream. It was the best.

The next night was our musical for the parents. I was nervous as I entered the auditorium in my Davy Crockett coonskin hat and fringed vest over my John Henry denim shirt, blue jeans, and suspenders. I sang like never before. I danced better, and I recited all my parts better than I ever had. When the play was over, the crowd yelled and hooted in appreciation. We all took a bow and had our pictures taken. I smiled and was so happy I could cry. That play was such fun to do that all the hard work was worth it.

91

Discussing the Model

Reading and Responding

- What did you like best about Anthony's story?
- Which of Anthony's two parts did he prefer? Explain your answer. (John Henry; he chose it; it was "very fun"; he gives more details about it)
- What was the hardest part of being in the musical for Anthony? (practicing)
- Have you ever performed before a large audience? Tell about it.

Reading As a Writer

- Why did Anthony's first two sentences catch your interest? (wondered why he was so happy)
- Does Anthony tell what happened in order from beginning to end? (yes) What happens first? (choice of parts) last? (performance) What main things happen in between? (choices announced, practices)
- What details bring Anthony's story to life? (Samples: jumped up and down, deep voice, fringed vest)

Characteristics of Personal Narratives

Elicit the following characteristics:

- *Purpose:* to tell about a true personal experience
- A clear beginning, middle, and end
- An interesting beginning
- Uses details that bring the story to life

SKILL FINDER

PROOFREADING

Theme Resources	Theme Resources
Grammar • Subjects and Predicates, pp. 59I–59J • Kinds of Sentences, pp. 81I–81J • Run-on Sentences, pp. 107I–107J	*Spelling* • Short Vowels, p. 59H • Spelling Long *a* and Long *e*, p. 81H • Words Often Misspelled, p. 91E • Spelling Long *i* and Long *o*, p. 107H

Reading-Writing Workshop *(continued)*
A Personal Narrative

MINILESSON

Good Beginnings

Resource: Anthology p. 89

- Read aloud the first sentence of *Childtimes,* and ask students what questions it raises. (Samples: Why was she famous? Why for only a day?)
- Invite students to work in pairs to review classroom resources, including this anthology, for examples of good beginnings. (The search can also include nonfiction materials, including newspaper articles, if available.) Ask each pair to share their two best examples. Discuss different kinds of beginnings with students and the appeal of each.

Ideas for Beginnings
• interesting dialogue
• a description of a person or a place
• an exciting action or occurrence
• an intriguing question

- Ask students whether a story must always start at the beginning of the action. Does *Childtimes?* (No, the writer first says she was famous and then goes back and tells why.)
- Caution students not to begin their narratives too far ahead of the main action. For example, they need not describe getting up in the morning unless it is important to the story.

Warm-up

Shared Writing

As a class, write a narrative about an experience the class has shared, such as a field trip or a humorous occurrence. Elicit the important events and details, including dialogue, that convey the experience and bring it to life. Lead students to generate sentences and paragraphs that tell their story in an interesting way. When finished, discuss strengths and ideas for improvement.

Prewriting

LAB, pp. 29–30

Choose a Personal Narrative Topic

Students brainstorm and list ideas, consider and discuss their ideas, and choose one.

- **Make a List** Have students list three to five personal experiences they would like to write about.
- **Think and Discuss** Have students discuss their topics with a partner and ask themselves these questions about each idea: Do I remember this clearly? Can I make this experience come alive for my readers? Would someone else enjoy reading about this?

Help with Topics

Place Webs

Demonstrate the webbing strategy, encouraging students to make their own webs of ideas for personal narratives: one web for *school* events, one for *home,* and one for their *neighborhood* or another place.

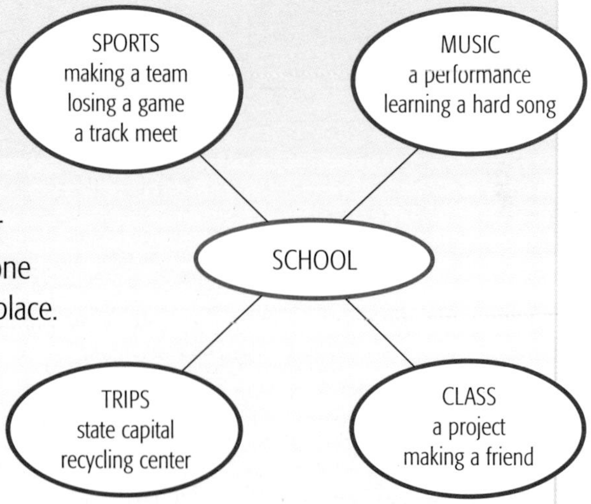

Students Acquiring English
This activity is especially helpful for these students.

MINILESSON

Supplying Details

Resource: Anthology p. 89

- Have students state in two or three sentences what happens in *Childtimes.* (A girl who does not like big parts in plays gets one anyway. She learns her lines, but her voice fails in the performance and she cannot be heard. The students talk about her, and the teacher is upset with her.)
- Ask students how the actual story differs from their summaries. (The story gives details and helps the reader feel what the experience was like.)
- Ask students to find details that the writer uses to help them feel what it was like to be in her position. (Samples: wanting to be one of the talking trees, sliding down in her chair and staring at her desk, children pointing, what the children said)
- Work with students to make a list of the kinds of details that make writing come alive, such as

  how things and people look
  what people say
  feelings
  sounds and smells

Prewriting *(continued)*

Plan the Personal Narrative

Students plan and discuss their personal narratives before they draft.

- **List Details** Have students list the events that make up the beginning, middle, and end, and brainstorm details.
- ***Cooperative Learning:*** **Audience Check** Encourage students to tell their experience to a partner or a small group. Listeners should tell what parts were most interesting and what else they would like to know.

Help with Planning

Personal Video

Have students imagine that their experiences were videotaped. Ask them to run the "video" in their minds. Encourage them to take notes on what they "see."

Interview

Cooperative Learning

Suggest that students interview each other to elicit details about WHO was involved, WHAT was said, and HOW people behaved and felt.

Literacy Activity Book, p. 29

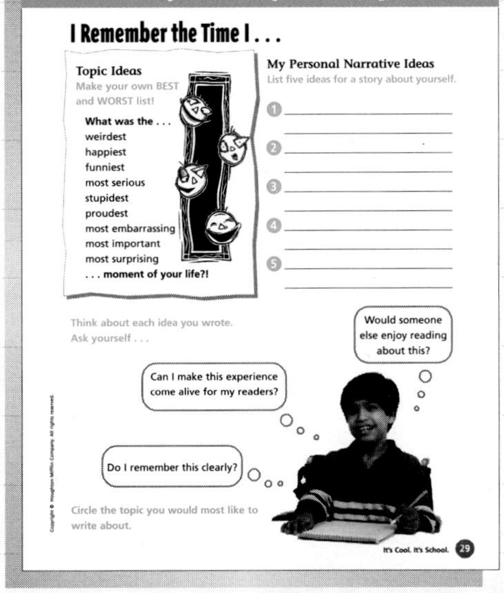

I Remember the Time I . . .

Topic Ideas
Make your own BEST and WORST list!

What was the . . .
weirdest
happiest
funniest
most serious
stupidest
proudest
most embarrassing
most important
most surprising
. . . moment of your life?!

My Personal Narrative Ideas
List five ideas for a story about yourself.

1. ______
2. ______
3. ______
4. ______
5. ______

Think about each idea you wrote.
Ask yourself . . .

Would someone else enjoy reading about this?
Can I make this experience come alive for my readers?
Do I remember this clearly?

Circle the topic you would most like to write about.

It's Cool. It's School. 29

Literacy Activity Book, p. 30

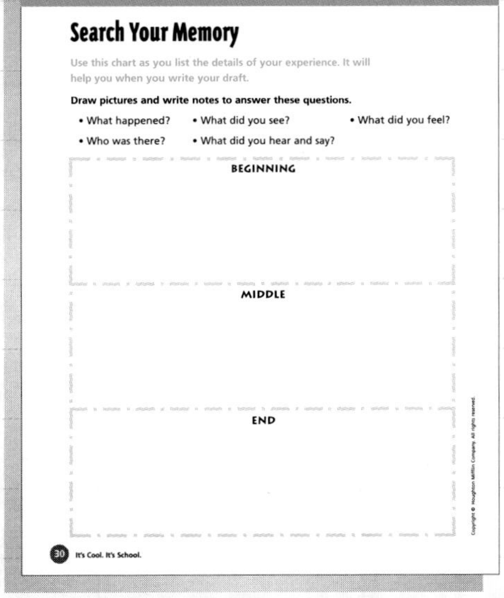

Search Your Memory

Use this chart as you list the details of your experience. It will help you when you write your draft.

Draw pictures and write notes to answer these questions.

- What happened?
- Who was there?
- What did you see?
- What did you hear and say?
- What did you feel?

BEGINNING

MIDDLE

END

30 It's Cool. It's School.

Reading-Writing Workshop *(continued)*
A Personal Narrative

MINILESSON

Dialogue

Resource: Anthology p. 89

- Ask students what quotation marks are usually used for. (to show that someone is speaking) Have them page through the stories in this theme, noting the words in quotation marks. Elicit that dialogue helps make stories real.
- Invite students to read aloud the words in quotation marks in *Childtimes* (paragraph 4). How many different ways can they read them?
- In the second and the last paragraphs, the writer summarizes what her teacher said. Ask students to imagine
  1) the words the teacher might have used
  2) what the writer might have said

  Write their suggestions on the chalkboard. Use quotation marks and start a new paragraph for each speaker.

Self-Assessment

Have students evaluate their stories, using the Revising Checklist.

Drafting

Students write the first drafts of their stories, using any pictures, graphic organizers, or notes that they have prepared.

Help with Drafting

Drafting Strategies

Encourage students to write without stopping to make corrections or to look up spellings. Tell them to skip every other line so that they have room to make changes later on.

Suggest that students set their word processors for double spacing to make revising easier.

Beginnings

Encourage students to write two or three different beginnings and save them for the writing conference. They might start with dialogue, with a description of a place, or with a feeling.

Revising

LAB, p. 31

Students revise their drafts and discuss them in writing conferences.

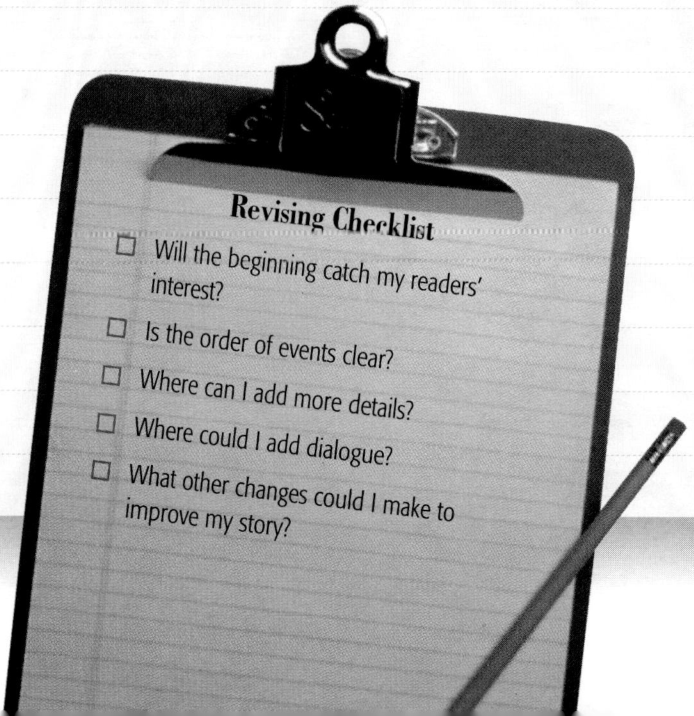

Revising *(continued)*

Writing Conference

Cooperative Learning Encourage students to read their stories aloud to you or to one or more classmates. They can use the Questions for a Writing Conference to guide their discussion. (*Note:* If this is the first writing process activity of the year, you may want to model a conference.)

Questions for a Writing Conference

- What is the best thing about this story?
- Does the beginning make the reader wonder what is going to happen?
- Is the story easy to understand?
- Are there places where more details would make the story clearer or more interesting?
- Where could dialogue be added to tell the story?
- How could the story be improved?

Help with Revising

Revising Strategies

Demonstrate ways for students to mark their drafts to show their changes, such as using carets to insert text, arrows to move text, and crossouts to delete text.

Details and Dialogue

Suggest that students circle two places where they could add details and two places where they could add dialogue.

Conference Strategy

Cooperative Learning

If students wrote more than one beginning, suggest that they first read all three beginnings to their listeners before reading the entire story. The listeners tell which beginning most makes them want to hear the rest of the story.

TECH TIPS

Suggest that students save their original drafts and revise on a copy to avoid deleting text they may want later.

Additional Questions for Writing Conferences

These questions may be useful during teacher-student conferences.

- What happened after. . . ?
- Why did you [or another person in the story] . . . ?
- Is this part really important to the story?
- Where were you at that point?
- What did [a person] say when . . . ?
- What did [a scene, a person] look like? Help me picture it.

Students can use The Learning Company's new elementary writing center to write the first drafts of their stories.

Literacy Activity Book, p. 31

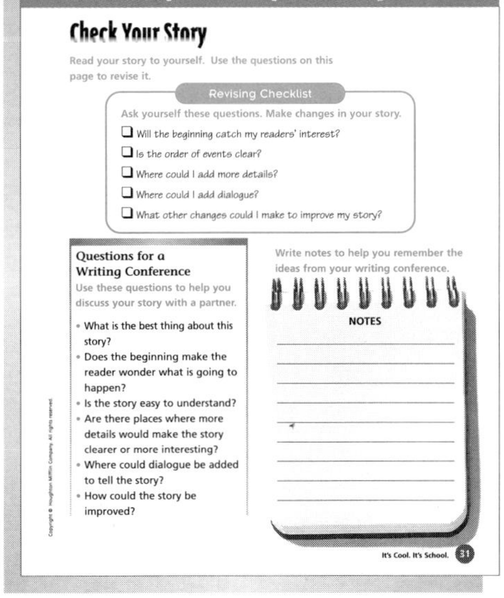
Check Your Story

Read your story to yourself. Use the questions on this page to revise it.

Revising Checklist

Ask yourself these questions. Make changes in your story.

- ❑ Will the beginning catch my readers' interest?
- ❑ Is the order of events clear?
- ❑ Where could I add more details?
- ❑ Where could I add dialogue?
- ❑ What other changes could I make to improve my story?

Questions for a Writing Conference

Use these questions to help you discuss your story with a partner.

- What is the best thing about this story?
- Does the beginning make the reader wonder what is going to happen?
- Is the story easy to understand?
- Are there places where more details would make the story clearer or more interesting?
- Where could dialogue be added to tell the story?
- How could the story be improved?

Write notes to help you remember the ideas from your writing conference.

NOTES

It's Cool. It's School. 31

Reading-Writing Workshop *(continued)*

A Personal Narrative

Students using **The Learning Company's Ultimate Writing & Creativity Center** software can spell check their documents before final printing.

Proofreading

Students proofread their stories, using the Proofreading Checklist and the proofreading marks in the Handbook of the *Literacy Activity Book.* Encourage students to make as many corrections as they can by themselves or by consulting with classmates.

Grammar/ Spelling Connections

- **Checking Sentences** Remind students to check to make sure that every sentence has a subject and a predicate, that they have used correct end marks, and that they have avoided run-on sentences. *pp. 59I–59J, 81I–81J, 107I–107J*
- **Spelling** Remind students to check the spelling of short and long vowel sounds and of Words Often Misspelled. *pp. 59H, 81H, 91E, 107H*

Publishing and Sharing

Students title their stories, make final copies in the format they have chosen, and present the stories to their audience. Remind them to double-check that they included all of their revising and proofreading changes.

Ideas for Publishing and Sharing

A Class Book

Bind stories together into a book and include it in the classroom or school library. Individual students can provide the art for their own stories, or class artists can become the official illustrators. Each student should provide a short self-description for an "About the Authors" page.

To make a class book, cover a piece of cardboard with wallpaper, contact paper, or other sturdy paper. Glue shapes cut out of painted watercolor paper, foil, or other printed papers to create an illustration. Punch covers and pages, and bind with decorative cord.

Taped Readings

Students can perform video- or audiotaped readings of their stories. Remind them to practice reading with expression. The tapes can be shared with any audiences the students choose.

MINILESSON

Spelling

Words Often Misspelled

Write the Spelling Words on the board, say them, and have students repeat them. Work with students to identify the part of each word that is likely to be misspelled.

Spelling Words

cannot	won't	I'll
can't	wouldn't	let's
don't	I'd	we're
haven't		

Challenge Words

minute	instead	divide
stretch	ninety	

Additional Spelling Words

I'm	o'clock	there's
didn't	that's	

SEE 5-Day Planner Spelling Plan p. 81H

Spelling Assessment

Pretest

1. There cannot be too many roles.
2. Both boys can't play John Henry.
3. They don't have long to wait.
4. Why haven't you picked a hero yet?
5. We won't be late to the play.
6. Why wouldn't you vote for this part?
7. I'd rather play Davy Crockett.
8. I'll let you know who acts this role.
9. Next, let's try on our costumes.
10. Now we're taking our bows.

Test Use the Pretest sentences.

Challenge Words

11. The minute seemed to pass quickly.
12. I took a stretch between classes.
13. We'll study now instead of later.
14. A score of ninety is very good.
15. Did you divide the number by two?

Challenge Words Practice Have students write an announcement for a school or classroom event, using the Challenge Words.

Literacy Activity Book

Spelling Practice: pp. 267–268
Take-Home Word Lists: pp. 313–314

More Ideas for Publishing and Sharing

Cards and Letters

Encourage students to share their accounts with the people who were involved in the incidents they describe, if that is appropriate. They might want to enclose the story in a handmade greeting card or write it on hand-decorated paper.

Reflecting/Self-Assessment

Use the Self-Assessment questions, or others of your own, to help students reflect on and evaluate their experiences writing their personal narratives. Students can discuss their thoughts or answer the questions in writing.

Self-Assessment

- What do you like best about your story?
- Do you like your beginning? Why?
- What was most difficult—putting the events in order? filling in the details? writing an interesting beginning?
- Which part shows the best use of details? dialogue?
- What did working on your personal narrative teach you about writing?
- What goals would you like to set for your next piece of writing?

Evaluating Writing

Use the criteria below to evaluate students' personal narratives.

Criteria for Evaluating a Personal Narrative

- The story is about a personal experience and is told in the first person.
- The story has a beginning, a middle, and an end.
- The beginning gets the reader's attention.
- Details, including dialogue when appropriate, are used to help the story come to life.

Portfolio Opportunity

- Save students' final copies to show their understanding of writing a personal narrative.
- Save students' planning aids and drafts to show their use of the writing process.
- Save the tapes from the Taped Readings activity to show students' oral fluency and expression.

Sample Scoring Rubric

1	2	3	4
The paper does not tell about a personal experience; or, if it does, there is no or little narrative structure.	The story is sketchy. There may be gaps in sequence that cause confusion. Details and dialogue are insufficient.	The story has a beginning, middle, and end. Details and dialogue are included but could be enhanced. Significant usage, mechanics, or spelling errors may keep the story from rating a 4.	The story has a strong narrative structure, including a good beginning, with realistic and well-distributed details and dialogue. It has a minimum of usage, mechanics, and spelling errors.

SELECTION: Koya DeLaney and the Good Girl Blues

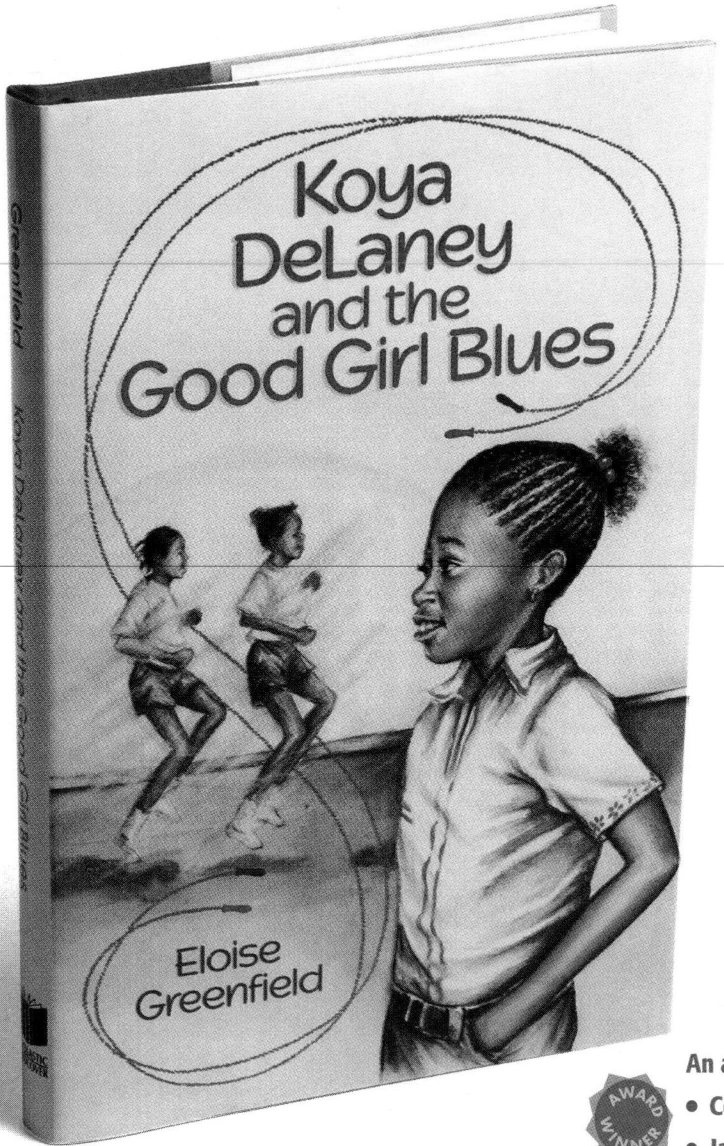

by Eloise Greenfield

Other Books by the Author

Childtimes: A Three-Generation Memoir

Mary McLeod Bethune

Under the Sunday Tree

William and the Good Old Days

An award-winning author

- **Coretta Scott King Award**
- **Jane Addams Children's Book Award**
- **Horn Book Fanfare**
- **Carter G. Woodson Award for Special Education**

Selection Summary

Koya DeLaney and her sister Loritha are best friends with Dawn. Loritha and Dawn are also teammates on the Barnett School double-dutch jump rope team. They've practiced long and hard for the upcoming championship.

Everyone admires Koya and Loritha because their cousin is a famous rock star. Dawn feels jealous and plays a trick on Loritha. She puts a new move in the freestyle routine and doesn't teach it to her friend. Loritha gets dropped from the routine but, for the sake of her team, outdoes herself in her other events. Barnett School comes in second, much to everyone's delight. Loritha and Dawn will patch up their friendship later.

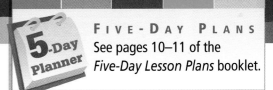

FIVE-DAY PLANS See pages 10–11 of the *Five-Day Lesson Plans* booklet.

Lesson Planning Guide

	Skill/Strategy Instruction	Meeting Individual Needs	Lesson Resources
1 Introduce the Literature *Pacing: 1 day*	**Preparing to Read and Write** Prior Knowledge/Building Background, 91I **Selection Vocabulary,** 91J • routine • competition • poised • rhythm • somersaulted • participants **Spelling Pretest,** 107H • rope • coach • know • side • spoke • high • blow • bright • wipe • goal	**Support in Advance,** 91I **Students Acquiring English,** 91I **Other Choices for Building Background,** 91I **Spelling Challenge Words:** 107H • microphone • surprise • recognize • narrow • approach	***Literacy Activity Book,*** Vocabulary, 32 **Transparencies:** Building Background, 1–13; Vocabulary, 1–14 **Great Start** CD-ROM Software, "It's Cool. It's School." CD
2 Interact with Literature *Pacing: 1–3 days*	**Reading Strategies** Predict/Infer, 94, 96; Self-Question, 94, 102; Think About Words, 100; Summarize, 102 **Minilessons** Making Inferences, 95; Writer's Craft: Thoughts vs. Dialogue, 99; Sequence of Events, 101	**Choices for Reading,** 94 **Guided Reading,** 94, 98, 100, 104 **Students Acquiring English,** 95, 99, 105, 106 **Extra Support,** 97, 104 **Challenge,** 107	**Reading-Writing Workshop:** Personal Narrative, 90–91F ***Literacy Activity Book,*** Selection Connections, 7–8; Comprehension Check, 33 **Audio Tape** for It's Cool. It's School.: *Koya DeLaney and the Good Girl Blues* The Learning Company's Ultimate Writing & Creativity Center software
3 Instruct and Integrate *Pacing: 1–3 days*	✓ **Comprehension:** Making Inferences, 107A **Writing:** Writing Messages, 107C ✓ **Word Skills and Strategies:** Structural Analysis: Compound Words, 107E **Building Vocabulary:** Vocabulary Activities, 107G ✓ **Spelling:** Spelling Long *i* and Long *o*, 107H ✓ **Grammar:** Run-on Sentences, 107I **Communication Activities:** Listening and Speaking, 107K; Viewing, 107L **Cross-Curricular Activities:** Health, 107M–107N; Math, 107N	**Reteaching:** Making Inferences, 107B **Activity Choices:** Role-playing, Character's Thoughts, Instructions, Cheers, 107D **Reteaching:** Structural Analysis: Compound Words, 107F **Activity Choices:** Exact Words for *good,* Words with *micro,* 107G **Challenge Words Practice:** 107H **Reteaching:** Run-on Sentences, 107J **Activity Choices:** Listening and Speaking, 107K; Viewing, 107L **Activity Choices:** Health, 107M–107N; Math, 107N	**Reading-Writing Workshop:** Personal Narrative, 90–91F **Transparencies:** Comprehension, 1–15; Writing Skills, 1–16; Grammar, 1–17 ***Literacy Activity Book,*** Comprehension, 34; Writing, 35; Word Skills, 36; Building Vocabulary, 37; Spelling, 38–39; Grammar, 40–41 **Audio Tape** for It's Cool. It's School.: *Koya DeLaney and the Good Girl Blues* **Spelling Spree** CD-ROM **Channel R.E.A.D.** videodisc: "The Ordinary Princess" The Learning Company's Ultimate Writing & Creativity Center software

✓ ***Indicates Tested Skills.*** *See page 40F for assessment options.*

Introduce *the* Literature

Preparing to Read and Write

Support in Advance

Use these activities for students who need extra support before participating in the whole-class activity.

Perform a Skit Have volunteers perform a skit featuring a character who overcomes disappointment.

Management Tip
During Support in Advance, the rest of the class can read independently.

Students Acquiring English
Make sure that students understand these concepts: gym, bleacher seats, basketball court, scoreboards, buzzers, locker rooms, and offices.

Transparency 1–13

TRANSPARENCY 1–13
TEACHER'S BOOK PAGE 911

IT'S COOL. IT'S SCHOOL.
Koya DeLaney and the Good Girl Blues
BUILDING BACKGROUND

Predicting Reactions

Situation	Ways the Character Might React	How I Would React	How the Character Reacted in the Story
Someone finds out at the last minute that she has been dropped from an event.	1. 2. 3.		
Someone has to cooperate with a good friend who has disappointed her.	1. 2. 3.		
A coach watches her team make a mistake.	1. 2. 3.		

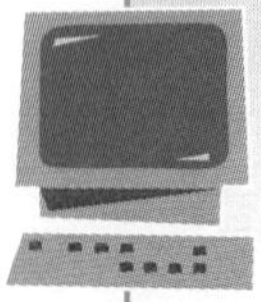

Great Start
For students needing extra support with key concepts and vocabulary, use the "It's Cool. It's School." CD.

INTERACTIVE LEARNING

Prior Knowledge/Building Background

Key Concept
Dealing with disappointment

Predicting Reactions Display Transparency 1–13. Discuss the situations presented, and ask students how they would react in such situations. Then ask how characters in a story might react. Record students' responses in the second and third columns of the chart. (Record what the characters actually did in the story after students have read the selection.)

Predicting Reactions

Situation	Ways the Character Might React	How I Would React	How the Character Reacted in the Story
Someone finds out at the last minute that she has been dropped from an event.	1. Answers will vary but should be supported by students' observations and experience.	Answers will vary but should be supported by students' experience.	Loritha is hurt and resentful but tried to put her feelings aside for the competition.

Other Choices for Building Background

Bilingual Discussion

Students Acquiring English Pair students acquiring English with native English speakers. Ask each pair to share words of consolation they might say in their primary language to someone who has suffered a disappointment.

Play Double-Dutch

Extra Support Ask volunteers to demonstrate how to play double-dutch. They should show how double-dutch is jumping rope with two ropes, and how jumpers can make up routines and do tricks.

Spelling

You may want to give the Spelling Pretest on page 107H before students read the selection.

Daily Language Practice

Use the sentences on page 107J as daily practice of the spelling and grammar skills taught in this theme.

INTERACTIVE LEARNING

Selection Vocabulary

Key Words

competition
participants
poised
rhythm
routine
somersaulted

Discuss the meanings of the key vocabulary words and how they relate to a *competition* such as a jump rope contest. Write *competition* in the first circle of the word web on Transparency 1–14. Then have students practice using the words by completing the word web and by including the words in a brief paragraph describing a sports contest.

Vocabulary Practice Have students work independently or in pairs to complete the activity on page 32 of the *Literacy Activity Book.*

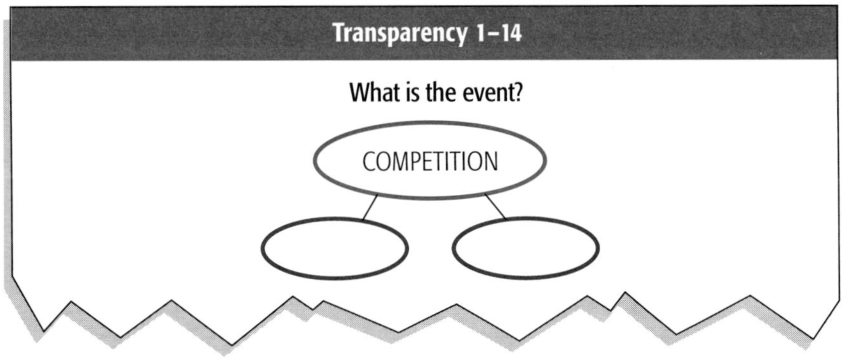

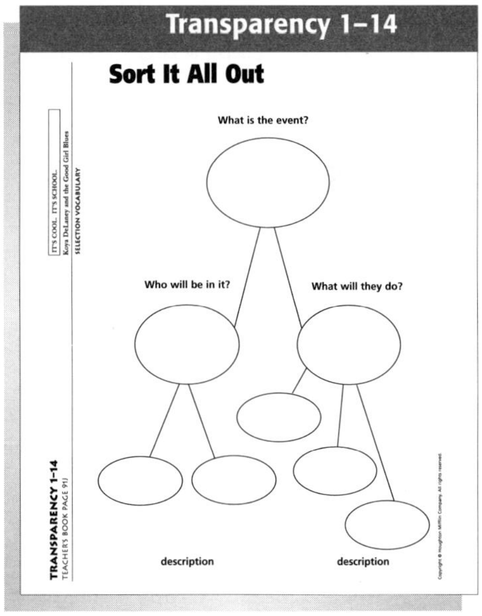

Social Studies

Teacher FactFile

Jumping Rope

- In the 1700s, rope skipping was mainly a game for boys. It was thought to be unladylike for girls and was made difficult by the long skirts that they wore.
- By the 1800s, as skirts became shorter and more girls participated in rope jumping, it became known as a girls' activity.
- Today both girls and boys jump rope. Rope jumping teams even compete internationally. Programs such as Jump Rope for Your Heart, sponsored by the American Heart Association, have helped promote the sport in recent years.

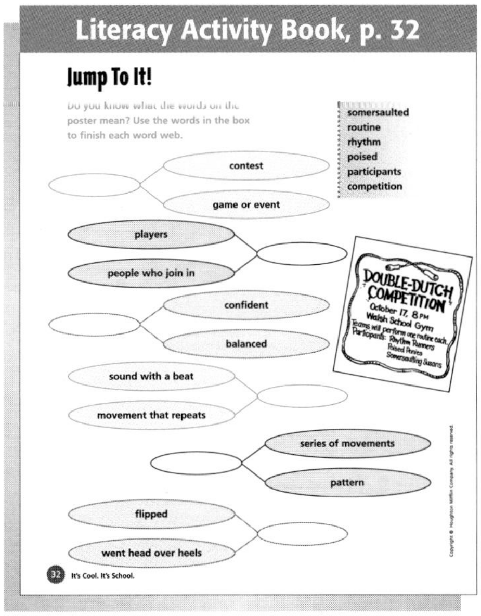

Interact with Literature

More About the Author

Eloise Greenfield

Eloise Greenfield was born in Parmele, North Carolina, in 1929 and grew up in Washington, D.C. In 1963, she joined the Washington, D.C., Black Writer's Workshop and focused on writing children's books "in which black children can see themselves and their lives and history reflected."

Later Greenfield became writer-in-residence for the D.C. Commission on the Arts and Humanities and began her biographies of Rosa Parks, Paul Robeson, and Mary McLeod Bethune. Although she felt that her biographical subjects "were people children needed to meet," Greenfield says she prefers "work that is totally my own creative effort."

Greenfield has won numerous awards, including the Coretta Scott King Award for *Africa Dream*. In addition, the students at P.S. 268 in Brooklyn, New York, have named their school library after Greenfield.

About the Author

Eloise Greenfield

Even though Eloise Greenfield has written over twenty books, she says, "Writing was the farthest thing from my mind when I was growing up. I loved words, but I loved to read them, not to write them."

Greenfield started writing only after her own children were born. When her first humorous rhymes and short stories weren't accepted by publishers, she "gave up writing forever." Her "forever" lasted five or six years, until her poem, "To a Violin," was published in 1963. Since then, writing has become part of her life and of her family's life. In fact, she often asks her children to read and talk to her about her stories.

About the Illustrator

Gil Ashby

Ever since he was in second grade, Gil Ashby has known that he would be an artist. He even attended a special high school, the School of Art and Design, in his hometown of New York City. Ashby says that when he illustrates a story, he does sketches first. Then he does research and takes photographs of real people doing the action of the story. He continues drawing from the photos, and "when that's done I put on music and paint." To do the illustrations on the following pages, Ashby spent a day with a double-dutch team from New York City.

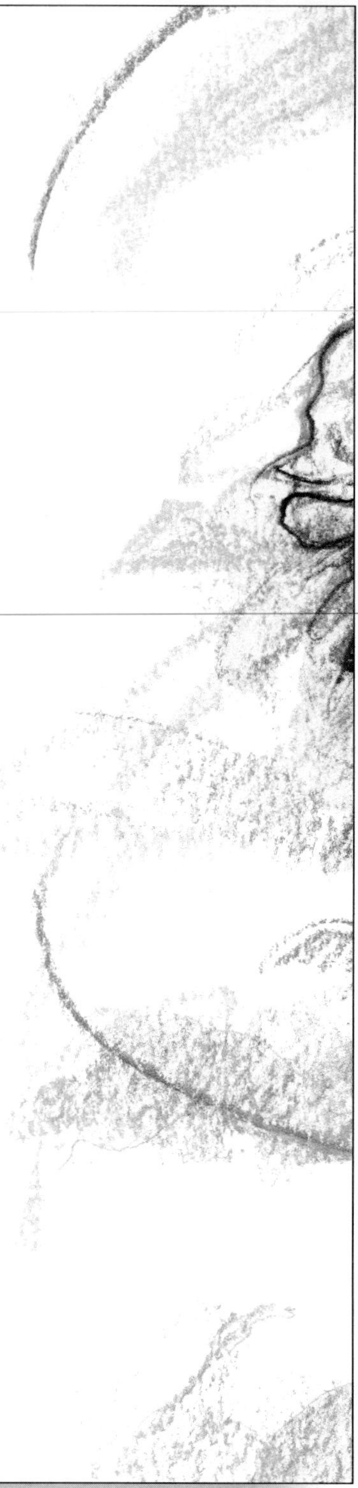

92

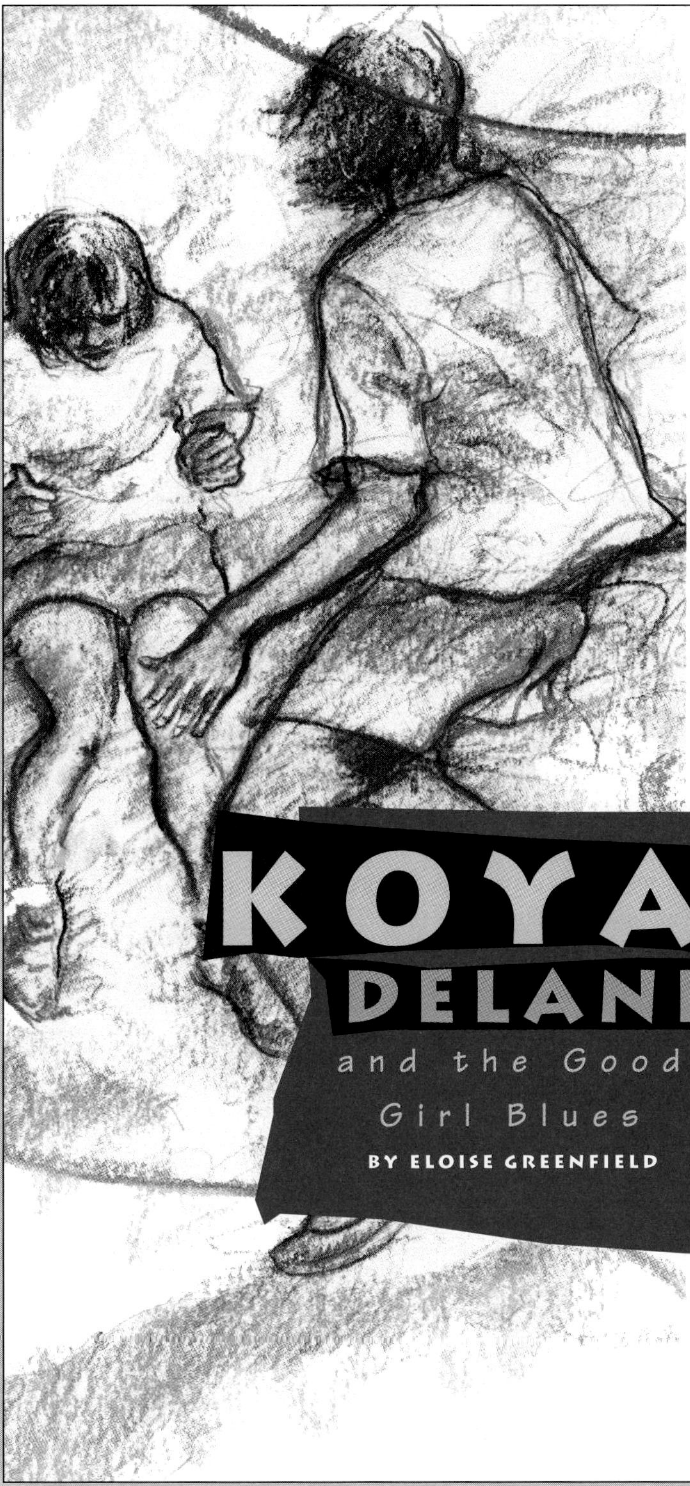

It's the day of the citywide double-dutch championship, and Koya DeLaney can't wait to watch. Koya's sister Loritha and her best friend Dawn are both on the Barnett School team, and they have a good chance to win. Little does Koya know that there's a surprise waiting in the gym.

KOYA DELANEY and the Good Girl Blues

BY ELOISE GREENFIELD

Interact *with* Literature

Reading Strategies

- **Predict/Infer**
- **Self-Question**
- **Summarize**

Student Application Ask students to recall strategies they used as they started reading other selections. (Sample: Read the title. Looked at the pictures. Guessed what the story was about. Asked questions about what might happen.) Then ask what strategies they might use with this selection.

Predicting/Purpose Setting Students might make predictions or ask themselves questions, then read to see whether their predictions were accurate or their questions are answered.

Choices for Reading

Independent Reading	Cooperative Reading
Guided Reading	Teacher Read Aloud

Meeting Individual Needs: Guided Reading

Have students who are using the guided reading option read to the end of page 99 to see if they find answers to their questions.

Koya's father found a parking space a block from the high school, and they all got out of the car and joined the other groups of people of all ages, from babies to grandparents, getting out of cars and buses, in the warm April sunshine, and moving toward the entrance of the school.

Koya loved looking at the double-dutch jumpers, in their many colors, walking throughout the crowd. They were from the six schools that would be competing to be the best in the city.

Inside, the large gym was packed and noisy. Koya had begged Ms. Harris to let her sit with the team, so while her parents headed toward the bleacher seats, she went with Loritha to look for the sign that said BARNETT. They passed the long table filled with trophies, gleaming gold and silver.

Ms. Harris saw them approaching and beckoned to them.

94

QuickREFERENCE

Journal

Encourage students to record their predictions and questions about the selection in their journals.

Background: FYI

The day before the competition, the principal announced that Koya and Loritha's cousin—a famous musician—would visit their school. Their schoolmates gave the sisters so much attention that their best friend, Dawn, felt left out.

"Loritha," she said when they reached her, "we tried to get in touch with you this morning. Dawn called several times, but your line was busy."

Koya didn't like the way Ms. Harris was talking. Her tone was too gentle, as if she were feeling sorry for Loritha. Koya couldn't imagine why.

"What was she calling me for?" Loritha asked.

"Well, she had thought up a new trick for our freestyle routine," Ms. Harris said. "As a matter of fact, she dreamed it. Isn't that something? She called me early this morning to tell me about it. So we all met at school to practice. It's fantastic. I think it could really put us over."

Loritha looked confused. "You all practiced this morning?" she said.

"I'm sorry we couldn't reach you, Loritha," Ms. Harris said.

Loritha's face looked stunned. "I'm not going to be in the freestyle?"

"I'm so sorry, Loritha," Ms. Harris said, "but you want to win, don't you? Wilson's going to be tough to beat, and this trick could do it for us."

Koya looked over at Dawn, sitting with the team. Dawn was watching them, and Koya could almost see the word *guilty* stamped on her face. She knew Dawn hadn't called.

Loritha was trying to hold back her tears. "But I could learn it now," she said. "We could go to another room . . ." She looked at the clock and knew it was too late.

95

MINILESSON

Making Inferences

TESTED SKILL

Teach/Model

Ask students what kind of person Loritha is. During the discussion, note that readers make inferences about characters by combining their own experiences with what is said directly and indirectly in a story. If necessary, model with a Think Aloud.

Think Aloud

As I read, I wonder what Loritha is like. The story says she tries not to cry when she gets bumped from the freestyle competition. This information, along with what I know about how people act, helps me understand Loritha. She feels hurt but is being strong for her team.

Practice/Apply

Draw the following character map on the chalkboard and have students make a copy to fill in. Show them how to use the map by writing "strong" under *Trait* and "held back tears" under *Evidence*.

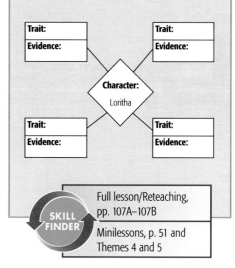

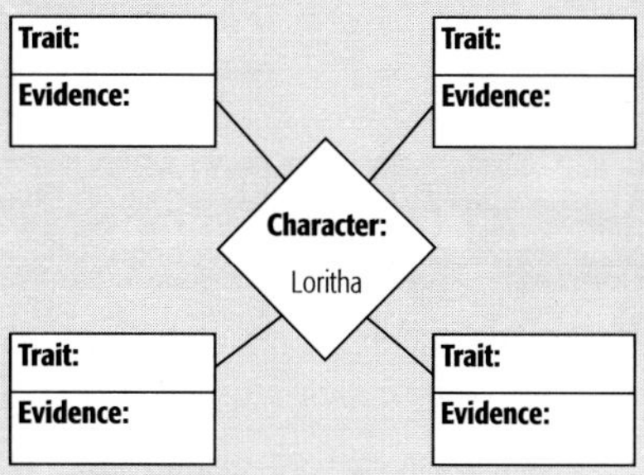

SKILL FINDER

Full lesson/Reteaching, pp. 107A–107B

Minilessons, p. 51 and Themes 4 and 5

Students Acquiring English

MEETING INDIVIDUAL NEEDS

Students acquiring English may not understand the phrase "Koya could almost see the word *guilty* stamped on her face." Ask for volunteers from the class to explain this expression.

Background: FYI

Starting a Team If students are interested in starting a double-dutch team, they can write to the American Double Dutch League; 4220 Eads St., N.E.; Washington, D.C., 20019.

Interact *with* Literature

Reading Strategies

Predict/Infer

The story reveals that trouble is brewing between Dawn and Loritha.

Ask students to explain how they can use this new information to update their predictions about the competition.

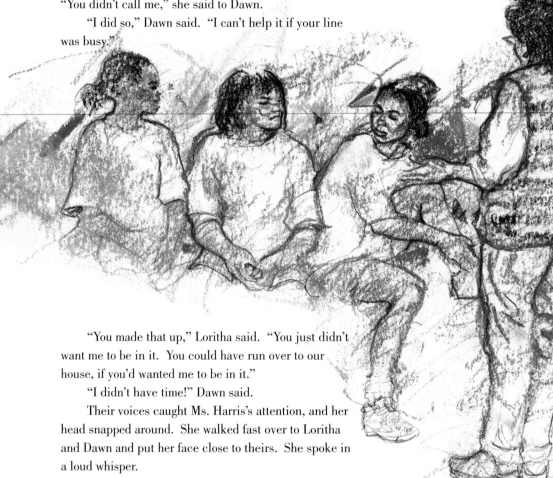

Ms. Harris was tired of being nice. "There's no *time* for that," she said. "You just have to *accept* this. You two take your *seats,* now."

Loritha asked one of the girls to move down one seat, so she could sit next to Dawn, and Koya took an empty seat two places away.

Loritha's disappointment had changed to anger. "You didn't call me," she said to Dawn.

"I did so," Dawn said. "I can't help it if your line was busy."

"You made that up," Loritha said. "You just didn't want me to be in it. You could have run over to our house, if you'd wanted me to be in it."

"I didn't have time!" Dawn said.

Their voices caught Ms. Harris's attention, and her head snapped around. She walked fast over to Loritha and Dawn and put her face close to theirs. She spoke in a loud whisper.

96

Self-Assessment

Encourage students to reflect on their reading using questions such as:

- How well have I understood the story so far?
- What information would help me understand the story better?
- How have I used strategies to help with my reading?

"*We are a team!*" she said. "I don't want you to say *another* word about this, or even *think* about it, until this competition is over. Now *concentrate* on what you came here to do, or you're going to embarrass yourselves, your families, the school, and *me*!"

As she walked away, there was a shrill whistle from the far end of the floor. The competition was about to begin.

"Take your seats, everybody." The announcer was Coach Dickinson, the high school basketball coach.

He held the microphone in his hand and let the whistle dangle from the chain around his neck. The shape of his stomach could be seen pushing against his bright-green T-shirt. "Take your seats, please."

The people in the audience who had been standing around talking walked quickly toward their seats,

Extra Support

Point out the italicized words on pages 96–97, and remind students that the emphasis on these words may indicate a particular tone of voice. Ask volunteers to read aloud the sentences with italicized words using various tones of voice. Which reading do they think the author intended?

QuickREFERENCE

Interact with Literature

Meeting Individual Needs: Guided Reading

Comprehension/Critical Thinking

1. What is happening at the high school? (jump rope competition) Why isn't Loritha participating in the freestyle competition? (She missed the morning practice.) How does she feel about this? (hurt, angry)
2. Do you think Dawn called Loritha? Why or why not? (Answers will vary but may draw from the text or students' own experiences.)
3. How do you think Loritha feels as she competes with Dawn as her partner? (Answers will vary. Students should recognize Loritha's determination to do the best she can even though she's hurt.)

Predicting/Purpose Setting

Have students recall the predictions they made or questions they asked before reading the story. Which predictions were accurate, or which questions have been answered? Encourage students to revise or add to their predictions or questions and then read to the end of page 100 to see what they find out.

holding the hands of their small children to help them up the bleacher steps. When almost everybody was seated, the announcer blew the whistle again, and the room grew quiet.

Koya was sorry now that she had asked to sit with the team. She wanted to be on the other side of the room with the families and her classmates and Dr. Hanley, where she couldn't see that Loritha was hurt and angry and struggling to keep from crying. And where she couldn't see the guilt on Dawn's face.

"Okay, we're ready to start," Coach Dickinson said. "I don't know about you, but I've been really looking forward to this day. Our first citywide competition. Sixth-graders only this year, but if all goes well, next year you won't be able to take two steps without bumping into a bunch of kids jumping double-dutch, everybody from fifth grade through twelfth. Now, I want you to welcome two people who are going to help us make this happen."

He introduced two school board members who stood up to be recognized. Then he introduced the six men and women who were going to judge the competition. Each of the judges went to one of the places on the floor where ropes were laid out. The teams followed. Twenty girls and four boys. Two turners and two jumpers at each place. The turners picked up the ropes. The jumpers stood beside them, ready to jump in. They waited, poised, for the signal that would tell them to begin.

"Take your mark!" the announcer said.

There was a hush in the room.

"Get set!"

Then he blew the whistle, and the jumpers went into the ropes, not jumping fast, but trying to do all the steps they had to do, in rhythm with their partners. Koya kept

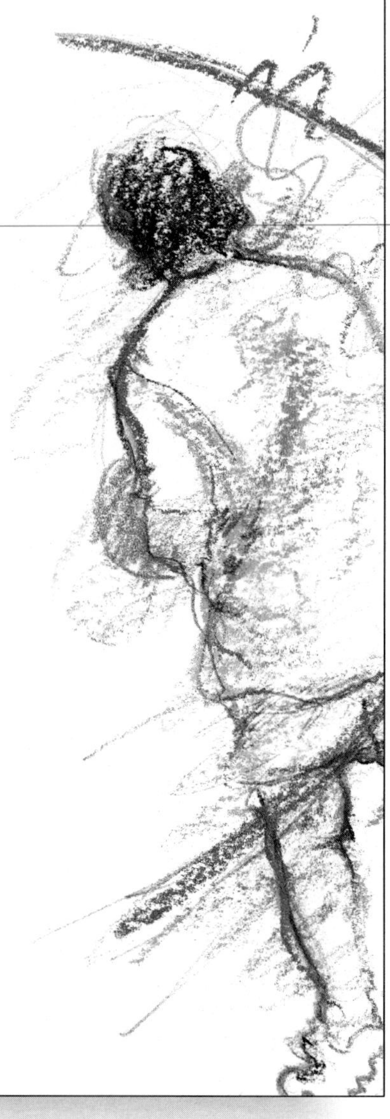

98

Informal Assessment

If students' responses indicate that they are understanding the selection, have them finish reading the selection independently or cooperatively.

Quick REFERENCE

Journal

Encourage students to use their journals to revise their questions and to comment on how their use of reading strategies has helped them predict and understand the selection.

her eyes on Dawn and Loritha. As she watched, her thoughts flowed in a rhythm of their own.

They move together like twins. Like best friends. Jump on the right foot, jump on the left, turn around, jump, jump on the right foot, jump on the left. They move together. Like friends.

MINILESSON

Writer's Craft

Thoughts vs. Dialogue

Teach/Model

Explain that authors often let readers know not only what a character says but also what a character thinks. This helps readers better understand the story. Eloise Greenfield has put what Koya is thinking in italics.

Ask students to list what they know about Loritha and Dawn. Then have them read Koya's thoughts about Loritha and Dawn in the full paragraph on page 99 and use this information to add to their understanding of the characters.

Practice/Apply

Encourage students to examine the use of italics throughout the story. How important to the sense of the story is the revealing of Koya's thoughts?

MEETING INDIVIDUAL NEEDS

Students Acquiring English

The use of italics can be confusing. Have students compare the italics at the top of page 97 to those on page 99. Help students see that sometimes italics show that certain words are spoken with emphasis, while at other times they show what a character is thinking.

SKILL FINDER

Writing Activities: A Character's Thoughts, p. 107D

Reading-Writing Workshop, p. 91A

Background: FYI

Speed Jumping Double-dutch competitions are divided into three sections: required moves, freestyle routine, and speed jumping. The world record for speed jumping is 425 jumps in 2 minutes.

Math Link

Have students describe a way to estimate the number of jumps they could make in 2 minutes if they counted the jumps they made in 10 seconds. Students' calculations should reflect the fact that there are twelve 10-second periods in 2 minutes.

Interact *with* Literature

Guided Reading

Comprehension/Critical Thinking

1. How did Barnett's team do in the first event? (Well) How do you know? (Ms. Harris smiled; the audience applauded.)
2. Do you think the teams are enjoying the competition? (Answers should reflect details from the story and students' experiences.)
3. What kind of friend do you think Koya would be? Why? (Answers should recognize Koya's sensitivity to Loritha's feelings.)

Predicting/Purpose Setting

Ask volunteers to read page 101 aloud. Have students predict how the event will end before reading to the end of the selection.

Reading Strategies

Think About Words

Context will help students figure out the meaning of *stomp* on page 101. You may wish to have a volunteer demonstrate what stomping is.

The judges were watching closely. Everything had to be perfect, or points would be taken off. The ropes couldn't touch. The jumpers had to go in and out of the rope correctly. Their posture had to be right.

The whistle sounded to signal the end of the first event. Ms. Harris was happy, smiling, as the audience applauded and the judges marked their score sheets.

"Freestyle, next!" the announcer said.

One minute of tricks the teams had created themselves. Loritha would have to sit down and let a substitute take her place. She left the floor and walked toward the chairs, smiling a stiff little smile, and Koya knew she was trying not to cry.

She wants to wait. Wait and cry at home. I won't look at her, I won't say anything, or she'll cry, and I'll cry, too.

Loritha took the seat beside Koya, instead of the seat she'd had before, as if she needed to sit close to someone she trusted. Koya leaned closer to her without looking at her.

"Okay, let's go!" Coach Dickinson said. "First team up is Parker!"

The girls from Parker School were nervous. They dropped the rope twice, and one girl slipped and almost fell, and finished jumping with tears rolling down her face.

Some of the other teams made small mistakes. But Wilson didn't make any. It was the team Barnett would have to beat.

Barnett performed last. Dawn and the girl who was taking Loritha's place jumped into the rope and began circling each other, exchanging places, jumping with knees

100

QuickREFERENCE

Physical Education Link

"Follow the Leader" is a rope-jumping game in which one person runs into a swinging rope, does a trick, and runs out of the rope. Everyone else must then do what the leader does. When someone makes a mistake, the next jumper becomes the new leader. Encourage students to play the game during recess this week.

high. Then they circled in the other direction. Hopped five times on one foot, then on the other. Then the turners began to stomp in rhythm with the jumpers, while still turning the rope. Koya had seen all of these tricks before. Now they were about to begin the new one.

Dawn and the other girl somersaulted out of the rope in opposite directions, jumped up and ran back in as the rope turned faster. Koya caught her breath. No other team had done anything as hard and as beautiful.

Thc girls somersaulted again, jumped up, and turned to run back in, but the ropes had touched and become entangled.

Koya heard Loritha gasp, and saw Ms. Harris close her eyes and give a small shake of her head. The turners quickly pulled the ropes apart, and the trick was finished, but the mistake had been made. Points would have to be taken off their score.

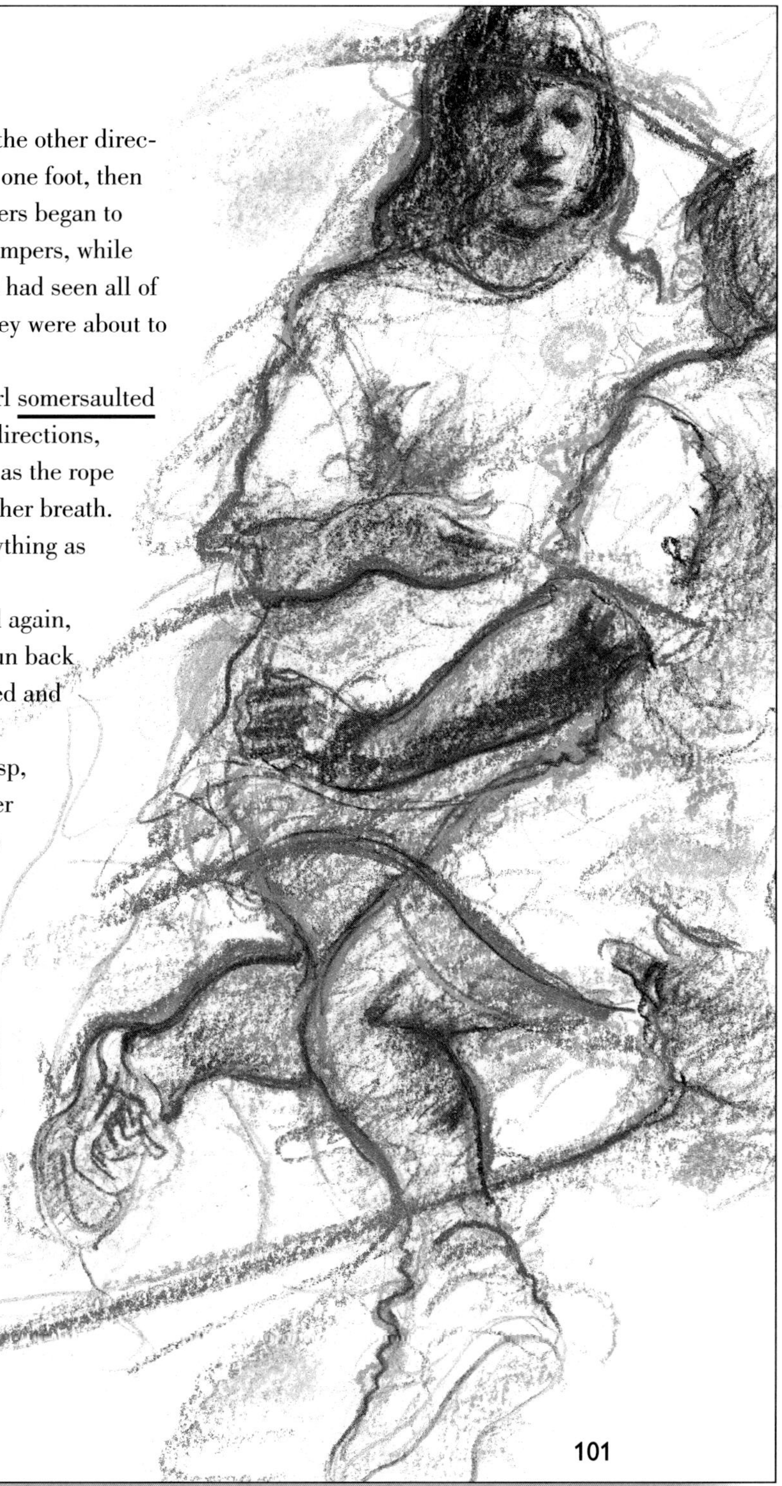

101

MINILESSON

Sequence of Events

REVIEW & MAINTAIN

Teach/Model

Ask volunteers to describe the events that lead up to this point in the story. Draw the following chart on the chalkboard, and use it to demonstrate how to put the events in sequential order. Note that the events don't make sense in the wrong order.

And Then What Happened?
1. The DeLaney family arrived at the school.
2.
3.

Practice/Apply

Have students copy the chart from the chalkboard and add to it as they continue listing the sequence of events. Consulting with a partner will help them decide which events are important enough to add to the list.

SKILL FINDER

Full lesson/Reteaching, pp. 81A–81B

Minilessons, p. 65 and Theme 5

Math Link

Compare the ways that various sports are scored. In this competition, points are subtracted from a perfect score; basketball scores generally increase by multiples of two; figure skating scores use decimals; and gymnastics scores are averaged.

Interact with Literature

Reading Strategies

Summarize

Ask students to tell what led to the tension that Dawn and Loritha feel at the double-dutch competition. Help them understand that this strategy, called summarizing, can help them remember and understand as they read.

Reading Strategies

Self-Question

Ask students to recall the questions they asked about the story before they began to read. Have them use the answers to those questions and information from the story so far to develop new questions about the rest of the story.

The last event was speed jumping. Two minutes of jumping as fast as they could. The judges would be counting the number of times the left foot hit the floor. This was Loritha's event. She would be jumping by herself.

The announcer gave the signal, and there was an explosion of movement and sound. Six ropes were whirring. Legs and sneakers flying. People in the audience cheering for their team. "Come on, you can do it! You can do it!"

Loritha jumped, left, right, left, right, left, right, speeding. She leaned forward at the waist, not moving her arms, almost not moving the top part of her body at all, as if her flying legs belonged to another person.

My sister is brave. Nobody knows she's really, really sad. Nobody but me.

"Go, Ritha!" Koya yelled.

The two minutes seemed more like two hours to Koya. She wondered if the whistle would *ever* blow. Loritha's eyes were narrowed, staring at a spot just above the floor. She was breathing through her open mouth, but once, for a moment, she pressed her lips together so tightly that deep lines dented her chin. The lost points had to be made up. Her legs kept churning.

102

Informal Assessment

Oral Reading Have one or two students read aloud pages 102–103 as a check of oral reading fluency. See the Oral Reading Checklist in the *Teacher's Assessment Handbook*.

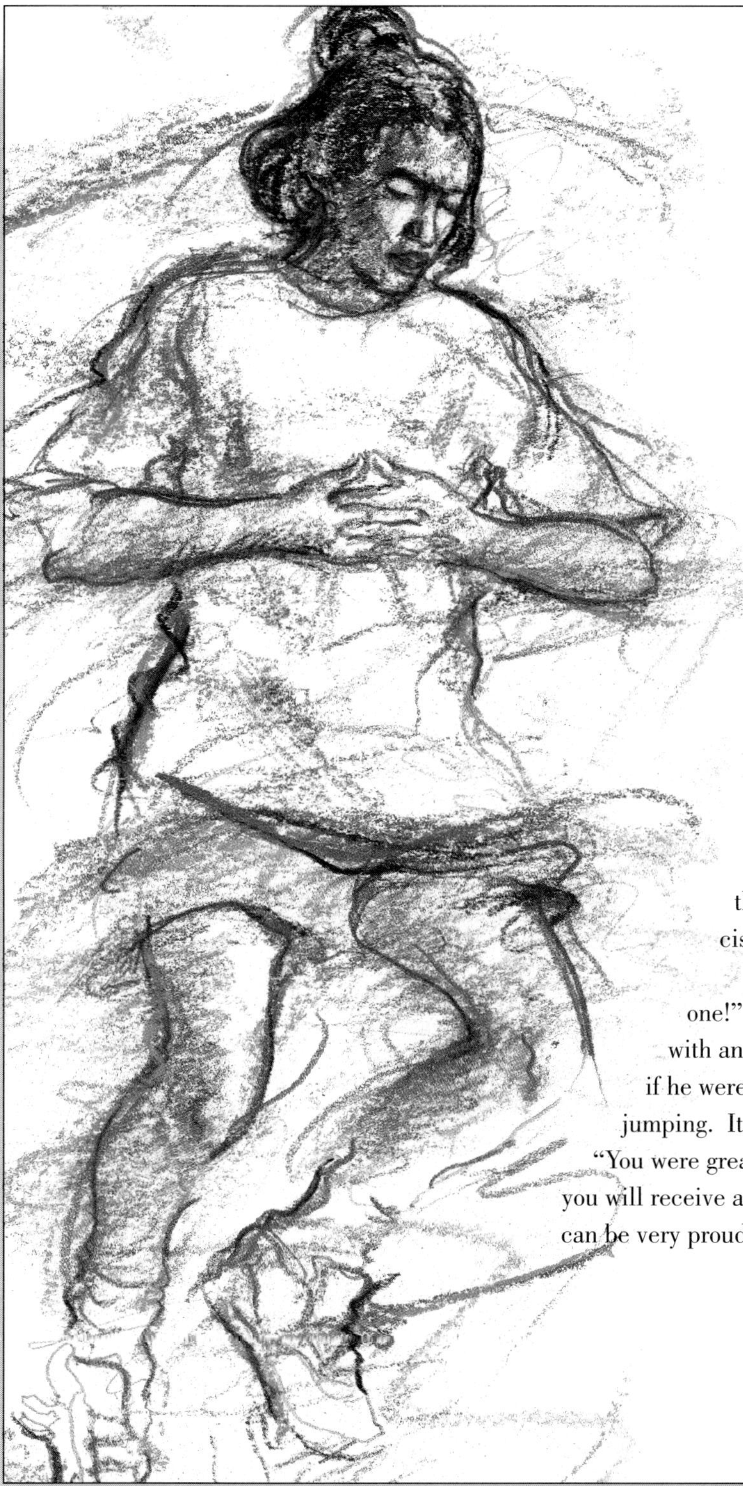

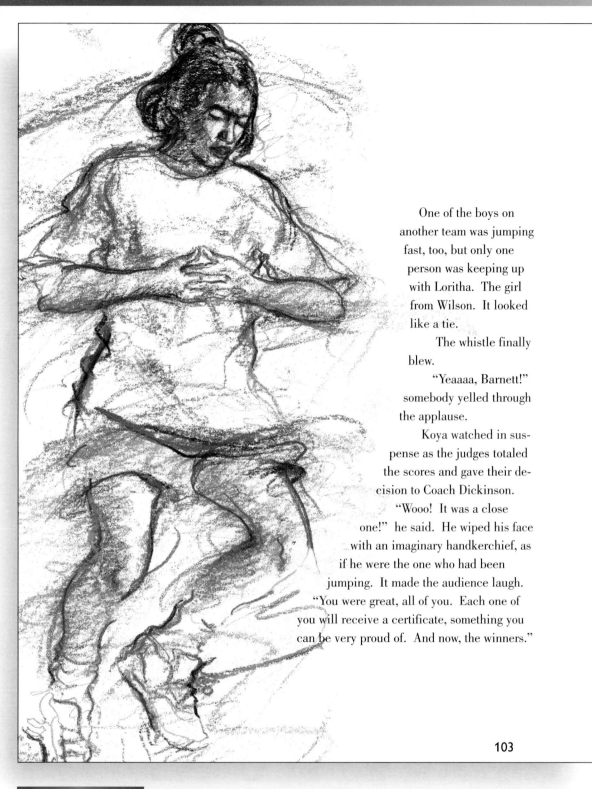

One of the boys on another team was jumping fast, too, but only one person was keeping up with Loritha. The girl from Wilson. It looked like a tie.

The whistle finally blew.

"Yeaaaa, Barnett!" somebody yelled through the applause.

Koya watched in suspense as the judges totaled the scores and gave their decision to Coach Dickinson.

"Wooo! It was a close one!" he said. He wiped his face with an imaginary handkerchief, as if he were the one who had been jumping. It made the audience laugh. "You were great, all of you. Each one of you will receive a certificate, something you can be very proud of. And now, the winners."

103

QuickREFERENCE

Multicultural Link

Invite a guest speaker from a local Youth Soccer League, Little League, or 4-H Club to come to class and discuss the various competitive events of their organization. Students who have lived in other places might wish to share their experiences of competition.

Interact with Literature

Guided Reading

Comprehension/Critical Thinking

1. Which school won the competition? (Wilson) Why do you think Barnett placed second? (The team made mistakes in the freestyle event.)
2. Do you think Ms. Harris is a good coach? (Answers will vary. Students should support their judgments with details from the story.)
3. What did you learn about teamwork from reading this story? (Answers will vary. Students should recognize that respect and cooperation, combined with individual effort, are necessary for a team to succeed.)

He read from the card the judges had given him. "First place, Wilson! Second place, Barnett! Third place, Merritt!" He clapped loudly. "Let's hear it for Wilson! Barnett! Merritt! And all the participants!"

The teams went to the front to receive their trophies and certificates. When it was over, relatives and friends came down out of the stands, and there was hugging and kissing, hand slapping and screaming. Koya ran over to where Loritha was standing with the team and hugged her tightly. Mr. and Ms. DeLaney rushed over, too.

"Girl, you were really something!" Ms. DeLaney said.

Koya looked around and was surprised to see Ms. Harris trying to comfort the girl who had made the ropes tangle. Koya wanted to go over and say something nice, but then she saw Dawn across the room. Dawn saw her at the same time, and came running toward her, laughing, reaching out to hug her.

Koya didn't know what to do. She didn't feel like hugging someone who had been so mean to her sister. But stepping back now, with Dawn's arms so close, would be like slapping the smile off her best friend's face. She couldn't bring herself to do it. She put one arm loosely around Dawn's shoulder.

And that's when she saw Loritha's eyes, looking at her from a few feet away.

Self-Assessment

Ask students to assess their reading using questions such as:

- How well did reading strategies help me understand the story?
- What strategies would have been more helpful?
- How hard or easy was this story to read?

QuickREFERENCE

Extra Support

Rereading If necessary, encourage students to ask questions during a rereading of the story to develop their comprehension.

Should Koya have hugged Dawn? What is Loritha thinking? How should Koya treat Dawn and Loritha now? More than anything, Koya wants the three of them — herself, Loritha, and Dawn — to be friends just the way they have always been. She struggles to make that happen in the rest of *Koya DeLaney and the Good Girl Blues.*

105

Home Connection

Urge students to finish the book as a shared family reading activity. Parents can also help their children find jump-rope books at their local library, such as *Red Hot Peppers* by Bob and Diane Boardman.

Meeting Individual Needs: Students Acquiring English

To ensure that students acquiring English understand the selection, suggest that they choose one of the three main characters and create a series of drawings that show the progression of that character's feelings through the story.

Interact *with* Literature

Responding Activities

Personal Response

In their journals students can write or draw their response to the selection.

Anthology Activities

Encourage students to choose an activity from pages 106–107.

Literature Discussion

How might Ms. Harris prepare the team for the next double-dutch competition?

Selection Connections

Have students complete the portion of the chart on *Literacy Activity Book* page 8 relating to *Koya DeLaney and the Good Girl Blues.*

Jump Right In!

Write a Newspaper Story

Sports Page

Here's your chance to be a reporter. Cover the double-dutch competition for the Barnett school newspaper. Write a newspaper story about the contest, including what happens, the way the contestants look, and how they seem to be feeling. Make your readers feel the tension and excitement.

106

Informal Assessment

Students' responses should indicate a general understanding of the selection.

Additional Support:

- Use Guided Reading questions to review and, if necessary, reread.
- Have students create a selection summary.

QuickREFERENCE

Students Acquiring English

MEETING INDIVIDUAL NEEDS

Students acquiring English might benefit from making a web of sports words before creating a news story in the Sports Page activity.

RESPONDING

Write a Diary Entry

Dear Diary

Loritha probably had strong feelings about losing her place in the freestyle event. How do you think she felt about what Dawn did and about what Koya did? What about her own behavior during the competition? Write a diary entry in which Loritha expresses her thoughts and feelings.

Hold a Debate

The Right Stuff

What does it take to be a double-dutch jumper? What athletic talents or skills do you need? Do you think other school sports, such as baseball or basketball, require more or less skill and strength? Decide which sports you think are the most demanding, and jot down examples to support your choice. Then meet with a group to debate your ideas.

Compare Two Teams

All for One and One for All

That sounds like a good motto for a team. Does it describe the way Loritha and her double-dutch team act? How about the way the Flying Train Committee behaves? Compare and contrast the behavior of the double-dutch team to the teamwork in *Tales of a Fourth Grade Nothing.*

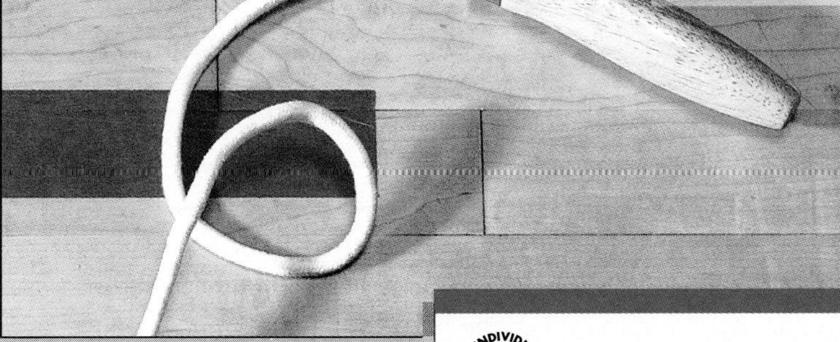

107

Comprehension Check

To check selection comprehension, use these questions and/or *Literacy Activity Book* page 33.

1. What did Koya think as she watched Loritha and Dawn jump together? (She thought they moved in rhythm together like twins or best friends.)
2. How do you think Koya felt about her sister? (Answers should be supported by the text.)
3. Have you ever played a sport or been in a competition? Compare your experiences to Loritha's. (Answers will vary but should focus on the experiences associated with competition.)

Literacy Activity Book, p. 33

You Be the Judge

You're a judge at the double-dutch competition. Answer the reporters' questions.

What is double-dutch?
I noticed Loritha Delaney did not take part. Why not?
Why did Barnett School lose points during the freestyle routine?
Who won?

It's Cool. It's School. 33

Home Connection

Encourage students to ask family members about field-day events they took part in when they were in school.

MEETING INDIVIDUAL NEEDS — Challenge

Interested students can present a play-by-play description of the rope-jumping contest to the class. Listening to sports announcers on television and the radio will give them ideas on presentation.

Portfolio Opportunity

- Comprehension Check: Save *Literacy Activity Book* page 33.
- Writing samples: Save responses to Sports Page and Dear Diary.

Instruct *and* Integrate

Comprehension

Transparency 1–15

Making Inferences

IT'S COOL. IT'S SCHOOL
Koya DeLaney & the Good Girl Blues
COMPREHENSION SKILL

Character Study

Name of Character ______

What we know about the character

A. What the author tells us:

B. What we can infer:

TRANSPARENCY 1–15
TEACHER'S BOOK PAGE 107A

INTERACTIVE LEARNING

TESTED SKILL

Making Inferences

LAB, p. 34

Teach/Model Ask students if authors always give readers a complete picture of their characters. Elicit in discussion that authors sometimes give only clues and that readers fill in the rest of the picture—or make inferences—by combining their own knowledge with those clues. For example, if a story character is a farmer, you might infer that he or she gets up early in the morning. (See minilesson, page 95, for an example from this story.)

Review the selection with students, and record on Transparency 1–15 information that the author gives about Ms. Harris. Then lead students to make inferences about her. Think aloud so that students understand your reasoning.

Character Study

Name of character: Ms. Harris

What we know about the character:

A. What the author tells us:
Ms. Harris lets Koya sit with the team; she sounds "too gentle" when she gives bad news; she sounds impatient when Loritha is disappointed.

B. What we can infer:
Ms. Harris tries to be kind to the girls; she is firm with her team; winning is very important to her.

Have students copy the transparency format and make inferences about Koya and Loritha. Ask them to explain the basis for their inferences using information from the text, their own experiences, and common sense.

Students Acquiring English You may want to pair students acquiring English with proficient English readers for this activity.

Informal Assessment

Students' responses during discussion and on *Literacy Activity Book* page 34 should reflect that they are making inferences based on evidence from the story.

Additional Support:

Reteaching, p. 107B
Minilessons, pp. 51, 95, and Themes 4, 5

SKILL FINDER
Minilessons, pp. 51, 95, and Themes 4, 5

INTERACTIVE LEARNING *(continued)*

Practice/Apply

- Have students use *Literacy Activity Book* page 34 to practice making inferences about story characters.
- Provide students with magazine advertisements, brief newspaper articles, or comic strips from which they can make inferences about people or characters. What can they tell about the person or character even though the writer doesn't say it?

Students can use the **Channel R.E.A.D.** videodisc "The Ordinary Princess" for additional support with Making Inferences.

Literacy Activity Book, p. 34

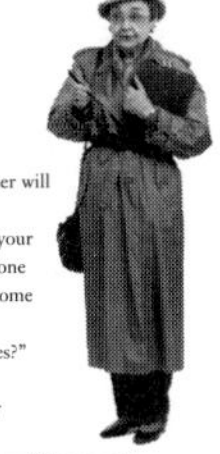

Where Are They Going?

Read the story. Then take a closer look at Ms. Robbins's class by filling in the chart.

"Okay, I want all of you to line up next to the wall with your partners," said Ms. Robbins. "Remember that you and your partner will stay together all day." Ms. Robbins put on her coat and hat.

"Now, I want you all to check that you have your bus money, your lunch, some paper, and crayons," Ms. Robbins added. "Did everyone remember to read the handout about paintings? We'll be seeing some beautiful paintings today."

"What about the mummies? Aren't there going to be mummies?" asked Koya.

"Yes, there will be mummies, too, and statues, and many other interesting works of art," Ms. Robbins replied calmly.

Koya was looking through her backpack. "I can't find my crayons." She started to search for another box, opening drawers and looking on the cubby shelves.

"You can share mine," said Koya's friend Aletha. They were going to be partners.

"That's a great idea. Thanks, Aletha," said Koya, looking relieved.

WHERE do you think the class is going?	WHY did Koya look relieved when Aletha offered to share her crayons?	HOW would you describe Aletha?	WHAT kinds of things will the students do today?

34 It's Cool. It's School.

Reteaching

Making Inferences

MEETING INDIVIDUAL NEEDS

Display the following chart for students. Ask them what information in the story tells how Dawn feels about her friendship with Loritha, and fill in the first space in the chart. Then ask students what feelings they have had in similar situations, and fill in the second space. Ask students to review spaces 1 and 2 and to make conclusions about Dawn's feelings. Explain to them that these conclusions are called *inferences*. Write students' inferences in the third space.

Have students work cooperatively to complete the chart. Ask them to come to agreement before they fill in each space. When they have finished, discuss the inferences they made about Dawn.

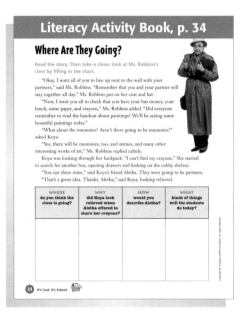

	Evidence from the story	Own Experiences	Inference
• How does Dawn feel about her friendship with Loritha?	Dawn doesn't call Loritha about the change in the routine.	Answers will vary.	Dawn doesn't seem to value her friendship with Loritha very much.
• How does Dawn feel before the competition?	Koya sees that Dawn has a guilty look on her face.	Answers will vary.	Dawn realizes that she has not acted like a friend.
• How does Dawn feel after the competition?	Dawn, laughing, runs to Koya and tries to hug her.	Answers will vary.	Dawn wants Koya to forgive her.

You may wish to have students use a similar chart to make inferences about other major characters in the story. Suggest that they also use this technique to make inferences as they read independently.

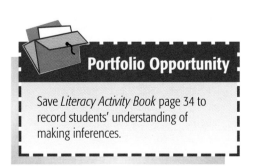

Portfolio Opportunity

Save *Literacy Activity Book* page 34 to record students' understanding of making inferences.

Instruct *and* Integrate

Writing Skills and Activities

Transparency 1–16

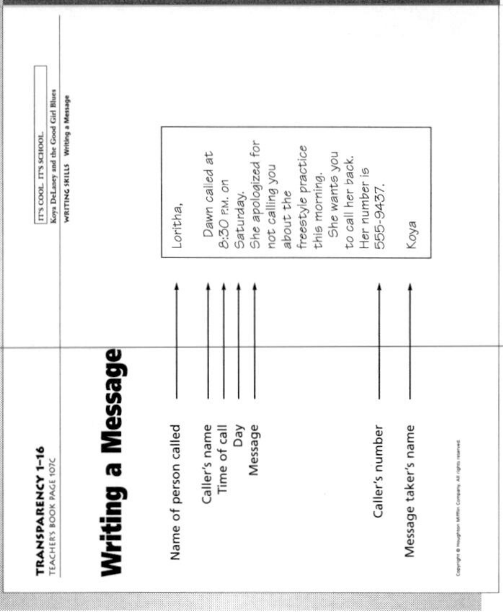
TRANSPARENCY 1-16
TEACHER'S BOOK PAGE 107C
Writing a Message
Name of person called
Caller's name
Time of call
Day
Message
Caller's number
Message taker's name
Loritha,
Dawn called at 8:30 P.M. on Saturday.
She apologized for not calling you about the freestyle practice this morning.
She wants you to call her back.
Her number is 555-9437.
Koya

Literacy Activity Book, p. 35

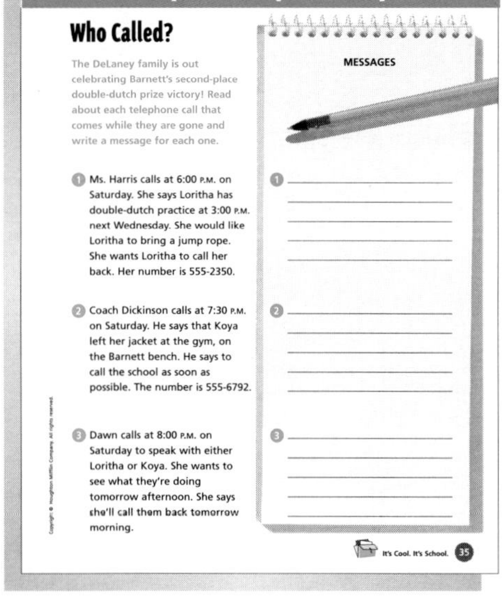
Who Called?

The DeLaney family is out celebrating Barnett's second-place double-dutch prize victory! Read about each telephone call that comes while they are gone and write a message for each one.

MESSAGES

1. Ms. Harris calls at 6:00 P.M. on Saturday. She says Loritha has double-dutch practice at 3:00 P.M. next Wednesday. She would like Loritha to bring a jump rope. She wants Loritha to call her back. Her number is 555-2350.
2. Coach Dickinson calls at 7:30 P.M. on Saturday. He says that Koya left her jacket at the gym, on the Barnett bench. He says to call the school as soon as possible. The number is 555-6792.
3. Dawn calls at 8:00 P.M. on Saturday to speak with either Loritha or Koya. She wants to see what they're doing tomorrow afternoon. She says she'll call them back tomorrow morning.

It's Cool. It's School. 35

Informal Assessment

Have pairs of students check each other's messages to make sure they are complete and accurate.

INTERACTIVE LEARNING

Writing Messages

LAB, p. 35

Teach/Model

Tell students that speaking on the telephone is a very important way of communicating with other people. Point out that taking messages is an especially big responsibility. Ask students what information they should include when they write a message. Write any suggestions on the board.

Display Transparency 1–16. Have students check their list of suggestions against the message on the transparency. Did they include the following items?

- the name of the person who was called
- the caller's name
- the time and day or date of the call
- the message: what the caller wants the person to know or to do
- the caller's number
- the name of the person taking the message

Remind students that it is important to write information correctly and completely in their messages. Encourage them to ask callers to repeat messages, spell names, or speak more slowly, if necessary. Suggest that they take notes while on the telephone and write out a complete message as soon as they hang up.

Remind students never to tell callers that they are home alone. Discuss with students how to take messages in that situation.

Practice/Apply

Assign the activity Take a Message.

Can you have
her call me?
I'll be home
until 3:00.

Writing Activities

Take a Message

Cooperative Learning

Have students role-play telephone calls, in which one student makes the call and the other writes a message. Have students prepare for the role-play by writing down the name of the person they want to call and what they want to tell that person. Encourage students to be imaginative. Then have students work in pairs to take turns being caller and message taker. Have volunteers role-play for the class and discuss the resulting messages.

Call him before 3:00.

Reveal a Character's Thoughts

Have students flip through *Koya DeLaney and the Good Girl Blues* to find the parts in italics. Remind them that these parts reveal Koya's thoughts. Invite students to write their own stories in which they include the main character's thoughts. Ask them to underline the thoughts or write them in a different color to set them off from the rest of the story. *(See Writer's Craft Minilesson , page 99.)*

Give Instructions

Have students work in pairs or small groups to plan a new trick for a double-dutch team to perform. If students are unfamiliar with double-dutch, have them choose a sport or activity they know more about, such as gymnastics, rollerblading, or dance. Once they have planned their trick, have them write step-by-step instructions, telling how to do the trick. Have volunteers demonstrate their tricks for the class.

Students can use The Learning Company's new elementary writing center for all their writing activities.

Write a School Cheer

Cooperative Learning

Have students work in small groups to write a school cheer for an athletic event or other school activity. Have them perform their cheers for the class.

Portfolio Opportunity

Save responses to activities on this page for writing samples.

Instruct *and* Integrate

Word Skills and Strategies

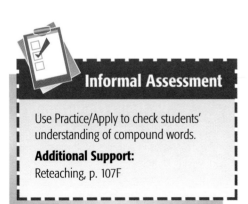

Literacy Activity Book, p. 36

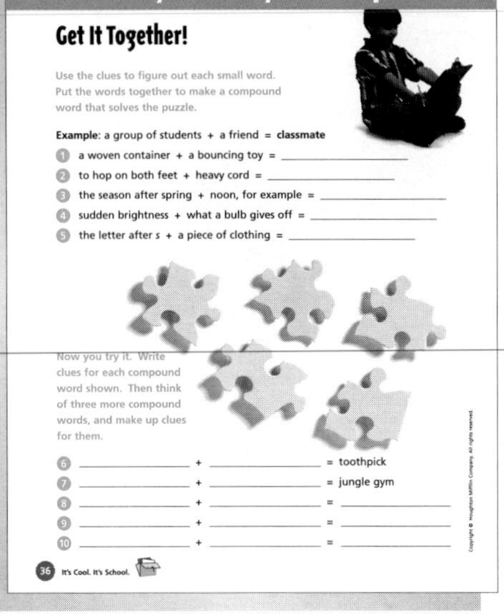

Get It Together!

Use the clues to figure out each small word. Put the words together to make a compound word that solves the puzzle.

Example: a group of students + a friend = **classmate**

1. a woven container + a bouncing toy = ____
2. to hop on both feet + heavy cord = ____
3. the season after spring + noon, for example = ____
4. sudden brightness + what a bulb gives off = ____
5. the letter after *s* + a piece of clothing = ____

Now you try it. Write clues for each compound word shown. Then think of three more compound words, and make up clues for them.

6. ____ + ____ = toothpick
7. ____ + ____ = jungle gym
8. ____ + ____ = ____
9. ____ + ____ = ____
10. ____ + ____ = ____

36 It's Cool. It's School.

Copyright © Houghton Mifflin Company. All rights reserved.

INTERACTIVE LEARNING

TESTED SKILL

Structural Analysis

Compound Words

LAB, p. 36

Teach/Model

Write these words from *Koya DeLaney and the Good Girl Blues* on the board.

high school	grandparents
sunshine	double-dutch

Tell students that these are all compound words, and ask them to define *compound word* based on these examples. Explain that a compound word contains two or more words. Point out that the words can be separated by a space, joined with a hyphen, or run together with no space. Ask students to identify an example of each kind of compound word on the board.

Tell students that knowing the smaller words can help them figure out unfamiliar compound words they come upon in their reading.

Practice/Apply

Have students search for compound words in *Koya DeLaney and the Good Girl Blues*. Have them record their words in a chart on the board.

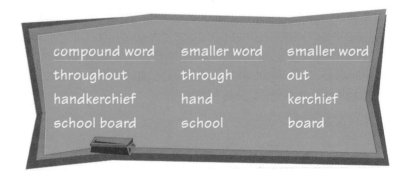

compound word	smaller word	smaller word
throughout	through	out
handkerchief	hand	kerchief
school board	school	board

Informal Assessment

Use Practice/Apply to check students' understanding of compound words.

Additional Support:

Reteaching, p. 107F

SKILL FINDER

Building Vocabulary, Theme 2
Spelling, Theme 4

Reteaching Compound Words

MEETING INDIVIDUAL NEEDS

Say each sentence and write the compound word on the board.

My sister is in high school.
Students do schoolwork.
They ride the school bus.

Ask students what two words make up each compound word. (*high + school, school + work, school + bus*) Discuss the meaning of each one. ("a school for students in the higher grades," "work that is done in school," "a bus that takes students to and from school")

Write these compound words on the board and have students use the objects to demonstrate how the two smaller words affect the meaning of the compound.

MINILESSON

Decoding Longer Words

Teach/Model Tell students that words that seem unfamiliar when they come across them in their reading might actually be familiar when spoken. Explain that one way to figure out how to pronounce new words is to look for phonics patterns that you know from other words. Write the word *somersaulted* on the board and use the example shown to model this process for students.

The first part of this word looks like the word *some*.

somersaulted

This part of the word reminds me of *fault*, and *ed* is an ending that I know., So if I put the parts together, I get some-er-sault-ed--somersaulted!

Practice/Apply Write the following words from *Koya DeLaney and the Good Girl Blues* on the board. For each word, have students note familiar parts, compare and discuss possible pronunciations, and then pronounce the word.

announcer imaginary certificate substitute recognized

Portfolio Opportunity

Save *Literacy Activity Book* page 36 to record students' understanding of compound words.

Instruct *and* Integrate

Building Vocabulary

Literacy Activity Book, p. 37

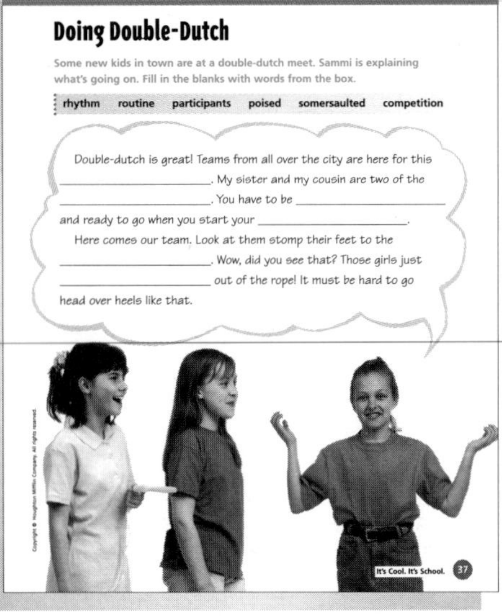

Doing Double-Dutch

Some new kids in town are at a double-dutch meet. Sammi is explaining what's going on. Fill in the blanks with words from the box.

rhythm routine participants poised somersaulted competition

Double-dutch is great! Teams from all over the city are here for this ____________. My sister and my cousin are two of the ____________. You have to be ____________ and ready to go when you start your ____________.

Here comes our team. Look at them stomp their feet to the ____________. Wow, did you see that? Those girls just ____________ out of the rope! It must be hard to go head over heels like that.

It's Cool. It's School. 37

Use this page to review Selection Vocabulary.

Vocabulary Activities

Exact Words for *good*

Cooperative Learning

Write the title *Koya DeLaney and the Good Girl Blues* on the board and circle the word *good.* Discuss with students what they think *good* means in the title. Point out that *good* has many meanings. Divide the class into five groups and give each group one of the sentences below. Have students brainstorm exact words that they could use in place of *good* in their sentence. Encourage them to think of as many as they can. Have each group share its words by adding them to a chart or word wall.

The movie was good.

We ate a good lunch.

Basketball is a good game.

The children were good.

You did a good job.

Words with *micro*

MEETING INDIVIDUAL NEEDS **Challenge** Remind students that Coach Dickinson used a microphone to announce the double-dutch competition. Write *microphone* on the board, explaining that it is made of two word parts from Greek: *micro,* which means "small," and *phone,* which means "sound." Ask students what a microphone has to do with a small sound. (It makes a small sound bigger.) Write the following words on the board and have students tell how each word is related to smallness: *microbus, microorganism, microfilm, microscope.*

Have interested students use a dictionary to look up other words with *micro* and create an illustrated microdictionary.

Selection Vocabulary Extension

Display *Literacy Activity Book* page 32, used to introduce the Selection Vocabulary (see page 91J). Review the Selection Vocabulary and encourage students to add words to the web. Use prompts such as the following to elicit words:

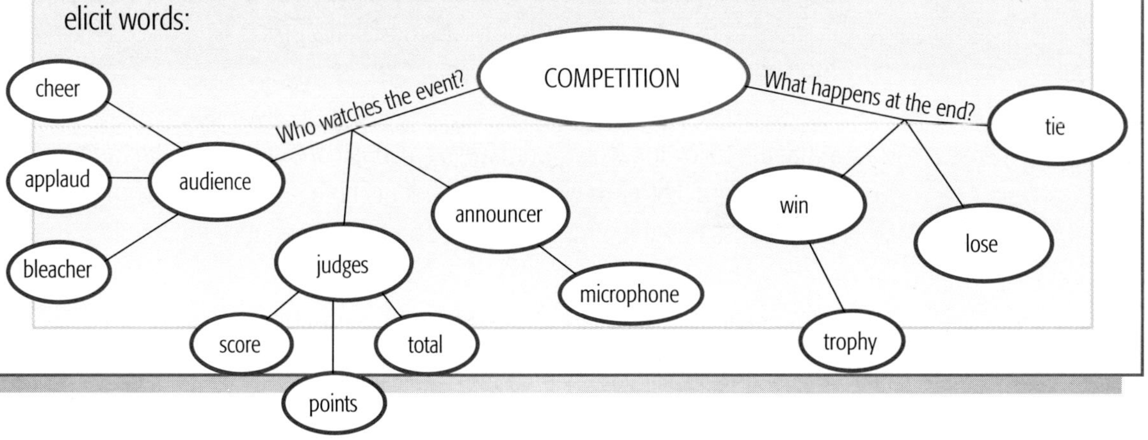

Spelling

FIVE-DAY PLAN

DAY 1	DAY 2	DAY 3	DAY 4	DAY 5
Pretest; Minilesson; Challenge Words/ Additional Words (opt.); Take-Home Word Lists (LAB)	First LAB page; Challenge Words Practice (opt.)	Check first LAB page; Second LAB page (except writing application)	Check second LAB page; writing application (LAB)	Test

Teaching CHOICES

MINILESSON

Spelling Words
*rope
*coach
*know
*side
*spoke
*high
*blow
*bright
*wipe
goal

Challenge Words
*microphone
*surprise
*recognize
*narrow
*approach

Additional Spelling Words
fright
wrote
blind
coast
glow

*Starred words or forms of the words appear in *Koya DeLaney and the Good Girl Blues.*

TESTED SKILL

Spelling Long *i* and Long *o*

LAB, p. 38, 39

- Write the word *side* on the board. Say the word aloud and have students repeat it. Ask them what vowel sound they hear in *side*. (/ī/) Write the word *bright* on the board, and say the word. Elicit that /ī/ can be spelled *i*-consonant-*e* or *igh*. Underline these patterns in the words on the board.
- Introduce the /ō/ sound in the same way, using the words *spoke, know,* and *goal.*
- Write the Spelling Words on the board. Tell students that each Spelling Word has the /ī/ sound or the /ō/ sound. Say the Spelling Words and have students repeat them.
- Encourage students to add to their Study List some words that they have misspelled in their own writing.

Spelling Assessment

Pretest

Say each underlined word, read the sentence, and then repeat the word. Have students write only the underlined words.

1. We jump rope at recess every day.
2. The coach made us run a mile.
3. I don't know the rules of the game.
4. Stand to the side until it's your turn.
5. The announcer spoke to the crowd.
6. How high can you jump?
7. I can blow a big bubble.
8. Our team uniform is bright red.
9. Here's a towel to wipe your face.
10. I scored a goal in the game.

Test

Spelling Words Use the Pretest sentences.

Challenge Words

11. The hikers followed the narrow trail.
12. I didn't recognize you in that hat.
13. First approach the net, then shoot the ball.
14. Losing the game was a big surprise.
15. Use a microphone to announce the winners.

SKILL FINDER

Daily Language Practice, p. 107J
Reading-Writing Workshop, p. 91E

Literacy Activity Book, p. 38

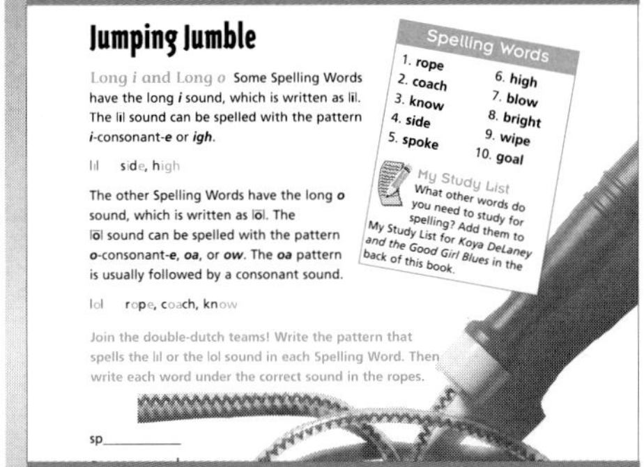

Jumping Jumble

Long *i* and Long *o* Some Spelling Words have the long *i* sound, which is written as /ī/. The /ī/ sound can be spelled with the pattern *i*-consonant-*e* or *igh*.

/ī/ side, high

The other Spelling Words have the long *o* sound, which is written as /ō/. The /ō/ sound can be spelled with the pattern *o*-consonant-*e*, *oa*, or *ow*. The *oa* pattern is usually followed by a consonant sound.

/ō/ rope, coach, know

Join the double-dutch teams! Write the pattern that spells the /ī/ or the /ō/ sound in each Spelling Word. Then write each word under the correct sound in the ropes.

sp________

Spelling Words
1. rope
2. coach
3. know
4. side
5. spoke
6. high
7. blow
8. bright
9. wipe
10. goal

My Study List
What other words do you need to study for spelling? Add them to My Study List for *Koya DeLaney and the Good Girl Blues* in the back of this book.

Literacy Activity Book, p. 39

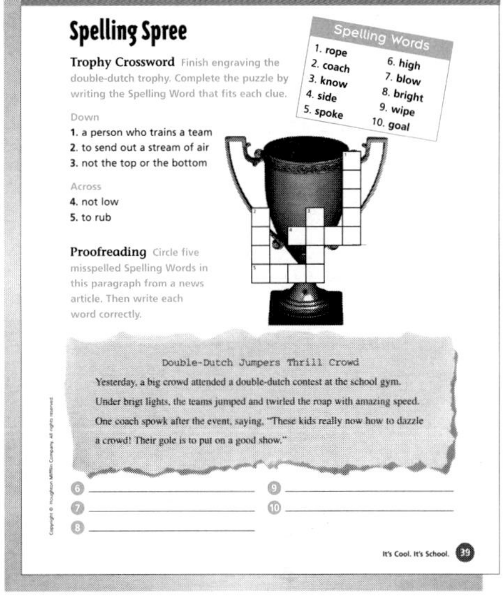

Spelling Spree

Trophy Crossword Finish engraving the double-dutch trophy. Complete the puzzle by writing the Spelling Word that fits each clue.

Down
1. a person who trains a team
2. to send out a stream of air
3. not the top or the bottom

Across
4. not low
5. to rub

Proofreading Circle five misspelled Spelling Words in this paragraph from a news article. Then write each word correctly.

Double-Dutch Jumpers Thrill Crowd

Yesterday, a big crowd attended a double-dutch contest at the school gym. Under brigt lights, the teams jumped and twirled the roap with amazing speed. One coach spowk after the event, saying, "These kids really now how to dazzle a crowd! Their gole is to put on a good show."

6. ________
7. ________
8. ________
9. ________
10. ________

Spelling Words
1. rope
2. coach
3. know
4. side
5. spoke
6. high
7. blow
8. bright
9. wipe
10. goal

It's Cool. It's School. 39

Literacy Activity Book

Take-Home Word Lists: pp. 315–316

Spelling Vocabulary

Students can use the **Spelling Spree CD-ROM** for extra practice with the spelling principles taught in this selection.

MEETING INDIVIDUAL NEEDS

Challenge

Challenge Words Practice Have students use the Challenge Words to write headlines for articles in the sports section of the newspaper.

Instruct *and* Integrate

Grammar

FIVE-DAY PLAN

DAY 1	DAY 2	DAY 3	DAY 4	DAY 5
Daily Language Practice 1; Teach/Model; First LAB page	Daily Language Practice 2; Check first LAB page; Cooperative Learning	Daily Language Practice 3; Writing Application	Daily Language Practice 4; Reteaching (opt.); Second LAB page	Daily Language Practice 5; Check second LAB page; Students' Writing

Transparency 1–17

Correcting Run-on Sentences

Run-on Sentence:	The next event began it was speed jumping
Correct:	The next event began. It was speed jumping.

Only one person jumped for each team the crowd was cheering hard.

The Wilson jumper was very good it would be hard to beat her.

The jumpers moved fast their ropes were whirring.

Koya waited for the whistle her sister was doing her best.

Wilson was in first place second place went to Barnett.

TRANSPARENCY 1–17 TEACHER'S BOOK PAGE 107I

Literacy Activity Book, p. 41

Koya DeLaney and the Good Girl Blues

Literacy Activity Book, p. 40

Double-Dutch Delight

Run-on Sentence: Contests do not just happen they take a lot of planning.
Correct: Contests do not just happen. They take a lot of planning.

Run-on Sentences A student committee is making up the schedule for the double-dutch contest. Use proofreading marks to correct their run-on sentences. Then write the events correctly onto the schedule in the correct order.

Proofreading Marks
≡ Make a capital letter.
⊙ Add a period.

Example: Everyone is ready the contest will begin.

The coach blows a whistle visitors take their seats.

The coach introduces the judges they walk to the jumping areas

The teams and visitors arrive all team members sign in.

The jumping begins a new event starts every fifteen minutes.

Winners are announced they receive their certificates.

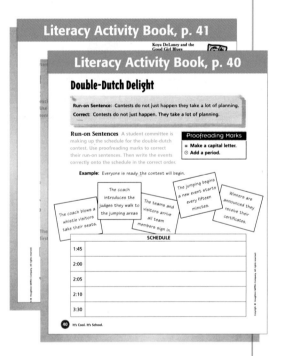

SCHEDULE	
1:45	
2:00	
2:05	
2:10	
3:30	

40 It's Cool. It's School.

Informal Assessment

Responses to the activities should indicate general understanding of how to recognize and correct run-on sentences.

Additional Support:

Reteaching, p.107J

INTERACTIVE LEARNING

TESTED SKILL

Run-on Sentences

LAB, pp. 40–41

A **run-on sentence** has two or more complete thoughts that run together. Correct a run-on sentence by writing each complete thought as a separate sentence.

Teach/Model

Write the run-on sentence below on the chalkboard, and read it aloud. Do not stop for breath; give no vocal cues to indicate where sentences end and begin. Ask students to determine how many sentences they hear.

Koya watched the girls jump together she thought they moved like twins they stopped when the whistle sounded.

Invite volunteers to try to read the run-on aloud without pausing. Then discuss the problem with the "sentence." Elicit that several complete thoughts are run together and that it is hard to understand what they are without pausing. Ask students how to fix this problem.

Read aloud the run-on sentence again, pausing at the end of each sentence. Ask students to listen for the sentence breaks and to mark them by adding capital letters and end marks.

Display Transparency 1–17. Have students add capital letters and end marks to each run-on sentence. Point out that this is how they correct run-on sentences when they proofread their writing.

SKILL FINDER Reading-Writing Workshop, p. 91E

INTERACTIVE LEARNING *(continued)*

Practice/Apply

Literacy Activity Book **Students Acquiring English** Read the run-on sentences aloud so that students can hear the intonation.

Cooperative Learning: **"Block That Run-on!"** Have students work in small groups to make posters or public-service announcements reminding others to avoid writing run-on sentences and showing how to fix them. Share their work with other classes.

Writing Application: Instructions Suggest that students write instructions for something they know how to do well. Ask them to proofread their instructions for run-on sentences.

Students' Writing Encourage students to check their work in process for run-on sentences. Suggest that they proofread for this problem by reading their sentences aloud and listening for the beginning and end of each complete thought.

More Practice

Houghton Mifflin English Level 4
Workbook Plus, pp. 17–18
Reteaching Workbook, p. 9

Writers Express
Writers Express SourceBook,
pp. 3–4, 5–6, 55–56, 117

Reteaching

Run-on Sentences

MEETING INDIVIDUAL NEEDS

Write the following run-on sentence on a large strip of paper.

Our school holds a Sports Day anyone can be in it.

Read aloud the run-on sentence several ways, pausing at different places, including the correct break. Ask students which reading allows them to hear two complete sentences. (If students need additional help, have them determine if each new "sentence" has a subject and a predicate.)

When students have identified the correct break, invite a volunteer to cut apart the sentences. Invite other volunteers to make the other corrections.

Organize students into pairs, and then give a different run-on sentence written on a strip of paper to each pair. Ask them to read aloud, together, the run-on sentence and to identify the separate sentences. Have them share their thoughts with the group, who determines if they have identified the sentences correctly. If correct, the pair can cut apart and write their sentences correctly. If incorrect, the pair should work with the run-on sentence again until they think they have the correct answer.

Daily Language Practice

Focus Skills

Grammar: Run-on Sentences
Spelling: Long *i* and Long *o*

Every day write one sentence on the chalkboard. Have each student write the sentence correctly on a sheet of paper. Tell students to correct any run-on sentences as well as any misspelled words. Have students correct their own paper as a volunteer corrects the sentence on the chalkboard.

1. We jump rope very well our gole is to be the best.
   We jump rope very well**. O**ur **goal** is to be the best.
2. Does our side have fast jumpers they can leap very hie.
   Does our side have fast jumpers**? T**hey can leap very **high**.
3. I know all the rules my job is to bloe the whistle.
   I know all the rules**. M**y job is to **blow** the whistle.
4. Our coche helped us get started she spoke to the parents.
   Our **coach** helped us get started**. S**he spoke to the parents.
5. What brite uniforms we have they are green with yellow numbers.
   What **bright** uniforms we have**! T**hey are green with yellow numbers.

Instruct *and* Integrate

Communication Activities

Listening and Speaking

"Apples, peaches, pears, and plums
Tell me when your birthday comes."

Rhyme and Rhythm

Invite volunteers to teach jump-rope rhymes to the class or to read several aloud from a book. Encourage students to move in rhythm to the rhymes by jumping a rope, clapping their hands, or tapping their feet. Then raise the following observations in discussion, and write them on the chalkboard:

- The rhymes have a definite rhythm.
- They are usually spoken rather than sung.
- They can tell a story or be nonsensical.

Have students compare jump-rope rhymes to football or basketball cheers and rap music lyrics. Then ask students to compose one of these kinds of rhymes to share with the class.

Tape-Recording

Students Acquiring English Make a tape recorder available to students and have them take turns reading a short summary or written response to the story through the microphone. They should discover the importance of modulating their voices and keeping a proper distance between the mouth and microphone. If possible, tape-record students reading part of a story and keep the tapes for comparison later in the year. Ask students to describe how it felt to tape-record their voices and to hear them played back.

Audio Tape
for It's Cool. It's School.: *Koya DeLaney and the Good Girl Blues*

Viewing

Games Demonstration

Have volunteers demonstrate playground games other than rope jumping that involve special skills and techniques. Encourage students in the audience to be polite if someone makes a mistake and to show their appreciation with a round of applause when each demonstration is over.

Body Language

Cooperative Learning

Using examples from the selection, ask students how facial expressions and body language communicate characters' feelings. (Sample: When Loritha gets dropped from the freestyle event, her face looks stunned; Koya thought that Dawn's face looked guilty.) Have groups of students choose an emotion and devise ways to show the feeling through facial expressions and body language. Then ask volunteers to demonstrate their group's feeling and have the other students guess what emotion they are portraying.

anger

delight

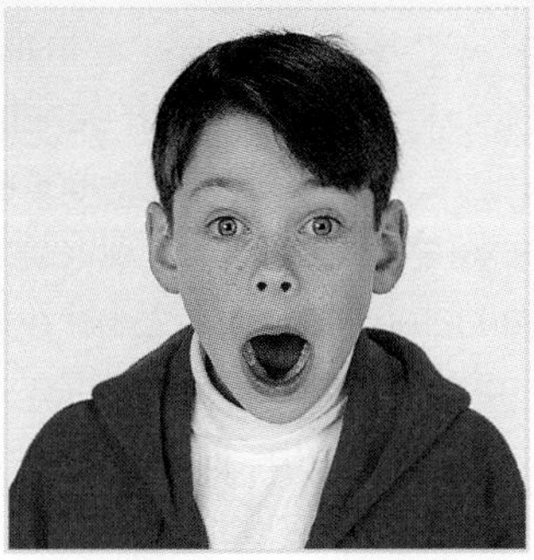

fear

Portfolio Opportunity

Make a video or audio recording of students' performances for Rhyme and Rhythm or other activities. Also save the tapes from the Tape-Recording activity.

Cross-Curricular Activities

Book List

Health

Red Hot Peppers: The Skookum Book of Jump Rope Games, Rhymes, and Fancy Footwork
by Diane Boardman

Health and Exercise
by Dorothy Baldwin

Outdoor Games
by David Buskin

Track and Field
by Donna Bailey

Choices for Health

Taking Your Pulse

Cooperative Learning

MEETING INDIVIDUAL NEEDS

Students Acquiring English Ask students what the word *pulse* means. Guide them to understand that it is a medical term for the regular contractions of the heart. Counting heartbeats is called "taking a pulse." Have students take their pulses using one of the methods shown and then record their heart rates in the "at rest" column of a chart like the one below.

Press two fingertips alongside the windpipe (larynx) to feel the carotid artery.

Next have paired students measure and record their heart rates after they run in place, jump, or climb stairs for a few minutes. They should discover that aerobic exercise increases the heart rate. A child's pulse is about seventy beats per minute at rest and about one hundred beats per minute after several minutes of exercise.

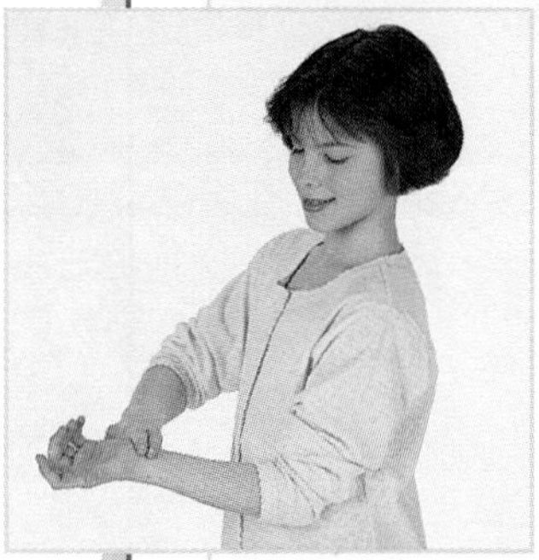

Press two fingertips against the wrist at the base of the thumb to feel the radial artery.

Activity	Jim's Pulse		Julia's Pulse	
	at rest	exercising	at rest	exercising

anaerobic

Fitness and Exercise

MEETING INDIVIDUAL NEEDS

Challenge Invite students to research the health benefits of regular exercise. Which activities are considered to be exercise? What is the difference between aerobic and anaerobic exercise? What does a good exercise routine include? How often should people exercise? What are some tips for getting in shape? Encourage students to choose a way to share the information they have gathered with the class, such as writing a handbook or holding a training clinic.

aerobic

Choices for Health *(continued)*

Having a Field Day

Cooperative Learning

Have students plan a field day of sports and games for their class or school. Some things they will have to decide include the following:

- Who will participate? Will younger and older students be invited too?
- What races and competitions will there be? Will the events be serious or fun?
- Will drinks and food be available to the participants?
- How will the scoring be done?
- What awards will be handed out?

Encourage students to make a list of the tasks that need to be done and assign people to each task.

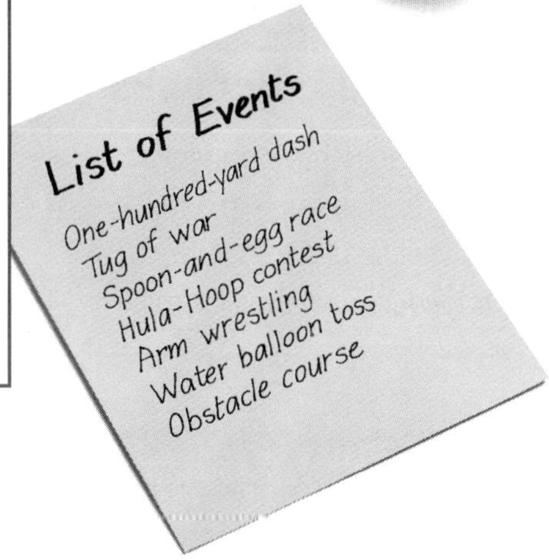

Math

Estimating Two Minutes

In the story, Loritha had only two minutes to jump rope as many times as she could. Ask students if they think two minutes is a short or a long time. Have them predict how often they will be able to do some simple activity in two minutes. (Suggest activities such as writing their names or reciting the alphabet.) Then invite them to work with partners; one partner can do the activity while the other keeps track of the time. Are students surprised by their results? How close were their predictions? Encourage students to share their results with others.

Alice & Alex
A play by Deborah Sussman,
based on the book
Alice's Adventures in Wonderland
by Lewis Carroll

Introduce the Literature

Activating Prior Knowledge

Use the following ideas to introduce the mood of the play:

- Ask students if they have ever moved to a new town or city. How did they feel the night before their first day at a new school?
- Ask students who have not moved to describe a typical first day of a new school year.

Meeting Individual Needs

Students Acquiring English

You may wish to have students acquiring English listen to a re-corded version of *Alice's Adventures in Wonderland* by Lewis Carroll.

Interact with Literature

Narration

Discuss what the word *narration* means and who a narrator is. During the discussion, elicit that a narrator speaks directly to the audience; helps tell the story; and gives the audience important information, such as how the characters are feeling and what events happened before the present time of the story. As a class, discuss why the narrator is important to the play *Alice & Alex*.

ALICE & ALEX

Characters

NARRATOR	**MARGE**, **MATT**, **DORA** (3 kids)
ALICE, **ALEX** (9-year-old twins)	**MS. QUEEN** (a scary person)
MOTHER	**MS. QUEEN'S GANG** (a group of two or more people)
MR. RABBIT (a white-haired man)	
CHESTER (the hall monitor)	

Scene 1 The Twins' Room

NARRATOR: Meet Alice and Alex. They're twins. They just moved to town. It's bedtime, and Alice is reading *Alice's Adventures in Wonderland* out loud to Alex. Their mother comes in.

ALICE *(reading)*: "The Cat only grinned when it saw Alice. It looked good-natured, she thought. Still it had very long claws and a great many teeth —"

MOTHER: Not too much longer, you two. Tomorrow is your first day at a new school. I want you to be bright-eyed and bushy-tailed!

ALEX: C'mon, just one more page.

ALICE: No! One more chapter!

MOTHER: Five more minutes, then lights out.

ALICE *(reading as Mother leaves)*: "Still it had very long claws and a great many teeth . . ."

Scene 2 At School

NARRATOR: The next thing Alice and Alex know, it's Monday morning and they're at their new school.

ALEX: Alice, there's no one else here.

ALICE *(calling out)*: HELLO! Is anyone here?

NARRATOR: Suddenly, a small, white-haired man with a pink nose rushes by.

MR. RABBIT: Oh, dear! Oh, dear! I shall be too late!

NARRATOR: The small man pulls a watch from his pocket and checks it. He hurries on.

ALICE: Quick! Let's follow that guy.

NARRATOR: The twins chase the man down the hall.

ALICE: Mister! Hey, Mister!

ALEX: Yo! Dude!

ALICE: Excuse me —

MR. RABBIT: Oh, there you are. Listen, Susan, and you, too, George. I need four gallons of lemonade right away.

ALICE: Um, I think you have us confused with some other children.

MR. RABBIT: Don't be silly. Now hurry up.

ALEX: No, really. We're new here. Who are you?

MR. RABBIT: Mr. Rabbit, of course. Now, let's see. New students. Well, you'll have to go to the main office.

ALEX: How do we get there?

MR. RABBIT: Follow the signs.

NARRATOR: Mr. Rabbit leaves.

ALICE: This school is weird.

109

Instruct and Integrate — MINILESSON

Genre
Play

Teach/Model

Ask students if they have ever performed in a play and what they know about plays. Elicit from discussion the following characteristics of a play, and list them on the chalkboard:

- It is a story meant to be performed.
- The action is divided into scenes.
- It has a specific format, including a cast of characters; indications of the time, setting, costumes, props, and a description of the stage or set; and stage directions and sound effects in parentheses.
- The characters' names appear next to the lines they are to speak.

Practice/Apply

Have students point out the characteristics of *Alice & Alex* that signal it's a play. Challenge them to describe how the information that these characteristics convey would be included if *Alice & Alex* were a story instead of a play. (For example, how would a story convey the cast of characters?)

Interact with Literature

Colloquialisms

Ask students what the words *check it out* mean in Alice's line on the bottom of column 1 on page 110. Then discuss what type of expression it is and what it reveals about Alice. During the discussion, introduce the term *colloquialism*, and help students understand that colloquialisms are words people use in everyday language. Ask students if they would identify more with a character who says, "Check it out," or one who says, "My, look at that." Lead students to see how writers use colloquialisms to reveal something about the character or to help the reader identify with the character.

Ask pairs of students to find more examples of colloquialisms in *Alice & Alex*. Have each pair make a chart like the one below, listing colloquialisms in one column and their meanings in another column.

Colloquialism	Meaning
check it out	"look at that"

ALEX: Yeah. Weirder than weird.

CHESTER: Says you.

ALICE: Who said that?

CHESTER: I did. Up here.

NARRATOR: Alice and Alex look up and see a boy standing on a tall chair, grinning.

CHESTER: I'm Chester Cat, the hall monitor.

ALICE: Do you know which way we're supposed to go?

CHESTER: That depends on where you're trying to get to.

ALEX: The main office.

CHESTER: You can go left. Or you can go right.

ALICE: What's the difference?

CHESTER: One's left, and one's right.

ALEX: You mean both ways lead to the office?

CHESTER: Sure, if you walk far enough.

ALEX: Are you trying to confuse us?

CHESTER: Not at all. I'm trying to help.

NARRATOR: The twins look around, trying to decide which way to go. When they look back at Chester, he has disappeared. There's a big grin on the wall where he once stood.

ALICE: Alex! That grin was in the book I was reading last night! The Cheshire Cat disappears, except for its grin.

ALEX: Yeah, yeah. But now what?

NARRATOR: Alice walks over to a little door. A sign on the doorknob says, "OPEN ME."

ALICE: Hey, check it out! A sign.

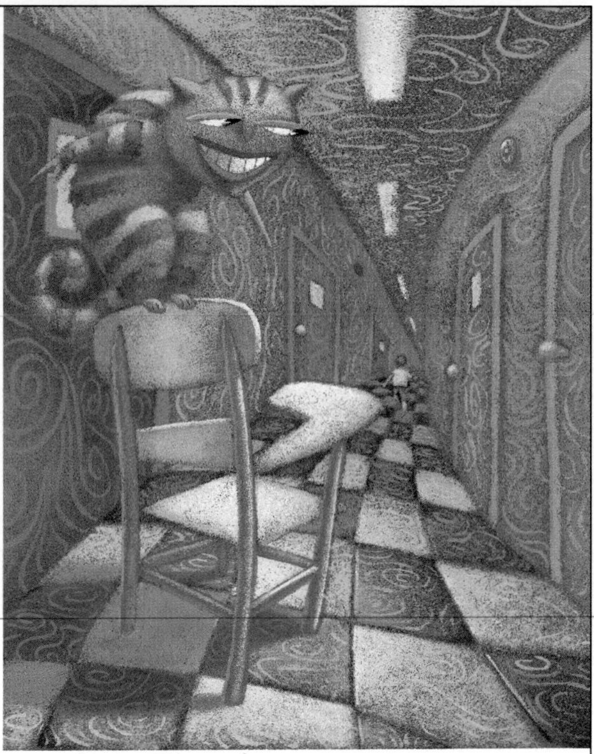

NARRATOR: Alice opens the door.

ALEX: Whoa! It's dark in there.

ALICE: Yeah, but I'm going in.

NARRATOR: Alice steps through the doorway and Alex hears —

ALICE: YIKES! I'm falling.

ALEX: Alice, are you okay?

ALICE: I'm still falling.

ALEX: You sound pretty calm about it.

ALICE: Still falling. Whooops! Hey! I just landed in a pile of humongous marshmallows.

ALEX: Really?

ALICE: Would I lie to you?

ALEX: Maybe.

ALICE: Come on down.

ALEX: Okay — if you say so.

110

Scene 3 The Lunchroom

NARRATOR: Alex lands next to Alice on a pile of huge marshmallows, in the corner of a large lunchroom.

ALICE: Look, we're not the only people here!

ALEX: You call those people?

ALICE: The one with the stack of hats. That's a boy . . . I think. That's a girl next to him — the one with the rabbity face and pointy ears.

ALEX: Oh. What's that sleeping on the table between them?

ALICE: It looks like a giant mouse.

NARRATOR: Alice and Alex walk over to the table.

ALICE: Hi. I'm Alice and this is my twin brother, Alex. What's with the mouse?

MARGE: This isn't any mouse. This is Dora Mouse. She's in third grade. Wake up, Dora! I'm Marge Hare and this is Matt Hatter. Now go away. There's no room here.

ALICE: What do you mean?

ALEX: There's plenty of room.

NARRATOR: The twins sit down at the table. Matt turns to Alice and looks at her hair.

MATT: You need a haircut.

ALICE: And you're rude!

MATT: Well, then, why is a raven like a writing desk?

ALEX: Is that a riddle?

ALICE: I bet I can guess that.

MARGE: You mean you think you can figure out the answer?

ALICE: Definitely.

MARGE: Then you should always say what you mean.

ALICE *(confused)*: I do. At least, I mean what I say. That's the same thing.

MATT: Not at all. Why, you might just as well say that "I see what I eat" is the same thing as "I eat what I see."

MARGE: Oh, dear. Dora is asleep again.

MATT: So, have you guessed the riddle yet?

ALEX: No, we give up. What's the answer?

MATT: I have no idea.

ALICE: Don't you have anything better to do than ask riddles that have no answers? What a waste of time!

MATT: If you knew Time as well as I do, you wouldn't talk about wasting it. It's him.

Interact with Literature

Idea Map

Ask students how they think Alice and Alex feel as they wander through their new school. Have students reread Scene 2 as though they were either Alice or Alex. Encourage students to "see, hear, and feel" each strange new person or room. When students have finished rereading the selection, ask them to create an idea map such as the one below. The center box should indicate how the character feels during Scene 2 (for example, confused). The surrounding circles should include details that contribute to these emotions (for example, being yelled at by Mr. Rabbit; Chester's strange directions; and falling down into the lunchroom).

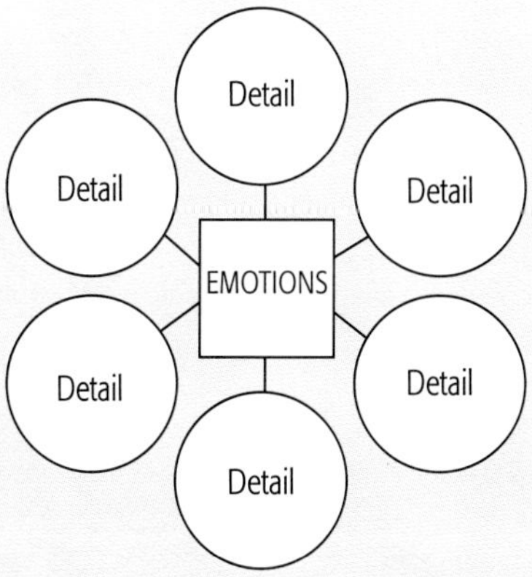

When students have completed their idea maps, have them write a paragraph as if they were the character, telling how they feel.

ALEX: I don't get it.

MATT: Of course you don't. You've probably never even talked to Time!

ALICE: And you have?

MATT: Oh, yes. We were very good friends, until . . .

MARGE: They quarreled.

MATT: It was last March, at the school recital. Since then, Time won't do anything I ask. It's always noon now.

ALEX: Is that why the table is set for lunch?

MARGE: Yes, that's it. It's always lunchtime, and there's no time to clear the table.

ALICE: Then you keep moving around the table, right?

MATT: Exactly, as things get used up.

ALEX: But what happens when you get to the beginning again?

ALICE: It must get disgusting!

MATT: Now who's the rude one?

MARGE: Let's change the subject. I vote that Dora tells us a story. Wake up, Dora!

DORA: I wasn't sleeping. I heard every word you said.

MATT: Tell us a story.

DORA: Once upon a time there were two twins, a boy and a girl.

MARGE: Twins! Yeah! Let's all have some more milk.

ALEX: We haven't had any yet. So we can't have more.

MATT: You mean you can't have less. It's very easy to have more than nothing.

DORA: If you two can't behave, I won't finish the story.

ALICE: Sorry. Go ahead.

DORA: So these two twins lived at the bottom of a well —

ALEX: What did they eat?

DORA: Honey.

MATT: I want a new carton of milk. Let's change places.

NARRATOR: Everyone stands up and moves one seat to the left.

ALICE: I don't understand. Where did they get the honey?

DORA: It was a honey well!

ALEX: Ha ha ha. That's so funny I forgot to laugh!

NARRATOR: Suddenly, Ms. Queen bursts into the lunchroom. She's wearing a dress

112

with red hearts all over it. A noisy gang follows her.

MS. QUEEN: There they are! Grab them!

ALICE: Wait! Is she talking about us?

MS. QUEEN: Someone has stolen the bologna sandwiches! You are all under arrest! Off with your heads!

MS. QUEEN'S GANG *(together)*: We'll get them!

ALEX: But we didn't do it!

MS. QUEEN: Do you like bologna sandwiches?

ALEX: Well, sure, but —

MS. QUEEN: Just as I thought. Guilty guilty guilty! Grab them!

NARRATOR: A big guy in a football helmet grabs Alex. A guy in a catcher's mask chases Alice.

MS. QUEEN'S GANG: *(together)*: Grrrr! Your heads are our heads now!

ALICE: No! Help!

ALEX: Get this creep off me!

MS. QUEEN: Off with their heads! Off with their heads!

Scene 4 The Twins' Room

NARRATOR: It's morning in the twins' bedroom.

MOTHER: Wake up, sleepyheads! Wake up!

NARRATOR: Alice and Alex open their eyes. They are safe at home. The book *Alice's Adventures in Wonderland* lies open on the floor.

MOTHER: You'll be late for school if you don't hurry.

ALICE: I had the weirdest dream.

ALEX: I bet mine was weirder.

ALICE: Oh, yeah? Did yours have a talking mouse in it?

ALEX: Yes, as a matter of fact.

ALICE: Really?

ALEX: And a disappearing —

ALICE: — hall monitor?

ALEX *(surprised)*: Yeah. How did you know?

ALICE: Let's just say I read the book.

The End

Instruct and Integrate

Art

Design In addition to actors, a play involves a set designer, who decides how the stage will look for each scene, and a costume designer, who decides how each of the characters will dress. Have students choose a scene or character from *Alice & Alex* and design either the set or the costume. You may wish to provide books about costume or set design for students' reference.

Theater

Reader's Theater Help students perform *Alice & Alex* as reader's theater.

- Arrange chairs in a circle, and assign a part to each student. (Students can trade off the lines of the narrator.)
- Remind students that while performing they should speak loudly and clearly; use voice to convey feeling and body language to convey meaning; and listen for their next line.
- After the performance, discuss ways in which students used their voices and body language.

Students Acquiring English Assign roles beforehand to students acquiring English so they can rehearse alone or with a partner before performing with the entire group.

Theme Assessment Wrap-Up

Time: About 1 hour

Evaluates

1. **Theme Concept:** School offers the challenges and rewards of life: friendship, problems, humor, and personal growth.

2. **Skills:** Making Inferences about Characters, Sequence

This is a brief, informal performance assessment activity. For a more extended reading-writing performance assessment, see the Integrated Theme Test.

PERFORMANCE ASSESSMENT

Creating a Skit

LAB, p. 42

Materials
- pencil
- paper
- props

Introducing Ask students to work in pairs to create a skit about the two *Tales of a Fourth Grade Nothing* characters, Sheila and Jimmy. Have students use *Literacy Activity Book* page 42 to plan their skit.

Character	What Each Character Is Like	Job(s) Each Character Will Do	Problems or Disagreements They Will Solve
Sheila			
Jimmy			

1. **Plan the events of the skit using the chart on *Literacy Activity Book* page 42.**
2. **Write a script or notes for the skit and practice performing it.**
3. **Perform or present the skit for the class or small group. (Optional)**

Evaluating You may wish to ask the student pairs to divide the two character roles between them so that each student is responsible for the dialogue and actions of only one character. Evaluate students' *Literacy Activity Book* pages and presentations using the scoring rubric.

Scoring Rubric

Criterion	1	2	3	4
Depicts a realistic challenge that can arise at school	Does not depict a realistic school situation	Partly depicts a realistic challenge at school	Generally depicts a realistic challenge at school	Develops and resolves a realistic challenge at school
Reflects inferential understanding of characters	Dialogue and actions do not relate to story characters	Dialogue and actions sometimes relate to story characters	Dialogue and actions usually relate to story characters	Dialogue and actions consistently relate to story characters
Relates events in logical sequence	Story events do not follow logical order	Some story events follow logical order	Most story events follow logical order	Story events consistently follow logical order

Literacy Activity Book, p. 42

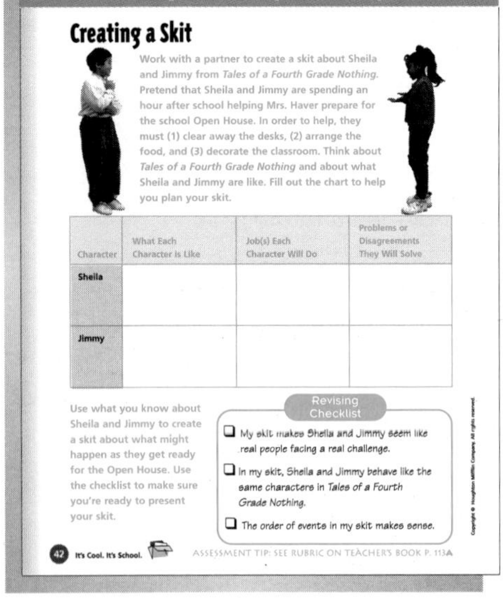

Creating a Skit

Work with a partner to create a skit about Sheila and Jimmy from *Tales of a Fourth Grade Nothing.* Pretend that Sheila and Jimmy are spending an hour after school helping Mrs. Haver prepare for the school Open House. In order to help, they must (1) clear away the desks, (2) arrange the food, and (3) decorate the classroom. Think about *Tales of a Fourth Grade Nothing* and about what Sheila and Jimmy are like. Fill out the chart to help you plan your skit.

Character	What Each Character Is Like	Job(s) Each Character Will Do	Problems or Disagreements They Will Solve
Sheila			
Jimmy			

Use what you know about Sheila and Jimmy to create a skit about what might happen as they get ready for the Open House. Use the checklist to make sure you're ready to present your skit.

Revising Checklist
- ☐ My skit makes Sheila and Jimmy seem like real people facing a real challenge.
- ☐ In my skit, Sheila and Jimmy behave like the same characters in *Tales of a Fourth Grade Nothing.*
- ☐ The order of events in my skit makes sense.

42 It's Cool. It's School. ASSESSMENT TIP: SEE RUBRIC ON TEACHER'S BOOK P. 113A

Portfolio Opportunity
- *Literacy Activity Book,* page 42
- Save students' skits.

Choices for Assessment

Informal Assessment

Review the Informal Assessment Checklist and observation notes to determine:

- How well did students apply reading strategies?
- Did students demonstrate adequate skills in writing?
- In what areas did students demonstrate a need for improvement?

Formal Assessment

Select formal tests that meet your needs:

- Integrated Theme Test for It's Cool. It's School.
- Theme Skills Test for It's Cool. It's School.
- Benchmark Progress Test

See the Teacher's Assessment Handbook for guidelines for administering tests and using scoring aids.

Portfolio Assessment

Introducing Portfolios to the Class

Explain to students that their portfolios will show samples of their work over the year.

- As a first step, have students create and decorate temporary collection folders to keep all their work for the theme.
- Partway through the first theme, have students create their portfolios for special work selected from the collection and decorate them to express their unique interests.

Selecting Materials for the Portfolio

Meet with students to review the work in their collections, and model the process of selecting work samples for the portfolio. Discuss your criteria as you pick samples that reflect important categories.

Grading Work in Portfolios

You may wish to grade formal tests, some student writing, and some *Literacy Activity Book* pages. Also see Portfolio Assessment notes in Themes 3, 4, and 5, and the *Teacher's Assessment Handbook*.

MINILESSON / ASSESSMENT

Spelling Review

Review with students the Spelling Words and, if appropriate, the Challenge Words from the spelling lessons on pages 59H, 81H, 91E, and 107H. Have volunteers summarize each spelling principle and explain how the words in each lesson illustrate the principle.

Pretest/Test

1. They <u>don't</u> <u>know</u> when the school play is.
2. We <u>can't</u> <u>wait</u> to act our parts.
3. Put the <u>rope</u> by the <u>side</u> of the stage.
4. I <u>won't</u> <u>knock</u> until you leave the stage.
5. Our <u>grade</u> placed at <u>least</u> second.
6. Your desks always <u>seem</u> so <u>neat</u>!
7. They <u>trust</u> us to meet our <u>goal</u>.
8. The wind will <u>blow</u> the leaves <u>away</u>.
9. The <u>bright</u> sun <u>wouldn't</u> last all day.
10. I <u>still</u> <u>haven't</u> read that book.

Challenge Words

11. In a <u>minute</u>, we'll take a <u>stretch</u>.
12. What a <u>surprise</u> your <u>sketch</u> is!
13. Be sure to <u>approach</u> <u>traffic</u> carefully.
14. We went to the <u>playground</u> <u>Wednesday</u>.
15. Do not <u>whisper</u> into the <u>microphone</u>.

SEE 5-Day Planner
Spelling Plan p.107H

Managing Assessment

Testing Options

Question: How can I assess students' overall progress at the end of a theme?

Answer: *Invitations to Literacy* includes a range of testing options for use at the end of a theme. Select options that best meet your needs:

Performance Assessment
The Performance Assessment on page 113A is a hands-on activity that can be useful with students acquiring English or with those who have difficulty in reading.

Integrated Theme Test
The Integrated Theme Test provides a new theme-related reading selection. It uses written and multiple-choice formats to evaluate reading strategies, comprehension, critical thinking, and application of theme skills.

Theme Skills Test
The Theme Skills Test evaluates discrete literacy skills of the theme. Sections can be used to evaluate specific skills that are areas of concern.

Benchmark Progress Tests
The Benchmark Progress Tests can be given two or three times a year to evaluate students' overall progress in reading and writing. They may be used at midyear and at year's end.

See also the *Teacher's Assessment Handbook*.

MEETING INDIVIDUAL NEEDS

Challenge

Challenge Words Practice Have students write bumper stickers, using the Challenge Words.

Literacy Activity Book

Spelling Practice: pp. 269–270
Take-Home Word Lists: pp. 315–316

Celebrating the Theme

Choices for Celebrating

Create Friendship Portraits

What qualities make a good friend? Ask students to list characteristics that they value in a friend. Then ask them how they could illustrate friendship in action. For example, they might draw and color a picture or cut and paste images for a collage. Display and discuss students' completed friendship portraits.

Write an Advice Handbook

Ask students to list three things they think first graders should know about going to school. For each of the topics, have students write one paragraph in which they explain the topic and give advice based on their own experiences. Assemble the responses into an advice handbook.

See the **Teacher's Resource Disk** for theme-related Teacher Support material.

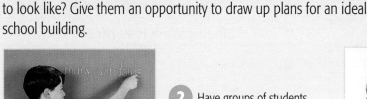

Design and Build a School

Cooperative Learning

If students could redesign their school building, what would they want it to look like? Give them an opportunity to draw up plans for an ideal school building.

Materials

- chalkboard or chart paper
- pencils, markers, crayons
- graph or other grid paper
- cardboard boxes

1. Ask students to list desirable features of a school building. Encourage them to think about the way a school must function as well as how it might look.

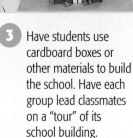

2. Have groups of students refer to the list as they develop layouts for the school. Ask them to devise a system for marking rooms, doors, and windows.

3. Have students use cardboard boxes or other materials to build the school. Have each group lead classmates on a "tour" of its school building.

Self-Assessment

Have students meet in small groups to compare and discuss their Selection Connections charts (*Literacy Activity Book,* pp. 7–8) using questions such as:

- What interesting ideas did I learn in this theme?
- What have I learned about how school relates to the rest of my life?

Glossary

GLOSSARY

Some of the words in this book may have pronunciations or meanings you do not know. This glossary can help you by telling you how to pronounce those words and by telling you the meanings with which those words are used in this book.

You can find out the correct pronunciations of any glossary word by using the special spelling after the word and the pronunciation key that runs across the bottom of the glossary pages.

The full pronunciation key opposite shows how to pronounce each consonant and vowel in a special spelling. The pronunciation key at the bottom of the glossary pages is a shortened form of the full key.

606

Full Pronunciation Key

Consonant Sounds

b	**b**i**b**, ca**bb**age	kw	**ch**oir, **qu**ick	t	**t**igh**t**, stoppe**d**
ch	**ch**ur**ch**, sti**tch**	l	**l**id, need**l**e, ta**ll**	th	ba**th**, **th**in
d	**d**ee**d**, maile**d**, pu**dd**le	m	a**m**, **m**an, du**mb**	*th*	ba**th**e, **th**is
f	**f**ast, **f**i**f**e, o**ff**, **ph**rase, rou**gh**	n	**n**o, su**dd**e**n**	v	ca**v**e, **v**al**v**e, **v**ine
g	**g**a**g**, **g**et, fin**g**er	ng	thi**ng**, i**n**k	w	**w**ith, **w**olf
h	**h**at, **wh**o	p	**p**o**p**, ha**pp**y	y	**y**es, **y**olk, on**i**on
hw	**wh**ich, **wh**ere	r	**r**oar, **rh**yme	z	ro**s**e, si**z**e, **x**ylophone, **z**ebra
j	**j**u**dg**e, **g**em	s	mi**ss**, sau**c**e, **sc**ene, **s**ee	zh	gara**g**e, plea**s**ure, vi**s**ion
k	**c**at, **k**i**ck**, s**ch**ool	sh	di**sh**, **sh**ip, **s**ugar, ti**ss**ue		

Vowel Sounds

ă	r**a**t, l**au**gh	ŏ	h**o**rrible, p**o**t	ŭ	c**u**t, fl**oo**d, r**ou**gh, s**o**me
ā	**a**pe, **ai**d, p**ay**	ō	g**o**, r**ow**, t**oe**, th**ough**	û	c**i**rcle, f**u**r, h**ea**rd, t**e**rm, t**u**rn, **u**rge, w**o**rd
â	**air**, c**a**re, w**ea**r	ô	**a**ll, c**au**ght, f**o**r, p**aw**	yōō	c**u**re
ä	f**a**ther, ko**a**la, y**a**rd	oi	b**oy**, n**oi**se, **oi**l	yōō	**a**b**u**se, **u**se
ĕ	p**e**t, pl**ea**sure, **a**ny	ou	c**ow**, **ou**t	ə	**a**bout, sil**e**nt, penc**i**l, lem**o**n, circ**u**s
ē	b**e**, b**ee**, **ea**sy, pian**o**	ŏŏ	f**u**ll, t**oo**k, w**o**lf		
ĭ	**i**f, p**i**t, b**u**sy	ōō	b**oo**t, fr**ui**t, fl**ew**		
ī	b**y**, p**ie**, h**igh**				
î	d**ea**r, d**ee**r, f**ie**rce, m**e**re				

Stress marks

Primary Stress ʹ: bi•ol•o•gy [bī **ŏl**ʹə jē]
Secondary Stress ʹ: bi•o•log•i•cal [bīʹ ə **lŏj**ʹĭ kəl]

607

alibi
Alibi comes from the Latin word for "elsewhere." A person with an alibi can prove that he or she was somewhere else.

ancestors

A

a•ban•doned (ə **băn**ʹdənd) *adj.* Left behind or deserted: *The **abandoned** puppy looked lost and hungry.*

ac•cu•rate (**ăk**ʹyər ĭt) *adj.* Exact, or free from mistakes: *Because she had never played before, her first shots were not very **accurate.***

a•dapt (ə **dăpt**ʹ) *v.* To adjust to fit changing conditions: *The Seminoles, who were used to living along streams, **adapted** to living in the swamps.*

a•larmed (ə **lärmd**ʹ) *adj.* Excited or disturbed: *The horses were **alarmed** by the noise of the approaching train.*

al•i•bi (**ăl**ʹə bīʹ) *n., pl.* **alibis.** An excuse for proving that a person was elsewhere when a crime was committed: *She was not in the cabin when the crime was committed, and this **alibi** kept her from being charged by the police.*

am•a•teur (**ăm**ʹə chər *or* **ăm**ʹə tər) *adj.* Relating to someone who engages in an activity for fun rather than for money: *Meg is an **amateur** detective, not a professional one.*

a•maze (ə **māz**ʹ) *v.* To fill with wonder: *The beauty of the land **amazed** the young man, and he could not look away.*

a•mend•ment (ə **mĕnd**ʹmənt) *n.* A change or added part to the United States Constitution: *An **amendment** to the Constitution gave women the right to vote.*

an•ces•tor (**ăn**ʹsĕsʹ tər) *n.* One from which another is descended: *His **ancestors** lived in the forest long before he was born.*

ar•range (ə **rānj**ʹ) *v.* To plan or prepare for: *We **arranged** to have our meetings twice a week at my house.*

as•ton•ish (ə **stŏn**ʹĭsh) *v.* To fill with a great feeling of surprise; amaze: *The size of the huge city **astonished** Grandfather.*

ă **pat** / ā **pay** / â **care** / ä **father** / ĕ **pet** / ē **be** / ĭ **pit** / ī **ride** / î **fierce** / ŏ **pot** / ō **go**
ô **paw, for**

608

a•tom bomb (**ăt**ʹəm bŏm) *n.* A powerful bomb whose great explosive force is a product of energy released by splitting atoms: *The **atom bomb** dropped on Hiroshima killed thousands of people.*

a•ward•ee (ə wôr **dē**ʹ) *n.* Someone who receives an award: *Each **awardee** will be given a trophy at the ceremony.*

B

be•wil•der (bĭ **wĭl**ʹdər) *v.* To confuse or puzzle greatly: *All the loud sounds and bright lights of the city **bewildered** him.*

be•wil•der•ment (bĭ **wĭl**ʹdər mənt) *n.* The state of being puzzled or confused: *He looked around at the many people in the yard, and a look of total **bewilderment** crossed his face.*

bored (bôrd) *adj.* Made discontented; weary from lack of interest: *Eric was **bored** by the dull speaker, so he tried to find another way to amuse himself.*

bus•tle (**bŭs**ʹəl) *v.* To move in a hurried or busy way: *People **bustled** along the sidewalks, in a hurry to get home.*

C

cas•u•al•ly (**kăzh**ʹōō əl ē) *adv.* Showing little concern; said or done without strong feeling or planning: *She mentioned the game **casually**, as if she didn't care whether or not they played.*

cham•pi•on (**chăm**ʹpē ən) *n.* The first-place winner in a competition: *The **champion** of the contest will win the biggest trophy.* —*v.* to fight for or support.

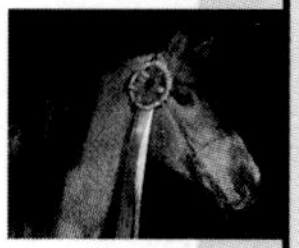
champion

charred (chärd) *adj.* Burned, but with parts still remaining: *The **charred** remains of the great trees stand guard over the burned forest.*

col•lect (kə **lĕkt**ʹ) *v.* To gather or bring together: *The men **collected** the garbage from the neighborhood every morning and took it to the dump.*

oi **oil** / ŏŏ **book** / ōō **boot** / ou **out** / ŭ **cut** / û **fur** / th **bath** / *th* **bathe** / ə **a**go, it**e**m, penc**i**l, at**o**m, circ**u**s

609

comfort
The Latin word *fortis* means "strong." If you comfort someone, you make them feel stronger.

Constitution of the United States

com•fort (kŭm′fərt) *v.* To make feel better when sad or scared: *I tried to* ***comfort*** *her, but she is still very sad.*

com•mit•tee (kə mĭt′ē) *n.* A group of people formed to complete a task: *Two* ***committees****, each with four members, will discuss the ideas this afternoon.*

com•mu•ni•ty (kə myoo′nĭ tē) *n., pl.* **communities.** A place where a group of people live: *The* ***community*** *of Spanish Harlem was a friendly, lively place.*

com•pan•ion (kəm păn′yən) *n.* One that keeps someone company: *A pet can be a good* ***companion*** *to keep a person from feeling lonely.*

com•pe•ti•tion (kŏm′ pĭ tĭsh′ ən) *n.* A contest; a struggle to win: *We finally beat Johnston in the double-dutch* ***competition*** *this year.*

con•clude (kən klōōd′) *v.* 1. To come to a decision or form an opinion: *After much thought, he* ***concludes*** *that his project is not a success.* 2. To finish; to bring or come to an end.

con•di•tions (kən dĭsh′əns) *n.* Events or facts that affect a situation or activity: *The weather* ***conditions*** *on Friday will have an effect on Holly's experiment.*

Con•sti•tu•tion (kŏn′stĭ tōō′ shən) *n.* The document containing the basic laws of government of the United States, adopted in 1787 and put into effect in 1789: *The* ***Constitution*** *guarantees certain rights to all people of the United States.*

cus•toms (kŭs′təmz) *n.* The process of inspecting goods and baggage brought into a country: *When we went to Mexico, we had to go through* ***customs*** *before we could enter the country.*

D

de•duce (dĭ dōōs′) *v.* To reach a conclusion by thinking and reasoning: *Can you* ***deduce*** *who stole the map by studying these clues?*

ă pat / ā pay / â care / ä father / ĕ pet / ē be / ĭ pit / ī ride / î fierce / ŏ pot / ō go / ô paw, for

de•feat (dĭ fēt′) *v.* To beat in a contest: *Did you* ***defeat*** *Olivia and win the contest today?*

de•pos•it (dĭ pŏz′ĭt) *v.* To put or lay down, to place: *The truck driver spent all day* ***depositing*** *loads of garbage at the dump.*

de•vel•op•ment (dĭ vĕl′əp mənt) *n.* Changes that take place as a result of growth: *We tracked the plants'* ***development*** *for three weeks to see how high they would get.*

dis•ap•pointed (dĭs′ə poin′ted) *adj.* Frustrated or let down: *The rainy weather* ***disappointed*** *the children, who wanted to play outdoors.*

dis•po•si•tion (dĭs′pə zĭsh′ən) *n.* One's usual way of acting, reacting, or behaving: *That friendly little puppy has a sweet* ***disposition.***

drear•y (drîr′ē) *adj.* **drearier, dreariest.** Gray and depressing, gloomy: *The* ***dreary*** *sky made Clara miss the bright colors of her island.*

E

ef•fect (ĭ fĕkt′) *n.* The way one thing acts upon another; the result: *Our class will study the* ***effects*** *of water and sunlight on plant growth.*

e•nor•mous (ĭ nôr′məs) *adj.* Very big; huge: *The side of the house was shaded by an* ***enormous*** *tree.*

en•vi•ron•ment (ĕn vī′rən mənt) *n.* Surroundings and conditions that affect how living things grow and change: *The hot, steamy* ***environment*** *of the rain forest supports many plants and animals.*

ex•cite (ĭk sīt′) *v.* To arouse strong feelings in: *The new land and all its opportunities* ***excited*** *Grandfather.*

ex•haus•tion (ĭg zôs′chən) *n.* Very great tiredness: *His muscles shook with* ***exhaustion*** *after the long race.*

deposit

environment
Environ means "in a circle" in Latin. An environment is what surrounds, or circles, living things.

exhaustion
The Latin word *exhaurire* means "to draw out." Exhaustion draws all the strength from a person's body

oi oil / ōō book / ōō boot / ou out / ŭ cut / û fur / th bath / *th* bathe / ə ago, item, pencil, atom, circus

science experiment

garbage

haze

ex•per•i•ment (ĭk spĕr′ə mənt) *n.* A test used to prove or find out about something: *Her* ***experiment*** *will show how vegetables grow in space.*

F

for•bid•ding (fər bĭ′dĭng) *adj.* Unfriendly or frightening: *The tall, dark buildings gave the city a* ***forbidding*** *appearance.*

foul (foul) *adj.* Dirty or unpleasant: *A* ***foul*** *odor reached Walter and made him wrinkle his nose in disgust.*

G

gar•bage (gär′bĭj) *n.* Unwanted or useless material; trash to be thrown away: *The* ***garbage*** *will be taken to the dump in the morning.*

gen•er•a•tion (jĕn′ ə rā′shən) *n.* 1. Offspring that are at the same stage of descent from a common ancestor: *Several* ***generations*** *of that family live in the same town.* 2. The act or process of producing or bringing about.

glare (glâr) *v.* To stare at in an angry way: *The man* ***glared*** *down at the children and demanded to know what they wanted.*

greet•ings (grē′tĭngs) *n.* Kind regards or best wishes: *They send* ***greetings*** *to you in their kind letter.*

H

haze (hāz) *n.* Dust, smoke, or other matter that makes the air less clear: *A brownish* ***haze*** *hung over the city, making it difficult to see the mountains.*

hes•i•tate (hĕz′ĭ tāt′) *v.* To pause or stop in uncertainty: *The man* ***hesitated*** *and looked back at the tree before he walked away.*

home•sick (hōm′sĭk′) *adj.* Missing one's home or a special place: *After traveling for three weeks, we were* ***homesick.***

ă pat / ā pay / â care / ä father / ĕ pet / ē be / ĭ pit / ī ride / î fierce / ŏ pot / ō go / ô paw, for

hon•or (ŏn′ər) *n.* Recognition, respect, or awards for showing special abilities or qualities: *They deserve high* ***honors*** *for all their good work.*

I

ig•nite (ĭg nīt′) *v.* To catch fire quickly: *The dry bushes* ***ignited****, and the fire quickly spread.*

in•te•grat•ed (ĭn′tĭ grā tĭd) *adj.* Having people of all races together: *Thurgood Marshall believed children of all races should attend classes together in* ***integrated*** *schools.*

in•ves•ti•gate (ĭn vĕs′tĭ gāt′) *v.* To study or examine closely: *Julian decided to* ***investigate*** *to find out who owned the dog in the car.*

J

judge (jŭj) *n.* A person who decides the winner of a contest: *The* ***judges*** *look for certain qualities as they choose the winner.*

K

kin•dle (kĭn′dl) *v.* To start a fire: *Sparks from the exploding trees* ***kindled*** *new fires.*

L

land•fill (lănd′fĭl) *n.* An area in which trash is buried beneath layers of dirt: *The trash is taken to the* ***landfill*** *every Thursday.*

leu•ke•mi•a (lōō kē′mē ə) *n.* A disease of the blood that is a form of cancer: *She is in the hospital with* ***leukemia.***

long (lông) *v.* To wish for something very much: *They* ***longed*** *to see their old friends.*

loom (lōōm) *v.* To appear, often seeming huge and threatening: *The buildings of the big city* ***loomed*** *in the distance, making her feel small and scared.* — *n.* A frame or machine on which thread is woven into cloth.

ignite
Ignite comes from the Latin word *ignis*, which means "fire."

landfill

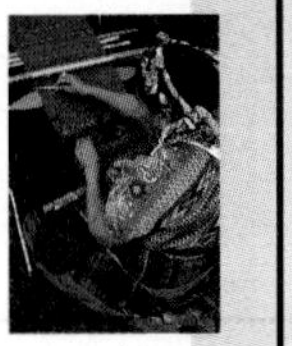
loom

oi oil / ōō book / ōō boot / ou out / ŭ cut / û fur / th bath / *th* bathe / ə ago, item, pencil, atom, circus

marvel/miracle
It's no wonder that *marvel* and *miracle* have similar meanings. They both come from the Latin word *mirari,* which means "to wonder."

monument

mound

M

mar•vel (**mär'**vəl) *v.* To be filled with surprise or wonder: *He **marveled** at the wonderful countryside and the busy new cities.*

me•mor•ial (mə **môr'**ē əl) *adj.* Acting to honor the memory of a person or event: *We had a **memorial** ceremony to honor those who were killed in the war.*

meth•od (**mĕth'**əd) *n.* A plan or process for doing something: *I think a monorail is the best **method** of mass transportation.*

might•y (**mī'**tē) *adj.* **mightier, mightiest.** Powerful, large, or strong: *Crumbles gave a **mighty** bark to show that he was feeling better.*

mir•a•cle (**mĭr'**ə kəl) *n.* An amazing or marvelous thing that seems impossible: *The people on the farm thought Charlotte's beautiful web was a **miracle.***

mir•a•cu•lous (mĭ **răk'**yə ləs) *adj.* Of or like a miracle: *The message in the spider's web was the most **miraculous** thing Lurvy had ever seen.*

mis•chie•vous (**mĭs'**chə vəs) *adj.* Naughty; causing trouble: *That was a **mischievous** prank he played on the man.*

mon•u•ment (**mŏn'**yə mənt) *n.* Something created to help people continue to remember a person or event: *The children helped raise money to build the **monument**, a statue of Sadako.*

mo•tive (**mō'**tĭv) *n.* A reason for an action: *The thief had no money, so we know that was one of his **motives** in committing the crime.*

mound (mound) *n.* A pile or hill: *The **mound** of trash grew so high it reached the windows of the house.*

O

op•pon•ent (ə **pō'**nənt) *n.* A person who is against another person in a contest: *My **opponent** in tomorrow's game is a friend of my brother's.*

ă pat / ā pay / â care / ä father / ĕ pet / ē be / ĭ pit / ī ride / î fierce / ŏ pot / ō go
ô paw, for

op•por•tun•i•ty (ŏp'ər **tōō'**nĭ tē) *n., pl.* **opportunities.** A good chance: *Going to Howard University is an **opportunity** to get a good education.*

P

pa•pers (**pā'**pərs) *n.* Documents telling who or what one is: *To sign up for school, we brought our **papers** to show our names and where we were born.*

par•ti•ci•pant (pär **tĭs'**ə pənt') *n.* One who takes part: *There were more than 100 **participants** in this year's soccer tournament.*

per•fect (**pûr'**fĭkt) *adj.* Without any faults; completely pleasing; excellent: *The beautiful stone was the color of a **perfect** white rose.*

pes•ky (**pĕs'**kē) *adj.* **peskier, peskiest.** Causing trouble: *Perhaps those **pesky** little dogs will leave the cat alone now.*

poised (poizd) *adj.* Balanced: *The runners stood **poised**, ready to start the race when the whistle blew.*

pol•lin•ate (**pŏl'**ə nāt') *v.* To transfer pollen from one flower to another: *Flying from flower to flower, bees **pollinate** the plants in the forest.*

pre•fer (prĭ **fûr'**) *v.* To value more or like better: *I like living on the prairie, but I would **prefer** to live near the ocean.*

prej•u•dice (**prĕj'**ə dĭs) *n.* Unfair treatment of a particular group; strong, unfair opinion: *Sending children of different races to separate schools is a kind of **prejudice**.*

proj•ect (**prŏj'**ekt') *n.* A task to be done or a problem to be solved: *The **project** is to write a report and draw a poster about transportation.*

poised

R

red her•ring (rĕd **hĕr'**ĭng) *n.* Something that draws attention away from the matter or issue: *The fake clue was a **red herring** that kept the detective from solving the mystery.*

red herring
A red herring is really a type of smoked fish. It was originally used to draw hunting dogs off the trail of their prey.

oi oil / ŏŏ book / ōō boot / ou out / ŭ cut / û fur / th bath / *th* bathe / ə ago, item, pencil, atom, circus

schedule

schedule
A sheet of papyrus, an ancient kind of paper, was called a *scheda* in Latin. *Scheda* became *schedule* over time. Many people write out their schedules on paper.

reg•is•ter (**rĕj'**ĭ stər) *v.* To place on an official list: *We met the principal when we went to **register** at our new school.*

re•lieved (rĭ **lēv'**d') *adj.* Freed from worry or discomfort: *He was **relieved** that Sonia understood the need to find the dog's owners.*

res•er•va•tion (rĕz'ər **vā'**shən) *n.* Land set aside by the government for Native Americans: *The government insisted that the Native Americans give up their own land and move onto the **reservation.*** 2. The act of setting something aside for later use. 3. Something that restricts or causes doubt.

re•spon•si•bil•i•ty (rĭ spŏn'sə **bĭl'**ĭ tē) *n., pl.* **responsibilities.** Something a person has to do; a duty: *Taking care of a pet is an important **responsibility**.*

rest•less (**rĕst'**lĭs) *adj.* Unsettled; unable to relax: *The children were **restless** after being stuck inside all day.*

rhythm (**rith'**əm) *n.* An action or condition repeated in regular sequence: *The girls jumped in **rhythm** to the beat of the music.*

ri•val (**rī'**vəl) *n.* Someone who competes with another for the same object or goal: *Sally and her **rival,** Phoebe, will compete against each other today.*

rou•tine (rōō **tēn'**) *n.* 1. An act that is part of a piece of entertainment: *We added five new steps to our dance **routine**.* 2. A series of usual activities; regular procedure.

S

sa•cred (**sā'**krĭd) *adj.* Holy; deserving of great respect: *During the ritual, even the small children were quiet and respectful of the **sacredness** of the occasion.*

schedule (**skĕj'**ōōl *or* **skĕj'**əl) *n.* A plan with a time line for doing something: *By the third week, we had made up lost time and were ahead of **schedule**.*

ă pat / ā pay / â care / ä father / ĕ pet / ē be / ĭ pit / ī ride / î fierce / ŏ pot / ō go
ô paw, for

scorch (skôrch) *v.* To burn the surface with great heat: *Flames moved quickly, **scorching** the grass and leaves.*

scurry (**skûr'**ē) *v.* **scurried, scurrying.** To rush around in a hurried manner: *People **scurried** from shop to shop, hoping to get home before dark.*

sigh (sī) *v.* To take a deep breath and let it out with a sound expressing boredom: *Peter **sighed** heavily and wished again for something to do.*

singe (sĭnj) *v.* To slightly burn surface features such as hair or fur: *Animals moved quickly to avoid **singeing** their fur in the flames.*

slouch (slouch) *v.* To droop lazily: *He **slouched** in his chair until a sudden noise made him sit up straight.*

smol•der•ing (**smōl'**dər ĭng) *adj.* Burning slowly without a flame: *The **smoldering** ruins of the cabins burned for days.*

so•lu•tion (sə **lōō'**shən) *n.* 1. The answer to a problem: *One good **solution** to the pollution problem is reducing the number of cars on the road.* 2. A mixture formed by dissolving a substance in a liquid.

som•er•sault (**sŭm'**ər sôlt') *v.* To roll the body in a complete circle, head over heels: *The gymnast **somersaulted** across the mat, carefully tucking her chin down onto her chest as she rolled forward.*

sort (sôrt) *v.* To arrange according to kind, size, or other characteristics: *Be sure to **sort** the garbage into piles for trash pickup and recycling.*

spe•ci•men (**spĕs'**ə mən) *n.* One of a group of things that can represent the whole group: *The huge vegetables were not the usual **specimens** of broccoli, avocados, and peas.*

spon•sor (**spŏn'**sər) *n.* A person or organization that helps plan and/or pay for an event: *The **sponsors** of the contest provided the prizes and the refreshments.*

slouch

oi oil / ŏŏ book / ōō boot / ou out / ŭ cut / û fur / th bath / *th* bathe / ə ago, item, pencil, atom, circus

strengthen

strength•en (**strĕngk'**thən) *v.* To make stronger: *Practicing every day for one hour has helped to **strengthen** my muscles.*

sus•pect (sə **spĕkt'**) *v.* To think that something is true without being sure: *He **suspected** that the water in the pond had already dried up.* (**sŭs'** pĕkt') *n.* A person thought to be guilty without proof: *We have questioned the seven **suspects** in the case of the missing map.*

T

territory
The Latin root *terra* is in *territory*. *Terra* means "land."

ter•rit•or•y (**tĕr'**ĭ tôr'ē) *n., pl.* **territories.** A geographical area owned by a government: *The government set aside **territory** in central Oklahoma for the Native Americans.*

the•o•ry (**the'**ə rē) *n.,* An opinion about what happened based on limited information or knowledge: *After studying the clues, Meg came up with a **theory** about who had broken into the strongbox.*

trea•ty (**trē'**tē) *n., pl.* **treaties.** A legal agreement between two or more countries or governments: *Both governments thought the agreement was fair, so they signed the **treaty**.*

U

up•town (**ŭp'**toun) *adv.* Toward the upper part of a city: *We took the train **uptown** after seeing the movie.*

W

won•der (**wŭn'**dər) *n.* Something very remarkable or unusual; marvel: *How Charlotte wove those words into her web is a **wonder**.* — *v.* To want to know; to be curious.

won•drous (**wŭn'**drəs) *adj.* Wonderful: *The sun reflecting off the spider's web made a **wondrous** sight.*

ă pat / ā pay / â care / ä father / ĕ pet / ē be / ĭ pit / ī ride / î fierce / ŏ pot / ō go
ô paw, for

ACKNOWLEDGMENTS

Selections

Selection from *50 Simple Things Kids Can Do To Save The Earth.*, by John Javna. Copyright © 1990 by John Javna. Reprinted by permission of Andrews and McMeel.

"A Play," from *Childtimes*, by Eloise Greenfield and Lessie Jones Little. Copyright © 1979 by Eloise Greenfield and Lessie Jones Little. Reprinted by permission of HarperCollins Children's Books, a division of HarperCollins Publishers.

"Alice and Alex," by Deborah Sussman from *Storyworks* magazine, January 1994. Copyright © 1993 by Scholastic, Inc. Reprinted by permission.

"Ali Baba and the Mystery of the Missing Circus Tickets," from *Hurray For Ali Baba Bernstein*, by Johanna Hurwitz. Copyright © 1989 by Johanna Hurwitz. Reprinted by permission of Morrow Junior Books, a division of William Morrow & Company, Inc.

Selection from *California Kids,* edited by Jim Silverman. Copyright © 1992 by The California Kids History Catalog. Cover art by Rick Wheeler. Reprinted by permission of Jim Silverman.

Selection from *Classroom Peanuts,* by Charles M. Schulz. Copyright © 1982 by United Feature Syndicate, Inc. Reprinted by permission.

"Earth Day Kids," from April, 1993 *3-2-1 Contact* magazine. Copyright © 1993 by Children's Television Workshop. Reprinted by permission.

"Elliot's House," by Lois Lowry, from *The Big Book for Our Planet*, edited by Ann Durell, Jean Craighead George and Katherine Paterson. Copyright © 1993 by Lois Lowry. Reprinted by permission of Harold Ober Associates, Inc.

Encyclopedia Brown and the Case of The Disgusting Sneakers, by Donald J. Sobol. Copyright © 1990 by Donald J. Sobol. Reprinted by permission of Morrow Junior Books, a division of William Morrow & Company, Inc.

"The Flying Train Committee," from *Tales Of a Fourth Grade Nothing*, by Judy Blume. Copyright © 1972 by Judy Blume. Reprinted by permission of Dell Publishing, a division of Bantam Doubleday Dell Publishing Group, Inc.

"Gluscabi and the Wind Eagle," from *Native American Stories,* told by Joseph Bruchac from *Keepers of the Earth,* by Michael J. Caduto and Joseph Bruchac. Copyright © 1991 by Michael J. Caduto and Joseph Bruchac. Reprinted by permission of Fulcrum Publishing, Inc., 350 Indiana St., #350, Golden, CO 80401, (800) 992–2908.

"Gotcha!" by John Shabe, from *Dynamath*. Copyright © 1993 by Scholastic, Inc. Reprinted by permission.

Grandfather's Journey, by Allen Say. Copyright © 1993 by Allen Say. Reprinted by permission of Houghton Mifflin Company. All rights reserved.

The Great Kapok Tree, by Lynne Cherry. Copyright © 1990 by Lynne Cherry. Reprinted by permission of Harcourt Brace & Company.

The Great Yellowstone Fire, by Carole Vogel and Kathryn A. Goldner. Copyright © 1990 by Carole Garbuny Vogel and Kathryn Allen Goldner. Reprinted by permission of Little, Brown and Company.

I'm New Here, by Bud Howlett. Copyright © 1993 by Bud Howlett. Reprinted by permission of Houghton Mifflin Company. All rights reserved.

Selection from *Julian, Secret Agent*, by Ann Cameron. Copyright © 1988 by Ann Cameron. Reprinted by permission of Alfred A. Knopf, Inc.

Jumanji, by Chris Van Allsburg. Copyright © 1981 by Chris Van Allsburg. Reprinted by permission of Houghton Mifflin Company. All rights reserved.

June 29, 1999, written and illustrated by David Wiesner. Copyright © 1992 by David Wiesner. Reprinted by permission of Houghton Mifflin Company. All rights reserved.

Just a Dream, by Chris Van Allsburg. Copyright © 1990 by Chris Van Allsburg. Reprinted by permission of Houghton Mifflin Company. All rights reserved.

"Keepers of the Earth," from the introduction of *Native American Stories,* told by Joseph Bruchac. Copyright © 1991 by Michael J. Caduto and Joseph Bruchac. Reprinted by permission of Fulcrum Publishing, Inc., 350 Indiana St., #350, Golden, CO 80401, (800) 992–2908.

Selections from "Kids Did It!" from February 1992 *National Geographic World*. Copyright © 1992 by *National Geographic World*. *World* is the official magazine for Junior Members of the National Geographic Society. Reprinted by permission.

Selection from *Koya DeLaney and the Good Girl Blues,* by Eloise Greenfield. Copyright © 1992 by Eloise Greenfield. Reprinted by permission of Scholastic, Inc.

"Leaving Home," from *All for the Better*, by Nicholasa Mohr. Copyright © 1993 by Dialogue Systems, Inc. Reprinted by permission of Steck-Vaughn Company.

"Look Ma! There's an Alligator in the Toilet!," from December, 1993 *3-2-1 Contact* magazine. Copyright © 1993 by Children's Television Workshop. Reprinted by permission.

"Lucas Cott Does Raisin Bread Arithmetic," by Johanna Hurwitz from *Storyworks* magazine, November/December 1993. Copyright © 1993 by Johanna Hurwitz. Reprinted by permission of Scholastic, Inc.

"The Marble Champ," from *Baseball In April and Other Stories*, by Gary Soto. Copyright © 1990 by Gary Soto. Reprinted by permission of Harcourt Brace & Company.

Meg Mackintosh and The Case of the Curious Whale Watch, by Lucinda Landon. Copyright © 1987 by Lucinda Landon. Reprinted by permission of Little, Brown and Company.

"The Miracle," from *Charlotte's Web*, by E. B. White. Copyright © 1952 by E.B. White. Copyright © renewed 1980 by E.B. White. Reprinted by permission of HarperCollins Publishers.

No One Is Going To Nashville, by Mavis Jukes, illustrated by Lloyd Bloom. Text copyright © 1983 by Mavis Jukes. Illustrations copyright © 1983 by Lloyd Bloom. Reprinted by permission of Alfred A. Knopf, Inc.

"On A Roll," by Donna M. Tocci, from *BAA Boston Marathon® Official Program*. Copyright © 1994 by The Boston Phoenix, Inc. Reprinted by permission. All rights reserved.

"Paul Bunyan, The Mightiest Logger of Them All," from *American Tall Tales*, by Mary Pope Osborne. Copyright © 1991 by Mary Pope Osborne. Reprinted by permission of Alfred A. Knopf, Inc.

"Playing Detective: Real Kids Portray TV Sleuths," from *Ghostwriter: The Team On and Off The Set*, by Joy Duckett Cain. Copyright © 1995 by Children's Television Workshop. Ghostwriter and the Ghostwriter Logo are trademarks and service marks of Children's Television Workshop. Reprinted by permission.

Sadako, by Eleanor Coerr, illustrated by Ed Young. Text copyright © 1993 by Eleanor Coerr. Illustrations copyright © 1993 by Ed Young. Reprinted by permission of G.P. Putnam's Sons.

Sarah, Plain and Tall, by Patricia MacLachlan. Copyright © 1985 by Patricia MacLachlan. Reprinted by permission of HarperCollins Children's Books, a division of HarperCollins Publishers.

Selections from *The Seminoles*, by Virginia Driving Hawk Sneve. Copyright © 1994 by Virginia Driving Hawk Sneve. Reprinted by permission of Holiday House, Inc.

"Smoke Jumpers," by Janice Koch from August, 1994 *National Geographic World*. Copyright © 1994 by *National Geographic World*. *World* is the official magazine for Junior Members of the National Geographic Society. Reprinted by permission.

Selection from *This Land Is My Land*, by George Littlechild. Copyright © 1993 by George Littlechild. Reprinted by permission of Children's Book Press.

Thurgood Marshall and Equal Rights, by Seamus Cavan. Copyright © 1993 by The Millbrook Press. Reprinted by permission.

"Who Stole The Cadillac," from *Clues & Suspects*, by Anne Civardi and Colin King. Copyright © 1979 by Usborne Publishing. Reprinted by permission of Usborne Publishing, Ltd.

Poetry

"74th Street," from *The Malibu And Other Poems*, by Myra Cohn Livingston. Copyright © 1972 by Myra Cohn Livingston. Reprinted by permission of Marian Reiner for the author.

"Birdfoot's Grampa," by Joseph Bruchac from *Entering Onondaga*. Copyright © 1978 by Joseph Bruchac. Reprinted by permission of Barbara S. Kouts for the author. Cover of *Native American Stories*, by Joseph Bruchac. Cover copyright © 1991 by Fulcrum Publishing. Reprinted by permission.

"Blossom," "Friendship," "Jeannie Had a Giggle," "Pride," and "Summer," from *Brown Angels*, by Walter Dean Myers. Copyright © 1993 by Walter Dean Myers. Reprinted by permission of HarperCollins Publishers.

"Dreams," from *The Dream Keeper and Other Poems*, by Langston Hughes. Text copyright © 1932 by Alfred A. Knopf., Inc. Copyright © renewed 1960 by Langston Hughes. Reprinted by permission of Alfred A. Knopf, Inc.

"I'm in Another Dimension," from *If You're Not Here, Please Raise Your Hand*, by Kalli Dakos. Copyright © 1990 by Kalli Dakos. Reprinted by permission of Simon & Schuster Books For Young Readers, an imprint of Simon & Schuster Children's Publishing Division.

"Jimmy Jet and His TV Set," from *Where The Sidewalk Ends*, by Shel Silverstein. Copyright © 1974 by Evil Eye Music, Inc. Reprinted by permission of HarperCollins Publishers.

"Last Night," from *Somebody Catch My Homework*, by David L. Harrison. Copyright © 1993 by David L. Harrison. Reprinted by permission of Boyds Mills Press.

"Listen to The Mustn'ts," from *Where the Sidewalk Ends*, by Shel Silverstein. Copyright © 1974 by Evil Eye Music, Inc. Reprinted by permission of HarperCollins Publishers.

"Ten Minutes Till The Bus," from *Somebody Catch My Homework*, by David L. Harrison. Copyright © 1993 by David L. Harrison. Reprinted by permission of Boyds Mills Press.

"We Are Plooters," by Jack Prelutsky, illustrated by Paul O. Zelinsky, from *The Big Book For Our Planet*, edited by Ann Durell, Jean Craighead George, and Katherine Paterson, published by Penguin USA. Text copyright © 1993 by Jack Prelutsky. Reprinted by permission of the author. Illustrations copyright © 1993 by Paul O. Zelinsky. Reprinted by permission of the artist.

Special thanks to the following teachers whose students' compositions are included in the Be a Writer features in this level:

Judy Thum, Paul Ecke Central School, Encinitas, California; Pamela Ziegler, Washington Elementary School, Fargo, North Dakota; Nancy Simpson, Friday Harbor Elementary School, Friday Harbor, Washington; Steve Buettner, Hammond Elementary School, Laurel, Maryland; Sandra Grier, Taylors Elementary School, Taylors, South Carolina; Cydelle Greene, Calusa Elementary School, Miami, Florida.

CREDITS

Illustration **18–33** John Dunivant; **43–57** Betsy James; **62–63** Charles Schultz; **84–87** Gregory Nemec; **88–89** Yvonne Brown; **93–105** Gil Ashby; **108–113** Will Terry; **146–155** Lark Carrier; **156–157** Piotr Kaczmarek; **158–159** Paul 0. Zelinsky; **160–182** Lynne Cherry; **198–223** Chris Van Allsburg; **234–258** Lucinda Landon; **266–274** Larry Johnson; **280–281** Michael McParlane; **282–291** Michael Chesworth; **305–332** Allen Say; **344–355** Sheldon Greenburg; **358–359** Patrick Gnan; **360–370** Leslie Wu; **382–390** Ronald Himler; **391** Chris Costello; **399** George Littlechild; **407–417** Mike Reed; **428** Beatrice Brooks; **454–481** Ed Young; **488–505** Lloyd Bloom; **510–511** Steve Cieslawski; **518–545** Chris Van Allsburg; **550–556** Kenneth Spengler; **560–561** Shel Silverstein; **562–582** David Wiesner; **586–589** Ethan Long; **590–593** Eric Petersen; **594–603** Garth Williams **Back cover inset** Steve Cieslawski (br)

Assignment Photography **278–279, 394–395, 396–397, 420–421, 427 (TR), 546–547, 548–549** Banta Digital Group; **192–193, 194–195, 276–277** Kindra Clineff; **292–293** Dave Desroches; **506–507** John Lei/OMNI–Photo Communications, Inc.; **371** John MacLachlan; **183** (inset) Katie P. McManus/*Teaching K–8 Magazine*; **34–35, 58–59, 60–61, 80–81, 90–91, 106–107, 183** (background), **186–187, 188–189, 196–197, 226–227, 228–229, 230–231, 232–233, 260–261, 298–299, 300–301, 302–303, 304, 333, 334–335, 336–337, 338–339, 340–341, 342–343, 380–381, 392–393, 400–401, 402–403, 404–405, 448, 516–517** Tony Scarpetta; **36–37, 38–39, 40–41, 114–115, 116–117, 118–119, 190–191, 224–225** Tracey Wheeler **Back cover insets** Tracey Wheeler (tl, tr); Tony Scarpetta (ml, mr, bl)

Photography **33** John Dunivant(tl); Johanna Hurwitz (t) **42** Mario Ruiz/Time Magazine (tl); Courtesy of Betsy James (tr) **60** C.A. Giampiccolo/FPG **79** Courtesy of Bud Howlett (bl) **82** Andrew Brusso **83** Beatriz Schiller (tl); Washington Post (tr); Cary Tolman (b) **90** Courtesy of Anthony Yengo **92** Courtesy of Eloise Greenfield (tl); Courtesy of Gil Ashby (bl) **120** ©Jerry Ferrara/Photo Researchers (background) **121** Robert Bower (mr) **122** Alan and Sandy Carey **123** Alan and Sandy Carey (t); Erwin and Peggy Bauer (m) **124–125** Boise Interagency Fire Center **126** National Park Service **127** Wyoming Travel Commission **128** Alan and Sandy Carey **129** Jeff and Alexa Henry (tr) **131** National Park Service **133** Alan and Sandy Carey **134** ©Robert Bower (l); Erwin & Peggy Bauer (tr, br) **135** Alan and Sandy Carey **136** Steven Dowell/Bozeman Chronicle **139** Wyoming Travel Commission **140** National Park Service **141** Courtesy of Carole G. Vogel (br); Courtesy of Kathryn A. Goldner (tr) **142–143** National Park Service (background) **144** ©Daniel R. Westergren/National Geographic Society (cover); ©Bill Moyer/National Geographic Society (inset); ©Micheal Yamashita/National Geographic Society (m) **145** ©Bill Moyer/National Geographic Society (m) **183** Katie MacManus/ Courtesy of Lynne Cherry **184–185** ©1994 Zefa Germany /The Stock Market **186** Courtesy of Megan Hunter **188–189** K.O.P.E. (t) **190** Courtesy of Melanie Essary **190–191** Intelligencer/Record (tr) **196** Susan Lapides **259** Courtesy of Lucinda Landon (t) **262** Richard Gray Gallery **263** Greg Hiens/Isabella Stuart Gardner Museum, Boston (t); Isabella Stuart Gardner Museum, Boston (l); Art Resource (r) **275** Das Anudas/Courtesy of Ann Cameron (tr); Courtesy of Larry Johnson **278** Courtesy of Bridget Hudson **282** Courtesy of Donald J. Sobol; Courtesy of Michael Chesworth (r) **294–295** Frank Micelotta/Children's Television Workshop **296** Barbara Nitke/Children's Television Workshop (tl); Michael Benabib/Children's Television Workshop (tm); Frank Micelotta/Children's Television Workshop (bm) **297** Don Perdue/Children's Television Workshop (br) Frank Micelotta/Children's Television Workshop (tr) **333** Courtesy of Allan Say **336** The Bettmann Archive (ml); The Granger Collection, New York (mr); Courtesy The Oakland Museum (bl); Wells Fargo Bank (br) **337** California State Library (bl); Courtesy The Oakland Museum (br) **338** The Bettmann Archive (tm); Wells Fargo Bank (tr) **340** Courtesy of The Bancroft Library (mr) **341** Courtesy The Oakland Museum (tl); Denver Public Library (tr) **342** Library of Congress (l); San Diego Historical Society, Photo Collection (mr) **343** Courtesy The Oakland Museum (ml) **344** Courtesy of Nicholasa Mohr; Mary Merrick/Courtesy of Sheldon Greenburg (b) **356** The Bettmann Archive **358** Museum of the City of New York (tl) **359** Comstock (t); UPI/ Bettman (bl); Christian Kempf/Musee Bertoldi-Colma (bm); ©Bill Backman/Photo Researchers (br) **371** Courtesy of Patricia MacLachlan; Courtesy of Leslie Wu **373** ©David Scott Smith/Stock Connection **380** Sharon McElmeel/ Courtesy of Virginia Driving Hawk Sneve (tl); Courtesy of Ronald Himler (tr) **394** Courtesy of Briana Taylor **406** Courtesy of Mike Reed (r); Courtesy of Gary Soto (l) **420** Courtesy of Nathan Cox **422** The Boston Phoenix (t) **423** Peter Travers **424–425** Boston Athletic Association (t) **424** Jeffrey Dunn (b) **425** Boston Athletic Association (r) **426** Boston Athletic Association(l); Peter Southwick/Stock Boston (r) **427** Kathy Tarantola/The Picture Cube (b) **430** NAACP **431** UPI Bettmann/The Bettmann Archive **432, 435, 438, 440** Marshall Family Photo **433** Library of Congress **434, 436** Courtesy Moorland-Spingarn Research Center, Howard University **437** Library of Congress; UPI Bettmann (t) **439** AP Worldwide Photos, Inc.(r) **440** UPI Bettmann/The Bettmann Archive (l) **441** AP Worldwide Photos, Inc.; The Bettmann Archive (l); UPI/Bettmann (bm) **443** AP/Worldwide Photos **444, 445** UPI/Bettmann **445** The Bettmann Archive (b) **446** Don Sparks/The Image Bank (m) **446–447** UPI/Bettmann (m) **447** U.S. Supreme Court Photo; UPI/Bettmann (tl) **447** AP Newsfeatures photo/AP Worldwide Photos, Inc. (b); ©Peter Chapman (br) **448** Courtesy of Sean Dolan (tl); Courtesy of Beatrice Brooks/PCI (r) **449** AP Worldwide Photos, Inc. (tl); Sandra Baker/Liason International (m); Virginia Blaisdell Photography (b); **450–451** Steve Dunwell/The Image Bank **453** Art Institute of Chicago **481** Courtesy of Ed Young (tr); Courtesy of Eleanor Coerr (tl)

483–484 Bruno J. Zehnder/Peter Arnold,Inc. **484** Gray Mortimore/Allsport (t); M. Greenlar/The Image Works (l); M. Greenlar/The Image Works (r) **485** Ronnie Fridthjor; Joseph H. Bailey/National Geographic Society **486–487** Uwe Lochstampfer/The Image Bank **506** Courtesy of Mavis Jukes **507** Courtesy of Mavis Jukes (b) **508–509** ©A.M. Rosario/The Image Bank **511–512** Tim Brown/Tony Stone Images/Chicago Inc. **514–515** Tony Stone Images/Chicago Inc. **516** Susan Lapides (tl) **548** Courtesy of Sophia Vilella **557** Courtesy of Lois Lowry (t); ©Susan Kennedy/Kenneth Spengler (l) **558–559** ©Ray Pfortner/Peter Arnold,Inc. **583** Len Irish/ Courtesy of David Wiesner (r) **603** Jill Krementz (t); Courtesy of Garth Williams (b) **604–605** ©Walter Bibikow/The Image Bank **608** David De Lossy/The Image Bank **609** Animals Animals **610** Jeff Hunter/The Image Bank **611** Paul & Karen Smith/Tony Stone Images **612** Terje Rakke/The Image Bank; Ulf Wallin/The Image Bank (b) **613** Steve Dunwell /The Image Bank (t); Louis Casteneda/The Image Bank (b) **614** Chris Hackett/The Image Bank (t); Mark Burnett/Photo Researchers (b) **615** Bob Daemmrich/Tony Stone Images **618** Ed Bock/The Stock Market

Special thanks **380–381; 392–393** Basket, doll, and skirt courtesy of Ah-Tha-Thi-Ki Museum, Seminole Tribe of Florida

Teacher's Handbook

TABLE OF CONTENTS

Study Skills

Graphic Information

TESTED SKILL

INTERACTIVE LEARNING

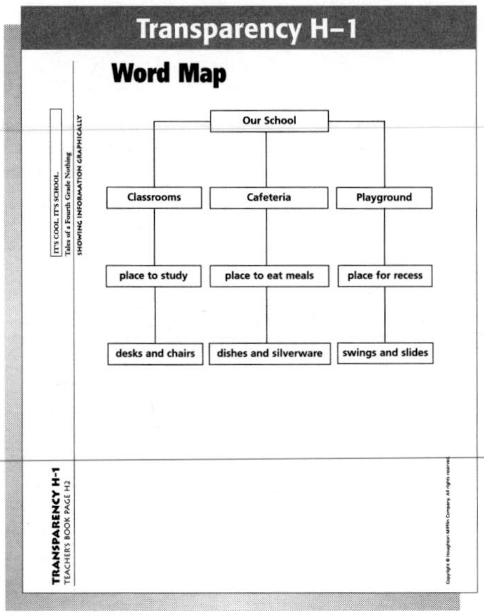

Teach/Model

Tell students that charts and graphs show information graphically, or as a type of illustration. Help students understand that showing information this way can help them understand and remember facts they read. It can also help them prepare for tests or research reports. Tell students that they will learn how to make a particular kind of graphic called a classification map.

Display Transparency H–1 and have a student read the three main heads aloud. Tell students that this is a classification map. It shows how facts can be organized into groups. A classification map makes it easy to compare how facts are alike and how they are different. Use the Think Aloud to model the skill of organizing information graphically. Point to the boxes on the classification map at the appropriate times.

Think Aloud

Suppose I am doing research for a report on our school. One way I can organize information graphically is to **classify**, or put into groups, what I have learned about the school. I will use a classification map to do this. I write the title at the top of my map. Then I write a heading for each item I have learned about. For example, our school has classrooms, a cafeteria, and a playground. These are the headings in my map. Under each heading, I write facts about the classrooms, cafeteria, and playground. I can keep adding boxes under each heading as I collect more facts about each place.

Practice/Apply

Write the headings *Library* and *Nurse's Office* on the chalkboard. Tell students that these are headings that can be added to the classification map on Transparency H–1. Lead a class discussion about these places and what they are like. Have students demonstrate how to show information graphically by asking volunteers to write facts from the discussion under the appropriate headings on the chalkboard.

SKILL FINDER
Minilesson, p. 49

Study Skills

Parts of a Book

INTERACTIVE LEARNING

Teach/Model

Choose a classroom textbook or reader that includes a glossary. Point out the title page, the copyright page, and the table of contents. Tell students that these are usually the first three parts found in any book. Use the Think Aloud to model finding information quickly by referring to these three parts of a book and to show how to find and use a glossary.

Think Aloud

To find out quickly the exact title of a book, the author's complete name, and the name of the book's publisher, I can read the **title page**. It is usually the first page of a book. If I want to find out the year the book was published, I read the second page of the book, the **copyright page**. The date I'm looking for comes right after the copyright symbol, which is the small circle with the letter *c* in it.

If I want to get a general idea about what's in a book, I turn to the **table of contents**. This lists all the chapters or sections in the order that they appear in the book. By reading the titles, I can quickly find out what topics or stories the book contains. The page numbers tell where each chapter or section begins. The table of contents also tells me the page on which the glossary begins. I see that the **glossary** of this book begins on page (name the page).

If I come to a word that I don't know as I'm reading, I can use the glossary. For example, I might want to find out what the word *instructor* means. Since a glossary is like a dictionary, I would look for the **entry word** *instructor* among the entry words that begin with *i*. To find the right page quickly, I can use the **guide words** at the top of the glossary pages to help me. I know that *instructor* comes between the guide words (name the appropriate guide words from the book you are using) in alphabetical order. So I would look for the entry word and the meaning on this page.

Practice/Apply

Have students use another book that contains a glossary to demonstrate using the parts of a book to locate information. Ask them to identify the information found on the title page, the copyright page, and the table of contents. Then have students demonstrate using the guide words in the glossary to help locate entry words and their meanings for words that you select.

SKILL FINDER Minilesson, p. 81N

Transparency H–2

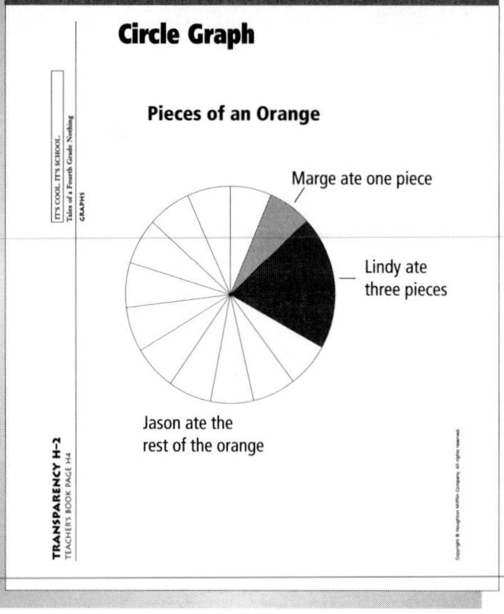

Transparency H–3

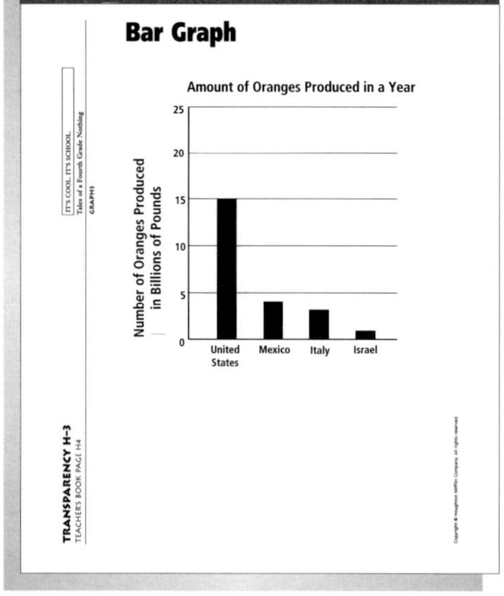

Transparency H–4

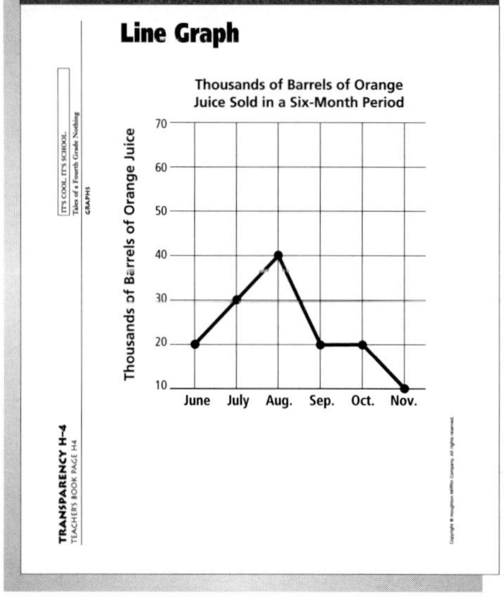

Study Skills

Graphs

INTERACTIVE LEARNING

Teach/Model

Discuss with students how graphs provide a way to share numerical information quickly. Display Transparency H–2. Note that circle graphs show how a part relates to a whole, and model reading the circle graph with a Think Aloud.

Think Aloud

The first things I read on a graph are the title and labels. The title tells me that the graph represents the number of pieces in an orange. By reading the labels, I know that Marge ate one piece, Lindy ate three pieces, and Jason ate the rest. By counting pieces I know that this orange had 15 pieces. Now I know that Marge ate 1/15 of the orange, and Lindy ate 3/15. From this information, I can determine how much of the orange Jason ate (11/15). The graph also lets me compare information. I can see that Jason ate more than anyone, and Marge ate less than anyone.

Display Transparency H–3, and ask students to read the title and labels of the bar graph. Point out that bar graphs compare numbers of items. Encourage students to discuss the numbers compared in the bar graph on Transparency H–3. Display Transparency H–4, and repeat this process with the line graph. Note that line graphs can show changes or differences in numbers that can be measured.

Practice/Apply

Have students take turns demonstrating how to read the three types of graphs. Ask questions like these:

- How many orange slices did Jason eat?
- What fraction of the orange did Jason eat?
- What country shown on the bar graph produces the most oranges? The least?
- In what month were the most barrels of orange juice sold, according to the line graph?

SKILL FINDER Minilesson, p. 87

INFORMAL ASSESSMENT CHECKLIST

Record observations of student progress for those areas important to you.

- **– = Beginning Understanding**
- **✔ = Developing Understanding**
- **✔+ = Proficient**

Tales of a Fourth Grade Nothing	Student Names								
Reading									
Responding									
Comprehension: Predicting Outcomes									
Writing Skills: Writing a Sentence									
Word Skills: Base Words									
Spelling: Short Vowels									
Grammar: Sentence Parts/Fragments									
Listening and Speaking									

I'm New Here									
Reading									
Responding									
Comprehension: Sequence, Noting Details									
Writing: Journal Writing									
Word Skills: Inflected Forms									
Spelling: Long *a*/Long *e*									
Grammar: 4 Kinds of Sentences									
Listening and Speaking									

Reading-Writing Workshop									
Spelling: Words Often Misspelled									

INFORMAL ASSESSMENT CHECKLIST

Record observations of student progress for those areas important to you.

– = Beginning Understanding
✔ = Developing Understanding
✔+ = Proficient

Student Names

Koya Delaney and the Good Girl Blues									
Reading									
Responding									
Comprehension: Making Inferences									
Writing Skills: Writing/Taking Messages									
Word Skills: Compound Words									
Spelling: Long *i* and Long *o*									
Grammar: Run-on Sentences									
Listening and Speaking									

Performance Assessment									
Spelling Review									

General Observation									
Independent Reading									
Independent Writing									
Work Habits									
Self-Assessment									

Audio-Visual Resources

Adventure Productions
3404 Terry Lake Road
Ft. Collins, CO 80524
970-493-8776

AIMS Media
9710 DeSoto Avenue
Chatsworth, CA
91311-4409
800-367-2467

Alfred Higgins Productions
6350 Laurel Canyon
Blvd.
N. Hollywood, CA
91606
800-766-5353

Audio Bookshelf
174 Prescott Hill Road
Northport, ME 04849
800-234-1713

Audio Editions
Box 6930
Auburn, CA 95604-6930
800-231-4261

Audio Partners, Inc.
Box 6930
Auburn, CA 95604-6930
800-231-4261

Bantam Doubleday Dell Audio
1540 Broadway
New York, NY 10036
212-782-9489

Bullfrog Films
Box 149
Oley, PA 19547
800-543-3764

Clearvue/EAV
6465 Avondale Ave.
Chicago, IL 60631
800-253-2788

Coronet/MTI
2349 Chaffee Drive
St. Louis, MO 63146
800-777-8100

Dial Books for Young Readers
375 Hudson St.
New York, NY 10014
800-526-0275

Direct Cinema Ltd.
P.O. Box 10003
Santa Monica, CA 90410
800-525-0000

Disney Educational Production
105 Terry Drive,
Suite 120
Newtown, PA 18940
800-295-5010

Encounter Video
14825 NW Ash St.
Portland, OR 97231
800-677-7607

Filmic Archives
The Cinema Center
Botsford, CT 06404
800-366-1920

Films for Humanities and Science
P.O. Box 2053
Princeton, NJ 08543
609-275-1400

Finley-Holiday Film Corp.
12607 E. Philadelphia St.
Whittier, CA 90601
562-945-3325

Fulcrum Publishing
350 Indiana St.
Golden, CO 80401
303-277-1623

HarperAudio
10 East 53rd Street
New York, NY 10022
212-207-6901

Houghton Mifflin/Clarion
181 Ballardvale St.
Wilmington, MA 01887
800-225-3362

Kidvidz
618 Centre St.
Newton, MA 02158
617-965-3345

Kimbo Educational
Box 477
Long Branch, NJ 07740
800-631-2187

Let's Create
50 Cherry Hill Rd.
Parsippany, NJ 07054
973-299-0633

Listening Library
One Park Avenue
Old Greenwich, CT
06870
800-243-4504

Live Oak Media
P.O. Box 652
Pine Plains, NY 12567
518-398-1010

McGraw-Hill
220 East Danieldale Rd.
Desoto, TX 75115
800-843-8855

Media Basics
Lighthouse Square
705 Boston Post Road
Guilford, CT 06437
800-542-2505

MGM/UA Home Video
2500 Broadway St.
Santa Monica, CA
90404-3061
310-449-3000

Milestone Film and Video
275 W. 96th St.
Suite 28C
New York, NY 10025
212-865-7449

Miramar
200 Second Ave.
Seattle, WA 98119
800-245-6472

National Geographic
1145 17th Street NW
Washington, DC 20036
800-368-2728

The Nature Company
P.O. Box 188
Florence, KY 41022
800-227-1114

PBS Video
1320 Braddock Place
Alexandria, VA
22314-1698
800-424-7963

Philomel Books
200 Madison Ave.
New York, NY 10016
212-951-8400

Premiere Home Video
755 N. Highland
Hollywood, CA 90038
213-934-8903

Puffin Books
375 Hudson St.
New York, NY 10014
212-366-2000

Rabbit Ears Books/Simon and Schuster
1230 Avenue of the
Americas
New York, NY 10020
800-223-2336

Rainbow Educational Media
4540 Preslyn Drive
Raleigh, NC 27616
800-331-4047

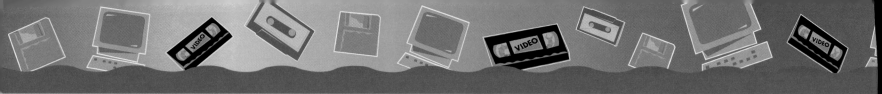

Audio-Visual Resources *(continued)*

Random House Media
400 Hahn Road
Westminster, MD 21157
800-733-3000

Recorded Books
270 Skipjack Road
Prince Frederick, MD 20678
800-638-1304

SelectVideo
5475 Peoria St., Unit 4C
Denver, CO 80239
800-742-1455

Silo/Alcazar
Box 429
Waterbury, VT 05676
802-844-5178

Spoken Arts
8 Lawn Ave.
New Rochelle, NY 10801
914-633-4516

SVE and Churchill Media
6677 N. Northwest Highway
Chicago, IL 60631
800-334-7830

Time-Life Education
P.O. Box 85026
Richmond, VA 23285-5026
800-449-2010

Video Project
200 Estates Drive
Ben Lomond, CA 95005
800-475-2638

Warner Home Video
4000 Warner Blvd.
Burbank, CA 91522
818-954-6000

Weston Woods
12 Oakwood Ave.
Norwalk, CT 06850
800-243-5020

Wilderness Video
P.O.Box 3150
Ashland, OR 97520
541-488-9363

BOOKS AVAILABLE IN SPANISH

Spanish editions of English titles referred to in the Bibliography are available from the following publishers or distributors.

Bilingual Educational Services, Inc.
2514 South Grand Ave.
Los Angeles, CA 90007-9979
800-448-6032

Charlesbridge
85 Main Street
Watertown, MA 02172
617-926-0329

Children's Book Press
246 First St., Suite 101
San Francisco, CA 94105
415-995-2200

Econo-Clad Books
P.O. Box 1777
Topeka, KS 66601
785-233-4252

Farrar, Straus & Giroux
19 Union Square West
New York, NY 10003
212-741-6900

Grolier Publishing Co.
P.O. Box 1796
Danbury, CT 06816
800-621-1115

Harcourt Brace
6277 Sea Harbor Drive
Orlando, FL 32887
800-225-5425

HarperCollins
10 E. 53rd Street
New York, NY 10022
717-941-1500

Holiday House
425 Madison Ave.
New York, NY 10017
212-688-0085

Kane Press
48 W. 25th St.
New York, NY 10010
800-528-8273

Alfred A. Knopf
201 E. 50th St.
New York, NY 10022
800-726-0600

Lectorum
111 Eighth Ave.
New York, NY 10011
800-345-5946

Santillana
2105 NW 86th Ave.
Miami, FL 33122
800-245-8584

Simon and Schuster
1230 Avenue of the Americas
New York, NY 10020
800-223-2336

Viking
357 Hudson Street
New York, NY 10014
212-366-2000

Index

Boldface page references indicate formal strategy and skill instruction.

A

B

D

E

F

G

H

I

Q

R